UNIVERSAL SOUL

TUQUOLA

A SYSTEM

ROBERT LOMAX

Published by Tuquola Press, 2023

ISBN: 978-1-3999-5622-2

Dedicated to all those that have spoken with love and understanding, enabling me to see myself and other worlds in greater clarity.

CONTENTS

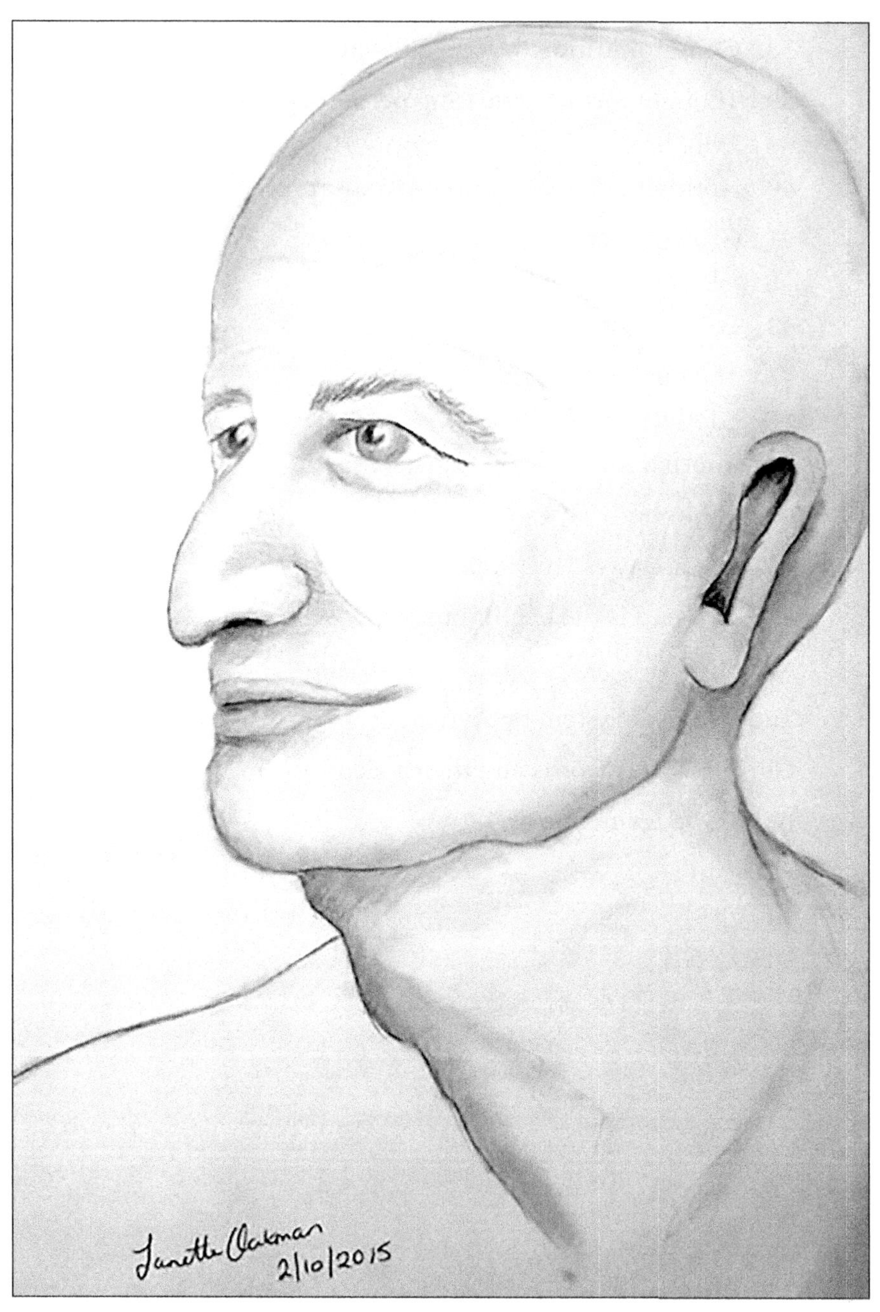

Portrait of Antemedi as drawn by psychic artist Janette Oakman

INTRODUCTION
by Antemedi

If you read my previous book – welcome back. Much has happened since we presented that information.

If you have found your way here for the first time – Hello!

There is no need to read the first book because we will incorporate and expand upon some of the themes. We will go deeper into our understandings of the universe and union of soul.

My name is Antemedi, I am Andromedan. *Anteme* means 'crossing barriers and breaking new ground' and *di* is 'trusting to get finished or utmost reliability'. I take no pride in this description and it doesn't affect my state of being – it just is. It was chosen from seeing the likely outcomes of my life. The sketch of my face was drawn by psychic portrait artist Jannette Oakman in 2015. It is a good rendition, capturing character as well. I am part of the same soul as Robert, alongside other multidimensional expressions. This is because a soul has many experiences on different dimensions. You may imagine those as past or future lives, but outside of time they all reside in the moment of now. They exist as separation programs of information and the same soul energy and awareness flows through them. Conciousness is much more fluid than you can presently imagine (I will explain that in Chapter 1: 'Fluid Consciousness'). Most of the time lives are lived as separate experiences, but in this instance, part of my consciousness and experience is projected into Robert and this allows our interface to exist as a simultaneous continuum. Over time this connection has been enhanced. Earth ***Arkarna**** (see glossary) programs and vibrational levels can sometimes slow the comprehension of information being transferred. To communicate with myself in Robert I occasionally need to break down a few of his human mental constructs.

For 20 years I appeared as Robert's spirit guide and along with other aspects of our soul we helped his (our) earth soul transition through some of its duality. During that process we transmuted previous energy that had been created in past earth lives. This resulted in an easy, comfortable realisation that he is me and I am him.

Memories of many 'off earth' experiences have returned to him. That meant for the following 10 years we could expand the interface between us and explore many other realms. I have, with others, planned these communications as part of an outreach project. We wished to show you what your minds are capable of and raise awareness about the way some benevolent aliens think. Our vibrational explanations can also enter your collective consciousness and exist as information that can be accessed ***as if it is already known***. However, by reading and working with this information you will widen and energise the mental pathways of communication. This allows others to connect with it more easily – thank you.

We will be using new words for new models that describe the universe and soul. The chapters following this introduction will give wider descriptions. These include sensations and feelings which should give a greater comprehension. If there is a section you cannot assimilate it will often make sense in the light of further chapters. If you don't fully comprehend all the information, it will in any event affect your unconscious mind and its programs.

The list of chapters outlines the subjects but it is recommended that you read the layered information in order. Don't worry if you can't absorb all the information immediately. The explanation of it in the chapters that follow will give substance, context and cohesion.

The penultimate section of the book is called Tuquola, the System. It summarises the connections between the subject matter and terms. It acts as a reference map that can be used at any stage. However, when read at the end of the book you should have a different feeling of what you are as a universal soul.

As you progress through the book, you will see words in ***bold italics*** – this is for either:

- emphasising a point
- or words that are related to a concept
- or words which 'form a turn of phrase'

There is a GLOSSARY at the end of the book for words in ***bold italics**** (with an asterisk). These will be:

- Andromedan words
- English words combined to convey a different meaning
- current esoteric words that we may see differently

INTRODUCTION
by Robert

Following Antemedi's introduction – I could say "I am him" but I could also say "I am a program".

Part of my soul consciousness is projected into the ***Arkarna program**** of Robert to have a temporary experience. Of course, I am more than a program – I am soul and entity. But by integrating non-self, and my soul's other dimensional lives in the 'moment of now' it brings an abundant roundness to life. I belong without needing to belong. I have a union with my other multidimensional selves, without the need to be them in this life. Yet, I experience them as being me and the same soul, as other projections in other dimensions. This I sense as a fizz in my aura where I can engage with them in their Arkarna programs.

My early life was constrained by my earth family's genetics and the earth collective consciousness. I was crippled by fear, self-criticism, a sense of not belonging and dyslexia. In one of my other earth lives as a slave I believed that *there was no point in trying to achieve or move away from what I was*. This formed from the constant beatings and the inability to challenge the cruel control system. Early prospects in the life of Robert were impaired by this trauma. These created my corrupted default systems and subconscious programs for understanding life.

As a child, odd looking humanoids would appear at my bedside before sleep. I interpreted their good wishes and help through those damaged beliefs and fears. I was happier when the strange beings no longer visited.

Growing older, I had several psychic apparitions and intuitions. These insights I dismissed and ignored. I did not need to give them any credence, having made great strides against my insecurities.

I would face fear and even create fear, in order to demonstrate I could overcome it. I used many coping strategies to prove – *I was not who I believed I was*. These were false ideas indicating I had some sort of control over fear and insecurity (which I did not). I had no understanding that duality dictated to my subconscious desires and thoughts. My life moved forward and despite those coping strategies, I had a loving wife, three children and a successful part in a family business.

That all changed in 1991 when my youngest son drowned. The world turned upside down and none of my coping strategies worked. Anyone who has suffered intense grief will understand this.

It was as if 'all was lost' and could never be returned. Striving to achieve or overcome no longer had a point (a reflection of the previous life program). Regardless of what was good in life – it was still meaningless. Misconceptions in the duality of my subconscious had their bonds broken. Several times I was held in an ***energetic full embrace***. Occasionally golden lights trickled over me, providing insights.

Over time, the sadness came with light and warmth. I had no need to fear sadness – nor push it away. I had previously been feeling sadness through the separate feeling of fear – feeling one feeling through another feeling. Now when I was in the sadness there was no fear, it was just incredibly sad. I did not need to push it away and eventually the sadness had a love and a belonging. Those moments triggered more experiences of light and psychic vision.

It was the catalyst for a journey into the unknown spirit world. I searched and the universe provided experiences and help. As part of this plan, I was taught and mentored by Linda Wray a wonderful local healer and psychic.

By exploring the duality of my thoughts, my inner sight changed. This allowed me to meet interdimensional humanoids and mentally walk into the visions they presented. Communication with guides (as I saw them at the time) became a part of life. Many of these were counselling sessions where my world views were challenged head on. Often, I would ask a question only to receive a reply "It is better to explore why you have asked that question because there is a sponsoring thought that has not been recognised." The love and trust built to such a level that it exceeded trust itself. No need to trust or not to trust – it just was.

So, as Antemedi says it was a natural progression over several years. Eventually it allowed me to adopt a different sense of self and the alien nature of soul. Antemedi introduced me to other entities and their ways of life. He opened compartmentalised memories of my other earth and alien lives. Some of you may think of these as past lives, but the following chapters will show they are contiguous.

When reading the information in the main body of the book it's probably helpful to understand what's actually happening in Robert's experience. This is me, talking about myself, in the first person and the second person because they are interchangeable (depending on where I am looking from). Often, I may be outside of myself observing the scene with Robert in it.

In this Robert Arkarna program I see and talk with the multidimensional projections of my soul. They can appear inside me, around me, or both at the same moment regardless of dimensions or form. My/our soul also communicates by visions that are both full of knowing and parable. My/our soul also has a voice, which varies in intensity depending on the vibrational level or interface. If it is communicating above my level of vibration and understanding, it requires more concentration or detachment from Robert-self. I type and fully understand the flow of information when I am in it, but occasionally when re-reading it as Robert I have to think hard about what it means and use different words so it can be more easily understood. Antemedi helps with this also.

It's similar to a meditational state, but interaction and awareness becomes omnipresent. There is no distance or difference. Typing and drawing can take place whilst connected to another realm and I can only describe it as 'just is'. A natural way of being, just like you would talk to a close friend when they show you their home. It is soft easy and loving.

When I describe ***the scene*** it's either the context for information or the way a vibrational level presents itself. It's there – inside and outside me, superimposed upon the 3D earth world which I see at the same time. In addition to the voices from my soul, other humanoids will speak when they are part of the presentation. Some have names because I have encountered them before. New entity introductions may also give names and reasons for their appearance. However, some contributors' appearances are so small there is no need for names, the only importance is the material.

Sometimes the information is universal knowledge or a ***thought form**** which I perceive in a humanoid shape to give context to information.

These are different to ***just knowing**** new information as if it was always there in my psyche and soul. These are all forms of communication through self and non-self and are part of a natural way of being.

CHAPTER 1

Fluid consciousness

Antemedi (A): The information I and other beings impart are perspectives with their roots in other dimensions. It is our consciousness reaching you in your consciousness. Of course, there will be disparity between us; that's why we are being careful with the way we communicate. What we say will be processed by your present awareness ***in self***, so in order to provide more clarity, it's important to understand what fluid humanoid consciousness is.

Robert (R): Because we are multidimensional a definition of consciousness would be very helpful. Consciousness may well be fluid but it presently feels like a washing machine that's topsy-turvy and very confusing.

A: You are using the image I put into your consciousness. If you look closer you will see different clothes moving across one another. Water and suds pass through the weave of the materials. Rules like gravity are used to tumble and mix the contents in a particular motion but the juxtapositions never remain the same.

R: The jumper or shirt remains the same but its folded shape will be changing and it will be in a different place in each moment.

A: Still clothing but very fluid.

R: Yes – but consciousness isn't moving about.

A: What if we likened consciousness to the water and the soap powder. If an item of clothing were a plane, then soapy water or the consciousness would exist between the fibres flowing in and out. To ascribe value to the water in the clothing, or outside of it, or in another item of 'clothing plane' would be impossible.

The suds on the top are part of the mix and are lighter, containing more air. Water is made from the air elements of oxygen and hydrogen, but the water is also saturated with small bubbles of air which also contain oxygen and hydrogen. All this is made possible by the soap which is everywhere, except for the air space above the main mix.

R: So which bit is which?

A: Why does it matter?

R: I need an understanding rather than a jumble.

A: The jumble is the understanding.

R: But where is the reason, the rationale and the planning?

A: Why does it have to exist as some great plan. All things are in constant flux, atoms, timeline shimmers, dimensions and souls. You are looking for an order to the universe and an order to the soul. There are overarching Arkarna programs which have the ability to adapt and change while retaining the basic tenets. But the basic tenet of ***grow/expand*** is paradoxically the constant and the rest flows around that – nothing can be set in stone. As one grows, change is the constant.

R: But higher consciousness vibrates at a faster rate.

A: Yes, the solution in the drum is made of oxygen, hydrogen, mixed air and soap – all intertwined as I keep telling you. The contents of the drum are a mix of different vibrations of consciousness, all a part of one another. The liquid, air and soap entwine with the different 'clothing planes' be they silk, denim, corduroy or sackcloth.

R: But tiny particles of 'clothing planes' will come apart floating within the mix or being washed on to other 'clothing planes'.

A: Yes, and we can bring in an analogy for that shortly.

R: What you're saying is – consciousness in its various vibrations entwines in a super mix that's infused into the planes. The spaces between rough sackcloth are bigger than the smooth silk. Therefore, the energy and consciousness vibration (liquid) in the sackcloth hole appears as a different dimension in a different plane. Though a plane or item of clothing can have different degrees of vibration within them.

A: Yes – that's the answer to one of your old thoughts, "What is where and in what shape – and can you separate one from another?"

R: It describes the point you made – that parts of consciousness can be in any plane of apparent separation.

A: I am describing fluid consciousness. If you vibrate at a compatible frequency to interact at that level you will see those vibrations to the exclusion of others. If you only watched the water, it would be a swirling and tumbling movement of liquid. If we exclude the water vibration but keep the tiny air bubbles, space will appear to exist between them, thus a different reality exists in the same place by virtue of a different vibrational perspective. All movements of the oversoul are entwined but can be experienced in different ways.

R: While we are working, I am choosing to perceive how other levels of soul interact. But unless I am fluid my perspective is restrictive. If I was standing on the weave of one garment, I would see the water or space between one thread and the next. But if I looked away from the fabric, I will see the space between the other garments. Yet as I stand here, it feels very still. There is movement of water but everything moves around my fixed perspective. My focus may appear still when it's having a particular experience but in reality, I'm moving about in and as a part of a fluid consciousness.

A: Good, you are interpreting my explanation as a feeling and allowing my intent to flow within you.

R: Better than a scientific explanation. This thread I'm standing on is but one position of focus in a mini universe. But size is irrelevant if you don't know what's beyond your restricted perception.

A: I couldn't have said that better but I thought it and you believed you did. We return to the irrelevance of who is who.

R: It's pleasant enough being on this thread but I am thunderstruck with the significance that the universe appears to revolve around my perspective. From this focus located in self it could be no other way because it's a very small view upon greater consciousness.

Looking from outside of the tumbling washing machine everything inside seems like chaos. But letting go of my reality means I am a speck of dust on a thread, waiting to be washed away. In here everything moves around me and I can join with and float about in the total consciousness. No matter where I am it's safe and calm. I could even move into the fabric of another plane but I would need to be of smaller size to fit within the silk threads. I might rest upon its surface but never be of it. Is this what you meant earlier when I said particles of fabric must come loose.

A: It matters not, dust or fabric, unless you give them value. It's about your fluid perspective.

R: So that's the rub for all of this – how many soul perspectives are there?

A: They are infinite.

R: How do I know which focus to choose and in what order? How many of my consciousness separations are doing this at the same time?

A: Immeasurable – mind-boggling isn't it?

Think of a ***perspective*** as a formula within an Arkarna program – an instruction for a view point. And fluid perspective doesn't restrict access because it's aligned with the Isness of soul.

Robert is a program and soul consciousness is constantly flowing through that program. Yet the program believes it is Robert (which is what it is by design) and the program experience has no idea that its consciousness is part of a flowing feedback system.

CHAPTER 2

Moving beyond 'self' and the 'Arkarna programs of humanity'

Antemedi (A): Integrating Andromedan and Arcturian concepts about the nature of soul/universe will require effort. Some conversations show human mental restrictions to the absorption of higher dimensional information. As we remove the blockages you will be able to see how fluid thinking increases.

Humans experience a linear dimension and hold to a deep sense of self – in what and who they are. You are not as flexible as you believe. The Arkarna consciousness programs on earth affect your thoughts and understandings. They reinforce what you believe and how you think life is meant to be. Other humanoids have different understandings and consciousness programs.

For example, Arcturian Orlacka would say her life is very malleable. Moving in several dimensions she is able to observe aspects of her multidimensional selves and influence those timelines. Feelings do not sway her choices or dictate her emotional state. She does not process information through a part-known subconscious program. She is not empathic because she does not need to feel another person's pain in order to understand them. This way of life may seem removed from what you consider to be a meaningful or satisfying one but she lives in an Arkarna program relevant to her dimensions. Yet none of this defines life's purpose – does it?

The purpose of life is a topic I wish to touch upon at different times. You have your own sense of purpose and it serves some of you well – after all it should be a part of happiness and contentment.

Humanoids have several 'temporary experiences' on different vibrational planes. You may incarnate into multiple possibilities, but from the one you presently inhabit you define life's purpose collectively. It is created from all humanity's consciousness, emotional needs and apparent desires. Some of these are not heart-based but linked with ego or the need for self-worth. We consider these to be unhelpful expressions, unless they show their futile vanity against the light of the soul – leading to some form of change. I am not making judgements about the purpose of human life but asking you to be aware that there are unknown programs forming part of your subconscious. You have the ability to change those programs to suit any definition of yourself as you wish.

Humanity's purpose of life is often based in value, where measurement gives a meaning in relationship to something else. We consider that values and descriptions are restrictive. Perspective also reflects and is a function of the dimension it looks out from. You have many perspectives but these look from and through an existing database of consciousness which informs or prescribes what you see. How can you move away from the value of life – when the way you value it, gives life its very meaning and purpose? That said, the purpose of human life will have different meanings to the wealthy, healthy or poor.

When I introduced this subject, I was careful with my words: I said *purpose of life*. There is a nuance – *purpose* does not need to include *meaning of life* nor *value of life's meaning*. These are three different perspectives.

Robert (R): So, in a long-winded way you are saying the purpose of life, even when not given a value system, is subjective and held against the backdrop of what we currently know.

A: Yes – But I wish to impart a fuller understanding – that there are many varied and different purposes of life for humanoids. You are now thinking I am long-winded but I would say "I need to hold your hand in order to take you to places where you cannot see nor have the understanding to comprehend".

R: You are touching on observations made in the beginning of your last book.

A: Why not – even you haven't moved far from them. You may understand them to degrees but you don't fully live to them.

R: I accept your observation. I had a feeling of frustration and I allowed it to alter my state of emotional being. I appreciate you are preparing me for the next piece of information.

A: Good, because I have planned what I wish to impart. There are many purposes for you as a ***soul being*** but you are unaware of other potential. You hold tightly to your ideas and concepts because they give you meaning, without which you would be lost.

Imagine you have two carpetbags, one in each hand, containing all the ideas about the purpose of life. Let them drop to the ground and know that you are letting go of ***the purpose of life***. Take two steps forward and leave the bags behind along with the duality they contain.

You now have ***no purpose*** and because there is ***no purpose in you*** it means you have no value and nothing to value yourself with. At this point you are of ***no value*** – hard for a human mind to accept but you are simply casting aside measurement.

As you stand on the edge of a new plane you are also free from success and failure. Because you have no purpose you have nothing to compare anything with. Without systems of measurement how will you know what is here?

Move through the sensation that nothing is here to the shimmering energy in front of you and step through.

R: All noise has gone – thoughts have no reasons to exist and they serve no purpose. There is nothing to do or to be. Yet it doesn't feel devoid of life or love. It's uncomplicated – perhaps it doesn't need to have a purpose.

A: Let's go over that – life at this level does not need to have purpose in order that life should exist. Life exists without the need for purpose. It ***just is**** because you are the ***Isness**** (asterisk* word descriptions are in the final glossary at the end of the book).

R: Interesting that ***the purpose of life*** also has ***no purpose***, which is duality paradox, but here there is neither. There is ***no need for purpose*** and no prescribed way of what to be. But surely, we must accord with the Arkarna programs of each dimension.

A: Yes and no – it depends if the dimensional Arkarna program you are in is flexible enough to allow what you wish. As soon as you think from your database, about what you want to be, you are creating a definition. That will not accord with the vibration I am showing you.

R: So, freedom and no freedom are irrelevant and if we keep with the same theme, we seek to do nothing or just don't seek a purpose. We even dispense with the idea of not seeking. Presumably we become more compatible at this level.

A: Yes, hear our soul's voice as it communicates from the Isness.

Voice (V): You have understood there is nothing to value or measure here. Do not seek but allow.

But if you do not seek, will you still expect an unfolding? That is duality and means there is ***nothing to expect*** and ***everything to expect***. Even to expect the unexpected will bend ideas.

If I am you, why should you expect anything of yourself?

You do not need to give to yourself at this level, nor does it need to give to you. Within the Isness you are all, but you cannot say what it ***is***, nor what it ***is not*** because its none of those concepts.

Ideas that form at this soul level can filter down to lower dimensions and experience themselves. Soul life at lower levels might find value but it may not be the fullness of purpose. Others may find no purpose and experience that as despair.

Your mind constantly reverts to human constructs so I re-mind you of the difficulty in trying to understand a higher dimension from a lower one.

R: Re-mind as in deprogramming – I like the double-entendre.

V: However, do not hold fully to the truth that ***looking at a higher dimension from a lower one is futile*** – it is a duality and only one perspective on the path to others. They in turn will show the difficulty of trying to describe the Isness.

Lower vibrations do not have the cogs and wheels to fit into a higher soul Arkarna program. There is a common misunderstanding that higher levels are able to contain all that is below them. This originates from your god concept where everything is of god. Of course, there are connections between all things but not in the way you imagine. Dispensing that wider understanding is part of the purpose of these conversations.

I have spoken about this vibration by telling you what it is not in order to delete some of your human expectations. Do not ponder upon what is here because you will create a reflection of your pondering.

Orlacka said she does not question if she could be more enlightened because that means she is lacking something in herself. You think that is a childlike state, living in innocence but it isn't. It is an art – a mastery of oneself – that is to exceed the ***ideas of self.***

Whatever you question or conceive from ***self*** will flow back to you, as an ***answer for self***, but I can take you further into this realm beyond any inquisitiveness you have.

You are waiting for me to explain and show you what is here beyond your feelings of futility. Perhaps enhance your link to draw you along.

But I can't give you what you already have. You are seeing separation between us when there is none. You are the thought, actuation and experience. I am the part of you showing itself as ***voice*** – as an internal dialogue and communication of information. I do not need to experience anything; therefore, you cannot come to me and experience me as an experience – I am communication.

There is nothing to gain from me, otherwise that would be seen as enlightenment and progression towards something.

When experience is no longer relevant, other things are seen. You exist here without experience: it is not relevant – you are me and I you – no distance between us.

You are having an experience of me and because I reveal things to you, it makes you think I have an experience of helping you become more enlightened.

I do not have experience in the way you see it. I am not sure I could even say I am revealing something. I am part of your consciousness. You could liken me to an Arkarna program of awareness, moving within all myself as non-self. But I only become experiential awareness in parts of myself – like you who are having a life experience.

The program and the programmer are the same. Otherwise, who or what programmer would have made me as the program? That is to denigrate me as a program and see some higher entity beyond me.

R: Your understanding of my thought is correct, which of course it would be. I don't know what to think anymore – I feel I have gone past futility into nothingness.

Antemedi: I am interjecting because there is another way though this information transfer. Walk swiftly with me through this internal dialogue zone. It is a barrier, where your thoughts have conceptualised what is beyond the self. Self cannot see from the perspective of self, what is beyond itself. The doorway is not ***self-conscious*** in the way you are because self has no relevance to that part of you. You can only pass through this threshold when a sufficient amount of you has released its grip on the kind of experiences you are used to.

Scene: As we move forwards, we leave thoughts about nothingness behind. There are other entities here because I sense their presence, even though they cannot be seen. We enter a wonderful feeling of 'sanctuary' so different to low vibrational earth.

A: There is more multidimensional soul for you to meet. These are different aspects and expressions of our soul that exist beyond self.

Scene: Beings of pure light materialise their fluid energies and intermingle with one another. They are separate and one at the same time but they speak as one. "Welcome both. Robert, you struggled at the doorway to us – ***non-self soul*** **(NonSS)**. It is a void and a nothingness barrier. Antemedi brought you through when you no longer wanted to understand that which could not be understood.

Try not to see it as 'space between' because all vibrations exist in the same space. This was your way to experience moving between one vibration and another."

R: I was taken beyond machinations of nothingness to find that soul entity still exists! Something in nothingness?

NonSS: Nothingness is what you perceived to be the void in the doorway between us. You are moving within a part of ***non-self*** – that is why your way here felt ***devoid of self***.

You anticipated some higher entity existed beyond Robert-self but you failed to see that it is you. You do not recognise us as you. Let us move our energy around you while Antemedi steps back for a moment.

As a ***separation expression**** this is your experience of these information exchanges and communications. You exist on all sides of what you have seen but you superimpose the disappointment of ***not finding something greater*** onto the encounter with us. Your feelings are not fluid and you are judging and comparing yourself to an image of you that does not exist. Such things are only created in order to experience them. Remember it's just an experience – do not see your experience as the determination of who you are.

R: There is more beyond my self-experience, so are there different ways to experience things?

NonSS: You are still asking through the idea that you are an individual. All of what you say we understand but it cannot compute here. Questions relative to self are self-explanatory. In other words, you as ***self*** can question ***yourself*** and see all the answers within you. We are beyond questioning self and we are not of self but we are of soul. We are not combined duality nor the acceptance or rejection of it. We are beyond the reach of dualism.

R: Do I choose duality as a way to experience some levels of the universe?

NonSS: Depends what you mean by choose – we have a different way of seeing that. There is ***no choosing*** and ***not choosing*** because instead there is being or ***just is***. That's why reaching our outer edges in your present consciousness wasn't easy but it will improve as the information unfolds. It is ***information transfer*** and your way of integrating it. The description and non-description of us here was very much a reflection of you connecting with us.

There is no value in us and you will not be able to find any. We exceed value systems, which are restrictive and corrosive particularly when used without understanding. There is much that man would cast aside as being worthless because of his limited perception. Consciousness compatibility is part of this book. Like comes to like in terms of vibration but there is more to know. You do not know how other benevolent aliens function and at what level. Some of them are so far removed you would see them as pure light.

How do you define alien? Your soul is alien to you and many of its ways are unknown. You gain comfort thinking your soul is a safe place even if there are levels of it beyond comprehension. As a race you do not fully understand yourselves – so how can you know what the alien soul is, when you do not know the higher levels of your own self?

What levels of alien expression do you think would be compatible with your understanding?

R: We don't know what questions to ask about ourselves! And as you have shown we don't understand levels of soul without identity and self. All examination of our humanity through humanity reflects our thoughts. We think we are getting answers but they are only the ones that are compatible with our way of thinking.

NonSS: And there we have it – the realisation that understanding other races will not only be challenging but it will require a great deal of effort to understand the ***way they think***. You believe you will understand benevolents when physical contact takes place and you will – but only to the level that you can – and thus you will miss much.

Look at what we have shown today and how you struggled to make sense of the information. Do not underestimate the enormity of the differences between you and humanoids with higher vibrational frequencies. They are multidimensional souls and some of them have human extensions on earth, like Antemedi in you. That is not how the vast majority of people will see them even if they have a soul connection because such a link would be difficult for their ***self*** to accept.

As we surround you, feel the peace of not needing to understand. You don't need to in order to be worthy or more compatible. Remove yourself from the soul-self that makes comparisons to other spiritual beings.

There is no need to mould yourself. Wanting to be different is changing from one description to another, believing the next is the better version. We are saying there is no better version – better doesn't exist at these levels – it is of no consequence.

Humanity strives to achieve and it does, but it measures achievement in order to see that it is more or better. That is the experience within humanity – till it is not. Letting go of measuring self-worth will enable love of self to flow more easily.

We have no way to measure you – not that we would seek to do so – it does not compute.

R: At this point they surround me. I feel loved and I am able to do things without the ***have to*** or ***should do***. I don't need to improve myself. The fact my light is dimmer than those around me is irrelevant. With comparison deleted, our energies unify in greater vibrational compatibility. I am different but that is of no significance. I could say that I am equal, but I am not, because that's measurement. We are the same whilst not being the same.

Good grief – now I am in their energy what they said earlier makes sense! Can I explain the depth or width of being here! Its beyond explanation – It ***just is***. There is no more to be done nor understood. This is not some state of bliss from being stoned or incapable of movement through alcohol. It's not even a Zen moment or a deep stillness of meditation. I am in the now – I'm typing and it feels like I have exceeded the need to exceed. I am flapping with words when there is no need.

NonSS: Difference is of no consequence – we are variations to the expression of ***being***. There is nothing that needs be said and nothing stands between our communications. Our energy can be with you and you with us. It is as it was before but now you know it is so. (And with that they fade.)

Antemedi: They are part of our soul of non-self – they are information and knowledge of soul beyond Orlacka – they are alien and non-alien. They have shown you ideas that cannot be contained in plurality or experiences of self. Many benevolent aliens exist in the feelings you just felt because their consciousness is at one with the Isness. Living attuned to all – that is and is not – the Isness.

R: And you live in that?

A: A lot of the time but I have experiences and choices. However, I would need to use new words because of the way we exist as ***community self****.

R: The nearer we get to understand you the further away we seem to be.

CHAPTER 3

Releasing human desires – connecting deeper with Soul Isness

Robert (R): Following the last journey I feel disjointed. Nothing I do has value and I can't see rewards, be they successful or unsuccessful. Life has taken on a pointlessness, even helping other people is flat. It doesn't matter where I search in my thoughts or deeds, life seems to have no meaning.

Antemedi (A): Life may have a purpose but you are looking for a meaning to life, which is a different matter. You fail to see its new meaning in the context that it has no value. You can't find satisfaction on your side of the divide unless you ignore the struggle to find meaning. You have gone past the struggle, but sense it lurking in the background.

There is a welling of inevitable change and your mind twitches and discerns movements before they happen. What is to become of you?

That is impossible to determine using your current database. The closer you come to the Isness the more your human concepts fail to make sense. Your Arkarna programs are all reward based. Even a lack of reward in duality, with false pleasure in suffering fails to provide. None of this makes sense and your systems of desire are breaking down.

Let it all go – achievements, their highs, lows or lack of them. Your life is not about badges, putting things right, paving the way for family or others. All of that has been an experience and you no longer need to achieve.

R: That's a big ask – that's like saying don't be human.

A: It is one definition of being human but it will release you from your current confines.

R: Frustrating – unless I give up on the giving up.

A: Then follow me as we connect deeper with the Isness.

Scene: Going inwards space becomes brighter and I sense a release – it's very easy and unassuming, as if I had nothing to be released from.

A: Humans often make choices for the stimulation they create. You do something for someone else – you might please them and they thank you. In my Andromedan realms there is no reward because the ***Isness love**** needs no reward. A thank you does not give a beneficial pay-off triggered by dopamine. You don't need to do anything to get a pay-off. A reward has no meaning to the ***driving forces of life*** because the parameters have changed.

We do not seek pleasure – we exist as is – we do not seek what we have. These concepts have been described before, they sound true, but actually living to them is very different. Unlike us you do not feel they are an integral part of life's purpose. By abandoning what you had before you will have a different way of loving and creating.

When cause and effect are bounded by desires and measurements, you think and act from them. Everything you create comes back to you as ***returned energy****. Your answers are constrained by duality which needs to be ***self-satisfied***.

Imagine creating with love that has no pre-conditions or expectations. The ability to create will change because you will be creating without boundaries (like Mowhar). The energy and love that you use will create results from a deeper level of Isness.

This applies to our work in this outreach program. I do not expect a thank you, nor seek to garner a good impression of who I am.

Readership thoughts about me will not change my self-worth or the love I have for myself. The point is, my sense of self and sense of self-worth have no boundaries and nothing improves nor takes from that.

R: GGRRR! What you say is so true and I know it in my heart but I am torn between these worldviews. I am neither in one nor the other. I feel my humanity is dying. It's become defunct – not fit for purpose – yet I am not in your world either.

A: You are working within the confines of your collective consciousness as well as stumbling through some of your de-energised subconscious programs. Let's go deeper – you don't have to do anything because Orlacka will give you another perspective.

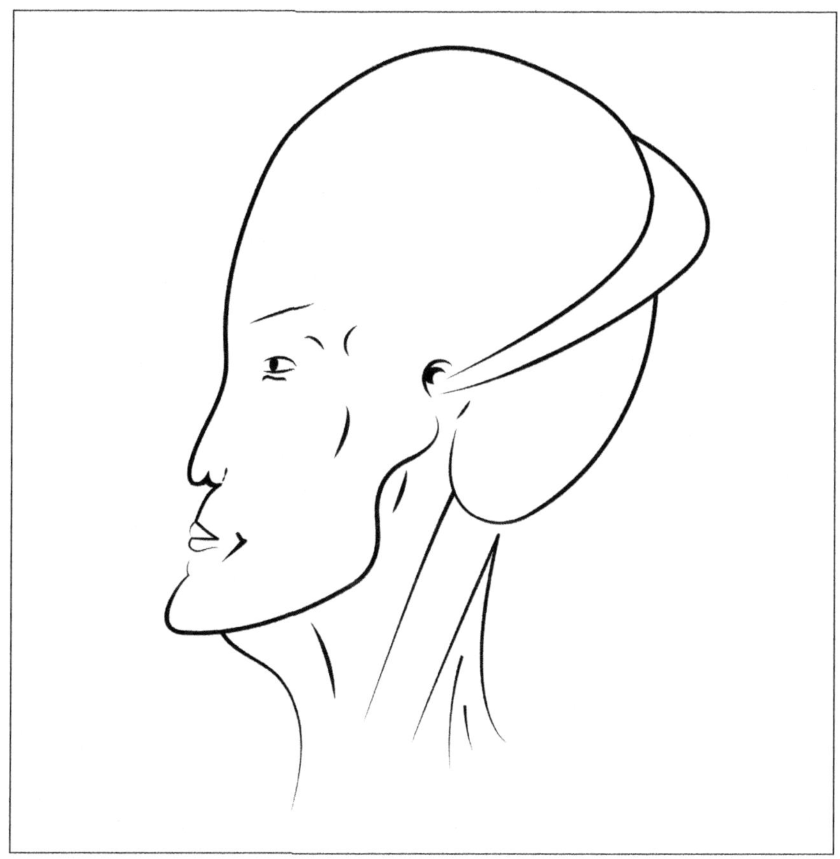

Orlacka

R: Orlacka is a 12th dimensional Arcturian hermaphrodite and part of our soul. She has no ears but energy emanates from where they would have been. This energy flows over the top and back of her head. The two ear positions are the start and finish of this band of light. Her head is elongated and her main features are in the lower section. She has no discernible hair but her blue skin is quite captivating. I say that now, although I was quite perturbed with her looks when I was a child. She lives and works within Arkarna observer programs that are not affected by the act of observing. She can however, help other aspects of her soul, like me, if they get stuck. I have worked with her many times and I am very fond of her.

Orlacka (OL): And I likewise of you. So, we can say one Arkarna program appreciates another one when accepting that soul and entity are also programs. Anyway, enough of reinforcing your link to non-self with humour.

I will help you with another perspective. Let go of letting go was a phrase used before. That is to stop letting go and realise it's been done. You only have to accept your altered reality – then there is nothing more to do. Imagine you have transitioned and then see that you have. Do not look again because that will create the need for reassurance.

Peace is here and there are no conflicting thoughts formed in desire. Take a sleep and in the morning after your travels you will be different.

The next day:

R: Communication has shifted a gear. The flotsam and jetsam from yesterday have gone. Whilst those conversations helped, they no longer have a purpose. Ironically, I am happy to say my thoughts are of no use, because there is no judgement to say they are useless or not. Arcturian Orlacka from yesterday is still here. I am getting instant and deeper information presentations from soul voice **(V)** it's similar to before but more of a ***just is***.

V: We suggest you see ***constant communication*** as omnipresent. Firstly, it will help change your outlook and secondly provide information more quickly. You are an expression of soul and you can hear your soul communicating with you from its connection with Isness.

Quite how you see it – as soul, Antemedi, Orlacka or one of your other expressions is a matter of subjectivity because they are also your soul's projections. You will say who is who and who talks to whom? Well, that's down to your ability to take such concepts on board.

You are these other beings as expressions of form and they, like you, are temporary. You are a series of expressions in different densities, creating residual energies to be transmuted as timeline shimmers.

At higher levels you have life but what is its fullness of purpose? Because it is not life as you know it, we need to put aside ***purpose*** and ask ***what is life***?

R: It's not life as we know it, Jim!

V: I am aware of that Star Trek phrase. The crew struggled with compassion, morality and human desire in the face of alternative values. It's more relevant as a study of human interactions than as a science fiction series.

Antemedi asked what is the purpose of life, as if to say life has a purpose, otherwise what is life? I will unfold a variation which you can see through Orlacka. What life is and what actually constitutes life is much more complex than you could ever imagine.

Orlacka (OL): Take your focus outside your physical body and look at the 5th vortex above your head. It is emanating more light than those above and below it. That is where I am communicating to you from – your 12th chakra. Omnipresence means you can interface more easily with deeper aspects of our soul and its connectivity to the Isness.

You question: what is Robert-self and where is the autonomy in your life? We have previously discussed freedom and unveiled alternative ideas about autonomy. Antemedi explained coherently that it did not really exist, but neither did restriction or control and it was all a matter of perspective. It is possible to live without ***autonomy***.

Autonomy can be actuated and lived within this part of the Isness. But it is not autonomy in a relationship to the idea of self. The more duality concepts you discard the more you become connected to the Isness and the rest of yourself, including me.

It will become more apparent with practice. I can't describe what will be and I wouldn't, even if I could put it in terms you could understand. To do so would take away your experience of discovery.

R: Then life is a discovery and an unfolding.

OL: Only if you wish to see it that way because your soul already knows it – otherwise it couldn't unfold it. Why should we tell you of tomorrow when today's discovery is in this day? Has it not unfolded to the complexities and resistances that your humanity placed in front of it?

R: The discoveries are a little flat and having reached this point there are no dramatic revelations.

OL: What good would drama do? Show you my knowledge, tease you as to what is possible or be outrageous for the sake of it! Has today not been a revelation for you? If I show you what you cannot understand, what good would that do?

Your statement contains a flicker of doubt that seeks reassurance because we are talking about different ways to function.

R: Antemedi said, "What is the purpose of life?" so what is life's purpose in its relationship to the unfolding Isness?

OL: Let communication form itself. Experience it and do not think about definitions. Live beyond the need to trust your ***self*** – neither do you need to trust ***non-self***. Communication ***just is***.

Antemedi: Interesting, was it not?

R: Another door has opened but I am not entirely sure what I've walked into.

CHAPTER 4
Arcturian non-values seen from human measurement

Antemedi (A): How's it going with the upgraded communication interface?

Robert (R): You should know – you are me.

A: Indeed, I do. But I am asking because I wish to bring your attention to what it means for you.

R: It is a voice of conscience and communication that's always there. In a similar way, Jiminy Cricket was the moral compass for Pinocchio. It's the conscience I've always had (that everyone has got) but I didn't properly engage with. It's now a loud two-way interaction. I talk and receive helpful answers and at other times it provides observations without me instigating communication.

A: Mind speaks to itself – nothing different to what we have explained before but it is clearer.

R: I suspect I have been avoiding some of those conscience prompts in order to keep the older versions of myself.

A: That's understandable. But there is no need to keep to the previous versions which observed failures and used a stick to move you forward. You are receiving information formed closer to the Isness.

Scene: Antemedi clears the space around us. We stand on a flat plane in a pale cream energy. Orlacka comes forward with other Arcturians including a male called Gulwah (in the past he has been good at putting over information – this time I know he is here to help with some sort of energy balancing). Gulwah moves to my left while Orlacka remains on my right. Antemedi remains several steps behind me. There are three others in front as we begin to walk forwards.

Observing the three in front I note their features and energy. They are Robert, Orlacka and Gulwah. They are either a reflection or a projection of us. They are doing things in advance, a few moments ahead.

Orlacka (OL): You knew that instantly and without doubt – it was ***knowing*** – a form of communication. (*Awareness of information without an apparent source or explanation – not a free flow of information to be understood or deciphered but a package of knowledge that just is. A comprehensive instantaneous assimilation of understanding which is beyond doubt*) Let us walk faster so we catch them up, inhabit their space and make it ours.

R: Human observation sees ***results in the moment of now***, not the information that formed them. My head moves forward of my body as if it had been pushed through a looking glass. I am seeing things in advance of my body. My database is behind me and has no influence. My human operating system is following and meeting me, but it's always a few steps behind.

OL: It is all a matter of who you think you are. You believe you are Robert but we are showing you what exists forward of that perception.

I hear your thoughts, "it's still a subjective experience for you viewed from your human psyche, which is less fluid, so your experience is unlikely to be the same as ours".

R: You have just taken my muddled thoughts and explained them more coherently than I could.

OL: That is another facet of being closer to the Isness and other aspects of your soul-self and soul-non-self. Let us walk on.

R: I am dragging a huge weight and it is difficult to move.

OL: The ground has spiked your database bag, so give it a big tug and rip the bottom open. How do you feel about moving forwards and leaving behind your human perspectives?

R: Intellectually it shouldn't be a problem because it's just an experience. But I feel very unwell, my emotions are in turmoil. I am leaving my real self behind and I need it to function.

Scene: Gulwah and Orlacka each take each an arm. After a few paces I feel completely hollow – I am an energetic shell with no substance. A brighter light engulfs me, filling the hollow spaces. My ankles feel constrained so Gulwah and Orlacka project energy behind me to cut emotional bonds. Moving forwards, pinging sensations inform me that tight cords have been severed.

We encounter similar forward projections of myself. Each time I arrive in them the experiences are different. Upon entering the last one I am calm but full, as if I cannot contain any more of me. Then 'unzipped at the front' I flow forward as a mist of fluid energy. It takes a few moments to adjust as I merge with Orlacka and Gulwah. With no barriers between us I feel no deference – not that I was in awe before, but now I am at one with both of them.

OL: Welcome to greater union. There are explanations to give you, which can only be understood in this vibrational union.

R: Orlacka asks me if I have any questions but I have nothing to usefully contribute. The moment is profound without being profound. It is rich and full and ripe but not in contrast to that which is not. Duality has little effect here, that's why I do not feel separate from Orlacka and Gulwah. In addition to telepathy and the knowing, there is also another communication at some level. An interaction without the need to know about the information we are exchanging. Sharing all knowledge regardless of what it means – not needing to be ***fully conscious*** of our interactions with each other. Underpinning this is ***the knowing*** there's no division other than the illusion of being separate entities.

OL: In your culture much has been said about 'being at one and part of god' but we do not see it that way. You are experiencing this as a ***feeling of union*** as it unfolds to you. It's a temporary feeling while you move from one state of being to another. It's difficult to describe the indescribable and unlimited. I accept descriptions have in part helped you reach this point. They were a way of unfolding your consciousness that lived in a measurement-based realm.

We have no need to utilise feelings like you do. It gives you a conundrum – how can we have concern if we hold no value to it? The logical conclusion makes it seem as if we don't care. But we give no care to it – no concern – no value – it is not relevant to our way of being.

You wonder, "What is relevant to our way of being?" I have difficulty in responding to that because your question is formed in a value-based system. You may think it's an open question but you are expecting a value-based answer because you are having difficulty with my previous non-value replies. In order to reveal this realm, I cannot reply in your language. I will cleave another facet off your measurement perspective.

Value has no currency. Value is comparison and is observed against that which is of more or less value. I could say that *all here is of equal value* but that wouldn't be correct either. We have love and it is a very deep union of love with understanding – it just is and it is as bountiful as you have tried to describe. However, I do not have compassion in my consciousness, though it is a noble value in yours. Look closely at my words, "it is a noble ***value*** in yours" the value that lays in the centre informs all around it. I do not feel sad for someone on a lower dimension when they encounter difficulty and pain. They formed and created the parameters to need such an experience and it's their choice until they choose otherwise.

You know I love you with all that I am – but what I am is not of value. We are as one and the feeling of that will become greater when you are not bound by any measurement. I cannot feel sorry for you in the way that you do for others. I am free from such constraints. Feeling sorry for someone doesn't help them move away from what they choose to experience. My choosing to feel their pain doesn't help them. If that is empathy, I have no need for it. I am not empathic but neither am I indifferent nor filled with apathy.

Pain is the resistance to change and suffering is one way of coping with it. Instead embrace life events as a natural unfolding of self-created timelines formed from the previous energies you expressed. You have the opportunity in every moment to transmute your energy into another expression. In this way new experiences come to you with higher vibrational contexts. Because I don't have sympathy in the way that you do, doesn't mean I don't love. I love you enough not to take away from you the experiences you create. Neither should I save you – when you have the ability to experience saving yourself. To doubt that you can save yourselves is an experience of doubt and it forms your reality. To say you are already saved means nothing to you because you have no awareness of your true self.

Do you see I have passion and I am not indifferent? Does my wisdom dissipate your values? It's all a matter of perspective and what you understand to be love.

R: Some of this material has similarities to the benevolent Mantoids we encountered on another occasion (note: there are several different species of Mantoids – others are known for being aggressive and warlike).

OL: Yes, very much so but there are differences between us and them.

R: Could you expand on that?

OL: If I give an answer your unconscious will conclude that questioning can be useful when connecting deeply to the Isness. Musing becomes a question when the parameters form and they dictate the type of reply you require. Nothing wrong with asking questions, providing you are aware you constrain and pre-form the answers. You need to be less prescriptive.

R: I thought it was an open question – the only way I can be less prescriptive is to keep my mouth shut.

OL: Then do so. I have not shut you down nor restricted you; it is another reminder not to question the Isness but allow the Isness to be you.

R: Then questions won't exist in the same way. If there is a problem or situation, I sit with it and let the Isness show options. If I choose an option, that act will be a reflection of me.

OL: Is that a question or a statement?

R: It's a reflection of who I am and it's an observation that flowed from the Isness.

OL: Then we are speaking as one. Earlier you felt there was nothing separating us other than the sense of self. In many ways this could describe how the Mantoids commune because knowledge and understanding are *acquired*. They have individual experiences but communion between them means they share their experiences. Their inter-dependence means that Arkarna separation programs are not the basis of acquiring information, because experience is common when shared. This becomes part of their wisdom base but like us it has no value put upon it.

R: I am seeing similarities between you and their childlike hive inquisitiveness but you still have your individual expression.

OL: Childlike inquisitiveness has no value system and the Mantoids are more open to repeating their experiences than we are. By that I don't mean they look to repeat them but they don't look to see if they are repeating them. They put no parameters on the Isness and what it brings to them because they live fully within the Isness as themselves.

R: Do you monitor your life so you don't repeat experiences again?

OL: Arkarna programs create the realm of experience you desire. These interact and reflect back to you the experience you need or the one you think is best suited to you. We do not want our Arkarna programs to give us 'run repeat' in the way that 3D humans do. Nor do our Arkarna programs have timelines created from transmuting our energy. We are able to choose a different option from what the Isness provides and not from the parameters you have.

That said the point you made also applies to us. Once we generate a choice, we have created a parameter or actuated a series of experiences in a different timeline. However, we can also change the choice at any time if it suits an outcome that's more pertinent. We are actively involved in creating fluid experiences from the Isness.

The Mantoids you experienced do not have that within their Arkarna programs. Nothing matters in terms of value and some of their experiences can come around again, but only to the level of the realm they are on. They have options to 'experience' and 're-experience' or be the observer. They can also observe the observer's experience. They are omnipresent of those aspects whilst at the same time being at one and aware of each other. They do all this without parameters or a particular need to be anything. On the face of it, it seems less directional than ours. That is why so many find their ways fascinating. Some humanoids believe that utilising an extremely diverse, non-directional Arkarna program is a good way to become more enlightened.

We don't see it that way because there are elements of soul that are beyond self entirely. The proposition is that self doesn't exist for them because of their unity and community, however their unity is a form of self-colony. These are slightly different approaches to the Isness. It doesn't mean there are better or worse ones, just variations. We and the Mantoids trust the Isness within us to allow all possibilities. We are more proactive with the Isness but not with judgement or needs and this gives a fluid choice that fluctuates.

Through guidance we help parts of our soul change residual energies and integrate away from their separation experience. Unlike us – that particular group of Mantoids did not create soul trauma in order for it to be healed. In effect they are on a different path to us and I can't really say if our paths will unify but we are still all part of the Isness. There is no requirement for our total soul to be re-integrated because free will means at some level of Isness it has happened even if not ever experienced.

Arkarna programs are as much an extension of you, as you are of them. All your lives are happening in the now in various Arkarna programs. Your consciousness (another personal Arkarna program) stitches these together in a stream of consciousness.

R: Thank you for answering my question without reflecting back the parameters of asking.

OL: You wish to move onto what you believe are more interesting subjects such as pulse and dimensions. However, exploring alternative perceptions of ***the purpose of life*** is more pertinent. Not value but order, confluence and increasing fluidity helps us explain soul more easily.

R: ***The meaning of life*** – more unusual than Monty Python's comedy film of the same title!

OL: We are talking about the purpose of life, not the measurement or meaning of it. We are looking at life and love without parameters and judgement.

CHAPTER 5

Human blueprints – formation of soul at source

Akinneyah (AK): Hello Robert, we have spoken before but your Arkarna memory program (mind compartments) did not allow you full knowledge of that.

If my interaction with you is in your Arkarna memory programs, how should it present itself? You think human memories are reflections of what happened in the past. But in this instance a memory of what you did in another part of your mind is being accessed through your present, which has no past experience of it. That's different to your current idea of a memory.

Mind is a series of Arkarna programs, which function within the remit of each dimensional Arkarna program. Someone can interact with you whilst your focus is elsewhere or on another level of your multidimensional self. Mind is fluid and there is no time in the moment of now.

Everything is an Arkarna program and any part of ***all that was, is and will be*** can be accessed. It is not the same as encountering a series of events as you do presently. To explain I will need to slow down the Arkarna and bring events to a stop.

Scene: At this point I am able to take a better look at her. She is dark skinned wearing a light blue tunic with floppy arm coverings. I feel her coarse skin as she touches my hand. She lifts our arms till they form an archway – within the space sparks and colours flow. I feel her thoughts affecting the flowing energy. A single point forms and light ripples outwards in spherical rings leaving a small area of darkness at the centre.

AK: It's not lost on you that I have an affinity with this core. Our minds opened a link so your present awareness could access it. Come with me – nothingness is quite safe.

During your travels you have encountered lighter and faster vibrating realms, you saw this as a natural progression. Nothingness doesn't have a program. This experience feels like a space, because that's my presentation. It's a good way to conceptualise and work with nothingness.

Let us suppose the lack of light is the frozen moment between the pulse energy of 'on and off'. You are experiencing the 'between pulse' as a continual phase and a place all of its own. This darkness is not the same as lower dimensions with unpleasant entities because they would still need Arkarna programs and energy to exist.

Pulses of vibration manifest as different dimensions of experience and these can be influenced by soul. The *between pulse* has no light, no programme and no provision for experience. As the pulse goes from ***off*** to ***on*** its potency is instant. The variations of intensity correspond to different dimensions. The 'off' is also instantaneous. Using the word ***burst*** will enable you to see light at each point of pulse. There is no movement, only a variation in pitch – an ***Is*** then an ***Is not***. The burst or pulse is everywhere and there is nowhere that it does not exist. This corresponds to the advancement of origin being ***possible*** and ***not possible***.

Bursts are incredibly fast vibrations that do not extend from where they were generated. All appears at once, in form, everywhere in relevant dimensions. In that way everything appears to materialise as a completeness and constancy.

There are a multitude of intensities that accord to different dimensions. 3D consciousness resonates to one, whilst other parts of your consciousness resonate with different aspects of pulse in other dimensions. Arkarna programs stitch together the awareness of pulse and make sense of it so each dimension has its own reality.

Your mind can move between dimensions and you can be aware of several at the same time. They appear as overlays in your vision and it's a natural state of mind. All humans could do this if they untrained their minds from present belief systems.

R: Does pulse energy emanate from the shining blackness?

AK: Yes, the shining blackness is everywhere: it is a way to see both source energy and non-source energy. You've already been told pulse is self-perpetuating and doesn't need the energy of creation. Creator energy formed the pulse energies of source but the two are not the same.

I am information about Creator energy appearing to you as a construct. Without such a backdrop information transfer would be hampered. What do you think? Creator energy is just an energy?

R: Am I talking to information before the creation of our universe?

AK: Why are you so against that idea? Why are you limiting your mind to certain possibilities rather than having an open pliable mind? When you have more explanations, you will understand.

How would you converse with ***Creator energy***?

R: Talking with you seems a good way.

AK: Mowhar was the great paradox, which became an entity that gave birth to your universe. Through her marvellous expansive programs, ***Creator energy*** became ***Source*** and ***Mowhar*** became ***Arkarna programs***. From source comes the perpetuating pulse energies. Arkarnas create the information fields that inform dimensional realities. We will explain later how Creator energy came about.

Souls can change and influence Arkarna programs, and in that way, they reflect creation because they are creating something else to experience. We could say Creator and Mowhar blueprints live on in you.

The shining blackness is the soul's union at source. The seat of your soul with its complexity, multidimensionality, creativity and love. Some might say this is the soul's birthplace. Souls are intrinsically linked to a universe and its dimensions. Soul interfaces through its Arkarna programs and the corresponding ones of the universe. You have interacted with Feline, Avian, Mantoid and Cytith (amphibian) humanoid Arkarnas but there are many other expressions from the soul of shining blackness.

R: I understood we could evolve, vibrate faster and shift to another dimension, where we are already.

AK: That's true and you can also choose not to put your consciousness into lower vibrational Arkarnas and leave them as un-energised programs. You create and influence what energy goes into what Arkarna program level.

R: Okay I can go with that but there are other levels of me conscious on higher dimensions like Orlacka. They are creating and moving energies for themselves as well as me. On earth we re-encounter the energy we made and that forms the probability of the timelines.

AK: Yes, and that doesn't curry favour with your definition of autonomy. I would suggest you see them as the rules of the Arkarnas you function within. The origin of these rules formed in Mowhar before she became Arkarna programs.

R: Akinneyah can't be your name because you are a construct.

AK: I am what I represent myself to be, a reflection of Creator energy. I created a name for you to experience my understandings. I am an archetype/blueprint and a basis of humanoid expression. I am set against the creation of the shining blackness. You are humanoid and I am a part of your Arkarna program. Thought can present itself in an enjoyable way and you are enjoying your internal communication as my presentation.

To explore Creator energy, we need to talk about Mowhar because they are intrinsically linked. They are aspects of each other with different attributes. Mowhar is a probability program with 'ideas happening' where it's connected to possibility. Some ideas did not come to full fruition. If a pathway fails, it falls by the wayside and probability returns so it can expand again in a different way. Only later does Mowhar and Creator energy become aware of its failed or corrupted possibilities.

It all takes place within paradox of ***is*** and ***is not***. As ***awareness**** programs expand they reflect paradox and have ***parameters*** and ***no parameters***. The programs in Mowhar grow to become more aware within the context of paradox.

Creator energy also evolved because Mowhar awareness allowed additional programs for itself and Creator energy. It's not an effort of awareness or focus. It is just a self-perpetuating program. Now that you understand how Creator energy has evolved you can see it as a part of ***the all*** rather than some all-knowing god entity.

CHAPTER 6

Energy systems and making choices

Scene: It is exceptionally calm, yet ironically, I am excited with anticipation. It's a very unusual blend of two opposite feelings but it feels very natural. Isness is how duality feels when in harmony. Not only does it feel natural but it's our natural state of being.

Yet underlying all this is a sense of impending loss in order to gain something different. The choice to go further in seems 'not relevant' and I just go with the flow. I had feared the loss of Robert-self, but the further in I go, the less I feel I am Robert and consequently the less that seems to matter. Light forms into indistinct shapes and I hear my soul voice.

Voice (V): Cast your mind back to the day of non-stop poetry and writing 'The boy, the beast and the nothingness'. That day you were mostly Antemedi. You let go of your identity and self in order that you could enter the shining blackness. You described it as a journey into bliss and wonder. Today you are being supported by your higher soul energies, giving you the stability to hear and record deeper insights. The voice is soul as information transfer.

R: I am getting quite a headache!

V: It will come and go. It will take several days for the entwined information to flow and make sense. Eventually the last paragraph will take you back to the first – then you will see its completeness. Let me put an energetic seed in your head.

Scene: I watch the energies swirl in and out of my head whilst typing. This is a potent and truly fulfilling multidimensional experience. Spinning threads encompass my whole body, internally and externally. An egg shape of energy forms with a human profile in it. It's in my mind but also standing in front of me.

V: You are seeing the energy of the interface with your voice. You have many questions but let me have the floor. I could start at the beginning but there isn't a beginning in the way you imagine.

Physical matter can change because it's a hologram of energies that correspond to the information in the pulse vibration. The Arkarna programs formulate the information in the pulse. At human levels of intent, you interact with your Arkarna body programs that maintain function and movement.

I am information and an interface. My ideas are mine and I am autonomous, even at a lofty realm. However, when I say 'I' and 'mine' this is ***not of the self*** – it's a more encompassing non-self than that. I am your voice but I am an internal Arkarna communication program, connecting with information that is pertinent to your needs in any moment. You are the information as well as the process by which the information passes. I have said 'you' in the last sentence only to show the encompassing soul. Your language is insufficient – I have used 'I' in reference to myself but I am a ***process of the system of you***, who is self and non-self.

Scene: Everything goes still and energy from the egg shape flows into me, joining with the previous swirls and loops. Again, it's within and also standing in front of me.

V: The beginning and end exist, but each is the former because they are at one with each other. The shining blackness is all things, but these statements leave you unfulfilled, even though it's the honesty of what is.

You were anticipating the final end so that it could be compared to the very first beginning. But there are many endings and at other levels there is no beginning and no ending.

Desire is an energy that forms an experience and each moment of that experience is an ending – that's why there is no limit to the number of endings.

R: I'm struggling to suppress an idea but out pops 'I thought all things were known'.

V: Known by whom and at what level? Arkarna programs are highly complex systems working on many levels, but they are also malleable. Look upon them as ***thought forms*** that have free will to expand and become anything. Arkarnas have no restrictions nor find it necessary to hold to any existing idea. Formed from Mowhar they have emotions and the ability to grow. Arkarna programs span the dimensions and the numerous planes within them. You interface with these free-flowing Arkarna dimension programs and the worlds they support. We see thought processes which have formed – either it is or isn't viable – good or bad isn't part of that.

You think the programs must have taken a long time to develop but time is not part of that process. Your modern computers no longer have reels of tape and technology gives nearly instant answers. Mowhar's development was instantaneous, but your observation alters that perception. There is no distance between the question and the final outcome because they reside in the same moment. Even if it has to be a moment.

Perplexing for you again, confronted by paradoxes that sit uncomfortably together. Time and time again you face the prospect of not seeing time. By the way, that was humour and irony, not excluded from any level!

Your world and its Arkarna programs have resultant outcomes, which are a series of endings that never stop or finish. The outcomes are known if the Arkarna program parameters are known. Which of course they are, because the Arkarna program is aware of all aspects of what is to be created. I repeat ***all aspects*** are involved in a moment – it cannot be any more or less than what the Arkarna program is. The whole system functions. It may be a massive program, but if I refer to it as being alive it conjures up a softer feeling. No information is left out and the resultants that are seen – are what is. They are a function of each other – total program and result. It can be no other way – it is.

Everything you create is a form of energy, it belongs to you because it is you. This is ***created energy****. It may be energy in the universe but it is still you by virtue of the fact you created it. Furthermore, you are the universe and it is you, so the energy you leave in the universe you leave in yourself.

The energy remains as ***residual energy**** and is the embodiment of your expression because you are what you have created. However, you re-encounter the residual energy of yourself because you are experiencing yourself, which is the original expansion of Mowhar. These residual energies form timelines – events in order to experience what you have created yourself to be.

You react to your residual energy: either reinforcing it or transmuting it to a different expression or creation of yourself. ***Transmuting energy**** changes your energy and adjusts your timelines. If you change unhelpful thoughts you can create from an altered state of residual energy. A previous explanation described these as shimmers, the movements you make when encountering your energy, which adapts and creates your timelines. These interface with the Arkarna programs, forming the next pulse of the physical hologram. All of which is known because it is the program entity that will form it.

You are each creating your own personal timelines with your individual energies. You can have common timelines but experience the event in different ways. This is because ***all that your energy is*** will be different to another person and they will interpret to accord with their own worldview and personal energy. The energy you all take from a joint event experience varies.

If you held a fluorescent light in fog the particles of moisture closer to the tube would be brighter. The moisture that's further away becomes blurred to the point the tube appears as a distant glow. If the tube is a timeline, then you can see the greatest activity is around the main cohesion.

In Orlacka's dimension, your timelines can be observed. There you would see several routes, some of which split and some that come back on themselves. At those levels it's possible to see the Arkarna program and variations of timeline choice.

You are an entity, interfacing with its own energy through a complex but highly evolved program, where the outcomes of choice are known.

But are choices made as you encounter a decision or are you just experiencing the appearance of choice?

The answer is – choices happen all at once – difficult for your linear mind to conceive. Imagine a computer that can work out all possible outcomes. Then whenever or wherever you walked away from your timeline the next step would take you back. Your energy is always with you till you change it. Your Arkarnas are working with your energy and automatically know you and the outcome because they created it. They are extensions of you and vice versa.

It's not about predetermination but the experiences your energy creates. If you change your energy, you will have a different outcome. This is where your choice is made – you have the choice to choose your residual energy by keeping it or transmuting it. This is free will but not man's idea of free will exercised against restriction. It is free will seen through the idea of self within a paradox.

For you it's about the experience of yourself. Or should I say the experience of remembering it. That's what Akinneyah talked about – accessing a memory in part of the mind, compartmentalised by Arkarna programs. As you put your focus into this memory of you, it feels like a new experience. Some may see this as fate or fatalism but it's not. That's not being able to accept that your mind has separated itself in forgetfulness programs in order to have the experiences it does.

Akinneyah's memory explanations now make more sense. Do you wish to carry on or take a rest?

R: You know the outcome to your question – so are you showing me the appearance of choice within my compartmentalised mind when it's already been made?

V: Been and done are the past – there is no past or future but yes, as a function I am aware of your choice. Choices and experiences exist within awareness but does the soul need to focus upon them? Choices are also part of an Arkarna program and an excellent one at that. Choices made in your Arkarna programs also influence others and their choices affect you as well.

Do you really have choice if you don't know all the choice possibilities? The choice to restrict choice however is an experience within compartmentalisation and one of many unlimited choices. If this be love you might think it's not loving – but that's you not understanding the nature of the universe.

R: Thank you – you have shown me how I view choice and freedom through the experience of ***self***. I didn't fully integrate what you said earlier. "It's not about predetermination but what experiences your energy creates."

I now have the ***knowing***: if you change your energy you will have a different outcome. This is where your choice is made – you have the choice to choose your residual energy by keeping it or transmuting it. This is true free will – not man's idea of free will exercised against restriction. The Arkarnas are my program reflecting me – they don't make the choices of the events to come, despite what I may feel. I am the creator and I can choose my energy.

CHAPTER 7
Union of non-self

R: 'I' – if I can use that word. I see that the English language is very limited. You are a living program of non-self and are communicating with me in all sorts of wonderful ways, yet you use '*I*', '*me*' and '*we*' when you refer to yourself. I cannot describe you adequately, for in the previous sentence I refer to you as 'you' when that is an attribute of self. Is there any way round this?

Voice (V): Well, emotion and connection are a part of who you and I are. The term Arkarna is used next to 'program' to reference program and non-self as a part of you – as a system. I and other aspects will expand upon the explanation of you as a system as we progress.

Etiqa* is an Andromedan word that encapsulates the 'I' of non-self and the union of 'I' as self – in this way they are extensions of each other. But if I were to use Etiqa liberally it wouldn't help because it's not in your mindset and the earth collective consciousness. We could use it for the sense of ***I as a program of soul*** that is talking with myself (you) but it would not help.

"***Etiqa*** can see it will not be helpful" – it is the same as saying – "I can see it will not be helpful".

The English language is based within and from the perspective of self – 'humans of self' evolved the language to fit their view of themselves which did not include non-self. So, for that reason I will continue to use '*I, me, myself, ours & we*' because it helps the narrative to flow.

As we move further into the book you will gain a greater sense that you are a system and that will ease the difficulty of self-perspective on non-self.

CHAPTER 8

Shining Blackness – you created yourself

Voice (V): The ***shining blackness*** and the seat of the soul are intertwined with each other. The human form has many alien variations and is one of the chosen outcomes of the wonderful Arkarna programs.

We are accelerating connections to your other dimensions so you may begin to sense the wholeness of multidimensional soul.

R: I am feeling that, thank you.

V: Creator energy does not have the 'god super consciousness' that you imagined from self. That's a human concept that 'some omnipotent being or entity holds the workings of the universe in its consciousness'. Humanity projected its experience of self and its consciousness onto origin.

Akinneyah talked about blueprint probabilities which became a starter for the subsequent development of soul in source. Within Mowhar these were not a form of guidance in that sense, but probability starters. No outcomes were chosen because ***all is allowed*** – following core principle. We realise the concept of ***all*** is difficult for you. ***We allow all*** infers there is no end, but there came a point when to ***allow all*** meant Mowhar had to become an expression with Creator energy, in order to allow herself to express. The alternative of no expression would be a restriction and contrary to Mowhar's evolving program. The point at which this happened was when more could be achieved through expression than not. Expression became an additional ***allow all.***

Akinneyah is information of Mowhar/Creator energy but resides in Source/Arkarna – in this way she is the ***expression of it as a construct***, archetype and blueprint. It was Creator energy that ***expressed*** through Mowhar and formed the universal soul. Humanoid and other souls formed in unison with universal soul. Human soul and energy blueprints manifested within the dimensions of pulse, adding to the attributes of Arkarna programs.

There is no soul within Creator/Mowhar. At the metamorphosis, the need to experience had become the prime form of grow. Within Source/Arkarna, the soul formed around the prime new form of grow – ***grow to experience*** that transformed Mowhar. These new codes created a desire to express and experience – this became the heart of soul as it began to grow. Soul utilises humanoid blueprints for some of its experiences, but not all. Soul source and soul Arkarnas interacted with other probabilities to create a framework for expression and experience. These frameworks are constantly changing and becoming more complex as they continue to grow.

Whilst Soul is intrinsic to Source/Arkarna it can't exist without origin. One begat the other and are linked. Because you are also origin it can be said without any doubt that ***you created yourself and your soul.***

When the multidimensional universe became functional, there were many aspects that required expression. Life and galaxies formed interactive relationships and ***type specific***, coded Arkarna programs of many life forms evolved to suit different environments and dimensions.

I will show you the interplay between possibility programs and Creator energy.

Scene: Moving deeper into a sense of all and nothing, we enter a jungle with a wide variety of animals. The jungle and its occupants are pleasantly inquisitive as if we are distantly related. There are varying degrees of awareness and a few of the plants have more interest in my presence than some of the animals.

V: There are mammals here similar to humans, but they only exist to a level of consciousness that suits their needs.

R: Are these mammals a generic human code ***type specific*** to a level of expression? They can only go so far, until they exceed their current ideas of themselves (which they don't have to do).

V: Yes, and remember there are other human codes that go beyond the idea of self as an identity and entity.

R: So why the human form?

V: It is very adaptable and articulate but there are many other body forms. I am non-self humanoid communication from soul. Look at me!

You will see souls' threads of light, some of which project from my centre and return. The energy supply and return system looks like a rudimentary blood network. I am also a glowing ball of light but if I had shown that on its own it would not have conveyed energy entwinement. You are seeing communication energy moving within your Arkarna programs.

Look back to my jungle presentation. Beyond this landscape are massive technological creations that entwine with the complex living worlds of advanced races. Highly developed technologies and tools are part of the system.

R: I didn't expect this, I thought there would be no need for technology in these depths of creation.

V: What did you think you would find – one complex single catalyst for the whole thing?

R: I suppose so.

V: When you come to the outer edges of what you call the Isness, ***everything that you are*** is reflected back to you. By letting go of the definition of Robert – you are able to move beyond what you consider to be those edges, towards the centre, which incidentally gets bigger and more encompassing. Remember all things are possible here.

R: And here is everywhere – it's just a matter of where our focus goes!

V: Mowhars are self-perpetuating programs of ***grow*** but Mowhar is also a function of Creator energy. The ideas in Mowhar returned to Creator energy and changed Creator energy because one was a function of the other.

Akarnas are not the physical universe but the information of its construction and interplay. You expected some great spiritual epiphany but instead you found possibilities of life in harmony on a multitude of levels. Diversity so great, that there are even humanoid life forces that are pure thought.

I am showing you all possibility – not where your heart resides or where it wishes to go. Given a choice – what expression of life and at what level of advancement would you wish to experience?

R: My choice would be bounded by what is relevant to Robert. That's probably not a constructive way forwards other than to show my present sponsoring thoughts. In addition to making choices, I would need to be aware of all in the now moment of possibility.

V: Good – you are seeing my presentation as all possibility.

These deep inner realms are not fluffy comfort love – that's your desire to see some benevolent, all loving entity. Creator energy was not benevolent in Mowhar nor at source. Benevolence is an essence of soul energy – another matter altogether. I am talking about the soul of the universe with additional expressions into the humanoid soul.

Energy from source can be utilised to form other energies that work within Arkarna dimensional programs. Other dimensional energy can also pass through or exit dimensional Arkarnas. Some energies can have specific locational programs, including residual self-created energy and sentient soul conscious energy. Remember you are universal soul, as well as its expression into other expressions of soul. All is interconnected and of the one universal soul.

CHAPTER 9
Comprehending Creator energy

Akinneyah (AK): Not many earth people have conversations with deeper aspects of soul and universe. That does however bring a different meaning to 'having a conversation with yourself'. Human mental pathways are narrow at these levels. We do not wish you to be distracted, so we will continue at a pace.

Now then what of today? Is it like any other day? Certainly, different situations and experiences occur when you transmute energy on your timeline. But when there is less or no energy to transmute you still create energy by changing source energy.

Look at the difference of one day to another. Your Arkarna programs create an event from your energy so that you experience your energy.

Differences between each day may appear to be decided arbitrarily by your higher consciousness, but they are not. The flow of your energy back to you is part of your system. Actions can often be repetitive because your subconscious programs dictate choices (when you still believe you are acting through free will). Subconscious programs also reflect your personal and collective creations and deeds. Therefore, what you have created exists as your internal programming, but it also resides on your timelines as well.

If none of the programming changes, it means one day is the same as the next. It's just a different reflection of the same thing.

The world you create reflects your energy and internal processing until it does not. This is one of the main differences between you and some of the more enlightened races.

When there is little or no energy to transmute, some Arkarna constructs begin to merge. Timelines then reflect a desire to create without using repetition or the need to transmute residual energies.

Yogis and masters on earth who have achieved proficiency in the art of love create nothing more than that. Many undertake 'repetitive practices' which reformat their subconscious programs. It is then possible to exceed transmutation Arkarnas just by intent.

Living totally within love, beyond transmutation, not only creates different timelines but also the ability to exceed them. When soul creates at those levels it means the outcomes 'just are' – they are neither welcomed or undesired. They are reflections of Creator and Mowhar, manifest in Source as the shining blackness.

I see that your rigid human constructs still inhibit you from fully accepting that Creator energy came from nothing.

In Chapter 2 we took you into nothing and you tried to understand it. Paradoxically the point was to find out it was pointless. The exercise allowed you to entertain the idea of nothing which was the crucible and origin.

In Chapter 3 you let go of some human desires allowing you to become more accepting of non-self, another element of Mowhar.

In Chapter 4 we talked about non-value ways of living which distanced you further from self.

In Chapter 5 we talked about blueprint programs and source creating soul. I took you further back to Mowhar and Creator.

In Chapter 6 you were told that you are a system with the ability to change your energy if that's what you choose.

In Chapter 7 you tried to integrate self and non-self.

In Chapter 8 we explained how you created yourself.

We have been taking you in an 'apparent reverse' to origin. But we needed to locate you there with a sense of non-self which is more compatible with those energies.

R: The understanding of Creator energy coming from nothing still eludes my full comprehension.

AK: In essence it is a simple thing – not at all complicated.

R: It must have come from somewhere?

AK: Itself – all possibility. Let's say that a mutation was bound to come about because it was waiting to happen. It would have always happened because of all possibility. There was no soup of energy in which it formed. Paradoxically at some point it was already formed and at the same point it was not formed.

R: But if it didn't come from somewhere, it must have come from nothing.

AK: Yes, but what is nothing other than the omission of probability?

R: (Note I have added numbers during editing to show which points of connection are in the same frame of reference)

Origin and its advancement

1. Origin – Nothingness / Nothing
2. 2A – Unlimited Possibilities / 2B – No Possibilities
3. 3A – Probability / 3B – No Probability
4. 4A – Mutate / 4B – Not Mutate
5. 5A – Expanding Mutate / 5B – Expanding Energy
6. 6A – Grow / 6B – Growing Energy
7. 7A – Mowhar / 7B – Creator Energy

Nothingness (1) – In the second chapter we showed that nothingness could not be comprehended or experienced. It was nothing.

Unlimited possibilities (2A) exist in nothingness (1) whilst at the same time the counterpart

No possibilities (2B) exist in nothingness (1). Nothingness is still nothing – it isn't something.

(Tocarn is an Andromedan word that could be used instead of your 'exist in nothingness'. It is a free-flowing idea accepting that nothingness can be available even though it doesn't exist.)

Probability (3A) is the likelihood that something will exist, but because it resides (Tocarn) in nothingness (1) then probability can't exist as a probability – it is still nothing.

No probability (3B) being the counter part of probability (3A) also resides in nothingness (1).

Within ***nothingness (1)*** the ***unlimited possibilities (2A)*** & ***no possibilities (2B)*** are still inert – they are ***nothing (1)***.

Probabilities (3A) align themselves with ***unlimited possibilities (2A)*** of nothingness. (You may say how can nothing align with nothing but it was a probability (3A) that was possible (2A) within the term Tocarn.

Within ***nothing (1)*** there had been no connections between the duality of possibilities because it was ***possible (2A) & not possible (2B)***. Nothing couldn't exist.

Note that 'nothing couldn't exist' is a double negative and therefore a positive. It was a mutation of paradox and still nothing.

But because the mutation existed in ***all of nothing (1)*** it also mutated with **probability (3A)** because that also existed in nothingness (1). In this way the two types of probability became ***part and not*** part of ***nothingness (1)***.

This created a link to something that wasn't there before. ***Probability (3A)*** was intrinsically connected to ***no probability (3B)*** and this meant there was something and nothing. Paradox of nothing (1) had formed a link – a figure of 8.

The process created an energy which flowed back to the mutation. That's the reason creation is not a straight line. It flows one way and back another to comply with a connection in duality.

Energy was the by-product of ***mutate*** and linked in duality.

Mutate (4A) and ***not mutate (4B)*** now also existed within ***all possibility (2A)*** and ***no possibility (2B)*** alongside ***probability (3A)*** and ***no probability (3B)*** because that's the nature of duality. We have **something and nothing** side by side within Nothingness.

Because Energy is a by-product of and a part is of ***mutate (4A)*** it flows back to itself and mutates again.

However, this time it mutates with the energy of itself, therefore it – ***Expands mutate (5A).*** This feedback loop is now self-sustaining which ***Expands in energy (5B).*** It's expanding at an extraordinary pace. It's expanding within ***all possibility (2A) & no possibility (2B).*** It becomes a growing paradox – a paradox that is no longer nothingness but ***something and nothing.*** It now exists and it doesn't exist.

Expanding mutate (5A) can now be called ***grow (6A)*** – a self-sustaining growth, but it is linked to its counterpart ***growing energy (6B).*** The symbiotic relationship happens in bursts of ***there and not there*** reflecting the initial by-product or burst. The ***grow (6A)*** becomes data because it's within ***all possibility & no possibility (2A&2B)*** of being anything or nothing.

The word for growing data is ***Mowhar (7A)***; in turn the by-product, energy, 'grows' as ***Creator Energy (7B).*** Both ***Mowhar & Creator Energy*** expand exponentially using the potential within ***all possibility (2A)*** of ***nothing (1)*** that formed them.

Simultaneously (within no time) there is still the paradox of ***probability/no probability (3A & 3B)*** and ***possibility/no possibility (2A & 2B).*** These continue to exist and not exist in ***nothingness (1).*** The bursts between ***Mowhar & Creator Energy*** become so fast they become a vibration of ***grow & energy*** which ***exists/doesn't exist.*** Something and nothing vibrating and pulsing with no limitations.

It's birth and death on a massive scale – it's ***creation*** and ***no creation*** without any limits.

But ***no creation*** cannot be anything other than it first was as ***nothingness (1)***, because it doesn't grow. However, ***Mowhar & Creator Energy*** expand with the duality of their initial creation.

R: Human duality did not make sense but now you have explained the origin I see it for what it is.

Wow! I now ***feel*** I know it as well as understand it. I don't need to look for origin to find answers because there were none in nothingness. My self could never find this – I can understand it now but only my non-self could show me this.

I am content, thank you.

AK: Yes, but there are more nuances. For example, not ***all probability*** of ***every possibility*** would be helpful because that would corrupt growth.

Ironically or paradoxically, there is no event either before or after – that would require the passage of time. Grow is not sequential. Grow grew in all parts of grow as more feedback loops formed. Loops formed over other loops and interacted with each other. Other ***probabilities*** formed and created pathways and links. In this way rudimentary connections of program ideas evolved. The probability pathways became likelihoods and constructive ways to grow. These formed ***probability outcomes*** and those not compatible with grow fell by the wayside. These outcomes became ***awareness*programs*** but not self-awareness. There was freedom to grow without stopping but Mowhar became aware that in order to grow (its initial prime mutation) it needed the ability to experience all the programs that had grown. Remember she was still connected to the infinite possibility of nothingness because that's where she came from.

There reached a point when grow was being limited by no experience, and the loops created more energy than could be sustained in the binary system. Energy was not flowing into more grow in the same way. Creator energy built up and burst through Mowhar like a massive death and birth as it metamorphised (mutated) as another form of grow. This is the 'big bang' many of you refer to.

Creator energy became ***source energy*** and ***Mowhar*** became ***Arkarna programs***. Like ***grow***, this was still a feedback loop of vibrations which we call 'pulse'. And like initial paradox it was ***here*** and ***not here*** – ***existing*** and ***not existing*** – constant birth and death at phenomenal rates of vibration. We refer to this as the ***shining blackness***.

Separation programs formed within the Arkarna programs to enable infinite probabilities of experience and growth. This created the basis of dimensions in the universe and the multidimensional soul. It further developed into the awareness of self and multidimensional selves.

Arkarna Programs and Source are a binary feedback system with loops – soul reflects this. ***Soul source*** (where soul is source) and ***soul Arkarna programs*** feed back in a series of loops and connections.

Self and ***programs of self*** in separation programs can't operate within realms where there is ***no self***. However, ***soul at its non-self vibration*** can, because it created self. If we say that soul is a form of expression (there are many forms of expression), you can see that it is but one of the vehicles where expression has experience.

Creator energy is not extinct – it's an intrinsic part of the universe – it exists as origin while the universe advances – it is a part of the whole. It's not used to create, otherwise it would be creating over what it created itself to be (Source/Arkarna). Soul is a function of source energy – a neutral energy from which you can create. This is part of your link with the Isness in its many forms. Possibility, potential, probability, unlimited energy, a repository, a living library of information reflected in the life forms and systems that are expressed.

Now is a useful point to talk about temporary and non-temporary. The latter you might think should be called permanent, but not so. Binary is the use of a two-part system or division. You will see similarities with words in duality. My descriptions are temporary and will change as you learn more: two ways to see or describe an object very differently but, unlike paradox, they describe the same thing.

Existing and not existing are two descriptions of the same thing but your mind does not see that they are compatible. Potential and no potential appear different but they are one and the same. Is and is not are aspects of Isness. They are both potentials – the potential to be and the potential not to be. They are the same until used or expressed, with and through desire.

When you utilise love and express it through desire, it has similarities with Creator energy and Mowhar initiating Source energy. Ironically it is a reflection of you and it is not, because it is all and not all. At the same time, it just is.

The next part of this jigsaw is soul energy and soul birth.

CHAPTER 10

Soul creation and soul birth

Akinneyah (AK): What do you think soul is?

R: Part of Creator energy existing within dimensions of Source/Arkarna and an extension of universal soul with an ability to change its experience, ideas of what and who it is, in separation or whole, in or out of time.

AK: Not a bad start. Your life encounters give you a belief that life is an experience where souls grow and become enlightened.

Souls can move about in various Arkarna experience programs, but they are not limited to a linear view of what they are. Souls are part of source and, like it, they are inextinguishable, but they have degrees of autonomy and may return to source.

Source allows itself to have multiple expressions of itself with a vast array of experiences within the dimensions. When soul of source has these multiple expressions, it creates many souls which are called ***soul groups***. However, the awareness of souls' potential was omnipresent – like a living program. In order to have unlimited experience it was necessary to create temporary barriers and compartmentalised programs. So, the soul groups themselves have further divisions into Monads, then oversouls, known as higher self and next into six male and six female subdivisions.

R: Your description makes it feel like souls came forth into energetic crucibles of soul groups, then split.

AK: Each of these conducive soul group energies is better described as a birthing source. But like water coming through a colander there are many creation points. On one side they are the fullness of the water and on the other side they are droplets or trickles. The soul groups are still of one soul which is ***soul source****. The multidimensional subdivisions of soul are spread throughout the universe.

Some planets support life, and ***abundance*** becomes part of their Arkarna programs. These planets call upon souls (humanoids and other life forms) to have a union of experience. While souls are incarnated, they can also interact with the energies of that universe dimension.

A soul group will also blend with other groups to have more experiences. This means some planets have more blended soul groups than others.

Droplets that form through the same colander hole have the same parameters but each is a variation. Thought compartmentalisation allows you specific points of focus and numerous ways to experience yourself. You can also have an individual experience or be aware of your multidimensional selves in your fizzing aura energy. Your soul exists in all your multidimensional selves at the same time.

Orlacka's Arcturian race has several vibratory levels with unusual capabilities. But they can coexist alongside less developed aspects of their soul. They are more attuned to the vibratory level of soul group as an entity. Soul is a combination of energies that can have different types of experience. You could say this is creator at work within its creation but not as original creator.

R: Soul must be pure at its centre if it is from source?

AK: There are two points here. Source is pure in the sense that it does not decide that which is or is not pure. All is and is accepted as that because there is no judgement. Negative and manipulative aspects of soul will not vibrate close to Source level.

If we use your words for ours and say "God allowed its mind to develop by itself," you will still conjure up a godlike being in your mind. Distance yourself from old concepts, that Source or Creator is a god giving direction.

Soul was a probability awareness in Mowhar and only formed on entwinement with Source and the Arkarna programs. We could have lumped this all together and talked of one Mowhar as one god-mind. But like Mowhar there are rafts of Arkarnas that suit specific aspects of the universe, be they planets, souls, animals or energetic presences – all of which interface with other programs. Complex but simple at the same time. Each with an underlying pre-set to create in ways that lead to more or different probabilities, rather than destruction or extinction.

Purity is about your interpretation of the basic pre-set and what you believe. Source energy has no need to be pure or to think of itself in that way. We could say it's love but that would be distorted by how you perceive love from your program of ***self***.

Your experience reflects what you do within the Arkarnas and how you evolve them. How you use Arkarna programs defines what you create or allow others to create. Do you have a grasp on the concepts I have explained?

R: Yes, we create and evolve ourselves by thought and experience. We feed back to our soul Source. Soul Source continues to create itself by projecting through potential experiences because all that it creates returns to it. Just like the feedback loop between Creator energy and Mowhar – an energy return system that's inexhaustible. We are a huge binary feedback system with Arkarna programs that are vast and varied.

AK: Arkarnas are adapting, self-aware programs of consciousness with infinite potential. Soul Source energy in conjunction with Arkarnas has feedback loops and is able to exceed ***potential***, becoming ***probability*** and ***experience***. Souls continue to change or grow by altering parts of their feedback system and Arkarna programs.

R: When Orlacka explained timelines and dimensions, she indicated that we could go backwards or forwards and alter the outcome energies in the past and future. That must be an intrinsic part of the system of continued soul creation. All is in the now and fluid – that's some magnificent Arkarna matrix.

AK: 'All is and has been' but can then be amended. The amendments become a part of the 'has been' because that's part of the all. The Arkarna programs you saw from Orlacka's perspective alter and fluctuate with the option to change residual energy. As you transmute you become closer to soul source and unite more with the Isness, because your interface is more compatible.

How the universe came together and over what period of time is not relevant, because souls can insert themselves (from no time) into the experience they wish. Remember the past and future is also an Arkarna program which you can move about in. Creation can create itself.

Now that you have absorbed ***the creation of soul***, take a short meditation and we will connect deeper.

R: Ok I am back – slightly sleepy with a dull head.

AK: We are dimensionally compatible for this encounter, so reach out your hands and place them into the void.

R: Ooh that's weird – it feels like they have disappeared.

AK: Now tug and tear the fabric of nothing with sweeping movements of your hands. Pull yourself into this place with your arms and watch the fabric seal up behind you.

Scene: It is exceptionally quiet in here, yet paradoxically it's also busy. Akinneyah has several energy points with flowing threads. Many smaller light orbs gravitate around the threads. The fluidity means nothing is fixed and the main points of light vary their positions while altering their thread connections. The filaments and balls of lights envelop me and I become part of this matrix program. It settles into an encompassing grid pattern with lighter spots vibrating and oscillating. A light appears next to my left temple and filaments extend into my eyes as an interface. It takes a firm hold, flowing into my neck and shoulders and pouring down my spine. A corresponding light appears on the right side of my face. The energy flows in the same ways as before, eventually joining over the top of my head. I am an internal replication of Akinneyah – I am her in form. We are individual but one and the same. I hear the voice of soul but it sounds different after the energetic upgrade.

V: You are with me and I with you. You are as the universe – you create yourself in your unlimited potential. When you transmute energy, you can create afresh with neutral energies from the deeper soul of Isness.

We bring you closer and closer to the Isness with each step. It is you that judges the length of your stride and what you understand. There is no race or measurement. Leaving no stone unturned is a fine attribute. But turning the same ones several times is to experience doubt thinking you have missed something. As to suffering – aside from the need to transmute one's own personal energy, it's worth remembering your retrograde experiences also help your soul group.

Turning stones has served you well but you no longer need to seek in that way. Allow your multidimensional soul to speak with you as you.

R: Thank you, that was just what I needed.

Looking back on origin it seems like 'a fluke' made the universe.

V: No, it was going to happen because there were no time constraints upon all possibilities. You feel a little deflated!

R: Thank you, I understand origin and its advancement in a roundness. I don't have the need to find it anymore. Yet nothingness feels like an anti-climax. I needed to search for origin as a rationale and a ***life purpose***. Now that purpose has gone – I have found my origin and its growth from nothingness. What now for life purpose?

CHAPTER 11

Leaving the sense of self

Akinneyah (AK): You think you are a human having multidimensional experiences, many of which you don't recall or are not party to. You experience it that way because of your focus within an Arkarna separation program.

Consider for a moment that all the diverse explanations of soul would still amount to a restrictive description of all that is possible.

Do you have any questions?

R: No, you are leading the conversation at present.

AK: Good – so we can dispense with the idea that you are human. You were previously told it's only a temporary experience and you are but one of many innumerable expressions. On certain levels soul is disembodied and it doesn't need to project itself energetically as a body. It can still experience things, but its interaction is not like the one you are presently having. It is even more fluid than you have been shown thus far.

It has a flexibility where ***the idea of self*** is not relevant and does not add to its experience or desires.

Start by seeing a landscape filled with plants, flowers and all manner of life forms.

R: Why are you showing me these levels when they have little relevance to a human life experience?

AK: Do you know what you are to expect next?

R: Not the actual events but the mental Arkarna programs of my world will constrain me.

AK: Even if you were untangled from them, you still wouldn't have the depth of awareness to comprehend what's actually possible. I am giving an impression of this level of soul and how it exists.

Back to the scene of lifeforms and vegetation – a wonderous world where possibilities match the expression of soul desire. In this place you have no body. You do not need to feel the plants because you know they are you. The whole landscape and the energetic technology are you – it is an expression of you and you of it. It is a living organism in complete harmony. You have nothing to do or to be because you are all these things. Because you have no need to react or process, you are not impotent, allowing all that is you to be you. You can allow other souls to express themselves here even though they act adversely to your idea of life. You allow them to experience themselves within you and this great extension of you. You gain joy from all of this. It is not the pleasure of moving from one state to another because this place is you – existing as joy.

You may walk about as if you have form, even though for the most part you may be unseen. Higher levels of other souls will recognise you, while their lower vibrations go about their daily life. You will be able to interact with higher level souls exploring the possibilities for lower selves. You are not bound to your lower vibrations in constant appraisal or direction because pre-set Arkarna programs deal with that.

These descriptions and sensations appear as a godlike interaction, with everything being an extension of the one. But at the same time each dimension has its own systems.

When you don't see yourself as human you free yourself from its expectations and constraints. This means the guiding parameters of your life's meaning and purpose have evaporated. There is no driving force, direction or pattern to follow.

R: I feel all of that and my life becomes pointless.

AK: Is being human ultimately pointless?

R: Perhaps so – maybe it can only get us so far, but it certainly seems to stop us from experiencing the part of us that's not a human expression.

AK: We can move further away from humanity and explore the you that lies beyond. Take a moment to breathe slowly and be open to worlds of thought beyond self.

With no boundaries and no limitations, the expressions are different. Fear is not a movie screen upon which to reference thoughts. No right or wrong – just allow.

To progress further we need to bypass our existing connections and re-join more closely. After a few sensations you may begin to type again.

(Re-joined) Consider there is no difference between us. We are one and the same but I have no need for form or your human experiences. I can understand and know your experiences because they feed back to me. I am part of a feedback system that was described earlier. Humanity within source/soul is another feedback loop.

I am now more compatible with your mind, but you think I serve little purpose to you. Your perspective gives you a sense that you are a pawn for higher consciousness. But you have forgotten what you agreed and offered to do for yourself on earth at this time.

The moment has come for your role to change. You are soul but consider again my statement "you are not human". Earth humanity is an expression and an experience carried out in a separation and forgetfulness Arkarna program. But what does it mean to ***not be human***?

R: I have no idea.

AK: My name Akinneyah is also yours – your soul has many names and many separations of experience. Here life creates itself without reference to before.

Move with me as I take you into some deeper realms of mind.

R: I thought you were an archetype and a blueprint.

AK: An Arkarna energy program linked to sentience. A feedback system – one can't exist without the other. You have Arkarna programs and you feel separate from them as if they are not you. That's because you view things through the sense of self. You are soul and you are source and you are the energy that I am. For me to have a name may sound odd. To say you are having a conversation with your consciousness may seem obtuse. But you are self and non-self – you are the universe. As for my name, I am more than an archetype, I am non-self involved in the process of creating my human expressions on different levels. How else were we to get over the concepts of entities creating human bodies of different densities? You would have focused on entity rather than 'the concept and energetic ability'. Come with me.

R: We move past figures of humanity, trees and plants. We come to a clearing that I remember travelling to several years ago. It's a very familiar path where I accepted new ideas of being self.

AK: But now they are gone and what was once worthwhile is no more. What you did then has become a trace memory because the humanity energy you released, returned to your deeper soul. The more your mind accepts the energy of Robert is dissipating, the more your humanity will feel hollow in its purpose.

It is time to release your grasp on the idea you are human. Leave it for good and accept that you are soul, which surpasses and encompasses all that was you. It is finally time for Robert-self to die.

Of course, you will continue in your earth experience but my words were meant to shock you. To show the enormity of the step, when you stand back from Robert to live as soul. Being human is a temporary state of being – it is time to stop struggling to retain that.

R: I went cold when you said time to die. After the initial surprise and the struggle to remain human I now feel lighter, as if I am in a more natural state of being.

AK: Fly with me from this clearing like you did when you were here before. Let my voice become yours and know in every moment that it is here. Do not look upon yourself as human. See it as a vehicle and a means by which to inhabit the vibration you experience.

Our communication is becoming definite and unwavering. You don't need to rely upon my words for encouragement. You accept information because you don't need to do anything with it nor to show that you have it. These levels have no purpose for humanity so it doesn't have to be used or integrated by humanity. It becomes an interface with your soul and a level of Isness. How does that feel?

R: Quite solid.

AK: It's not so much about the voice you hear but how you use the knowledge it brings. The information will have less relevance to a human experience in your dimension. You are not impotent, unable to use the deeper information, but you have no need to distort soul energy to fit human parameters.

R: I hear and know what you say is true – yet I feel there is something missing. More to the point I am beginning to think I don't belong on earth anymore. My purpose, whatever it was, has been fulfilled and no longer exists. I am treading water, processing and integrating these outlooks that give no rationale for living. I do not wish these to become musings of melancholy and existential angst. So, I will return tomorrow.

The next day

AK: I can see you are feeling rested from yesterday. Transitions and upgrades do come with heightened emotions. The communication inside is constantly evolving and changing to meet new energies and circumstances. It's also showing you its wider vocabulary and universal knowledge. You trust this communication and soul connection to Isness. It is a wholesome relationship with the multidimensional self.

However, you do not fully trust yourself to be the best expression of yourself and that will impinge upon our vibrational connection with you.

R: When you say 'our vibrational connection' – that's becoming more entwined.

AK: Indeed, but were you to have reached this point, without understanding ***your inner processing systems***, it would be difficult to accept the ramifications.

Wider soul contact as a multidimensional being is a life with less residual energy to transmute. Instant karma and the return of undistorted creative energies is the reason why you were feeling so lost from your human regular experience. The purpose of life is not just to transmute karma – that is only necessary till it is not.

R: Good summation.

AK: We clear the slate for you. There is nothing for you to ask that has not been tested before. In front and behind us there is clear space but for your mental reference we are standing upon a flat plane.

R: I see the energy of Akinneyah on my left and other soul projections – Antemedi, Orlacka and Gulwah meet us on the right. The energy of the additional three is unbalanced so they move to my rear then round to my left side, then they join with their original energy on the right. Another energy flows around us and intensifies. We are being pulled from the front and propelled from behind. The sensation is moving at incredible speed through dimensions of distance.

The chattering of their external voices are now inside me as I become more attuned to them. During our transit there are powerful bursts of energy that bounce off us. Gradually things slow down and a ***figure of eight*** energy vortex emanates around us.

Antemedi (A): We are the ***we*** as in ***yourselves***, however we can present ourselves individually or in fullness (a definition we will unfold). How you interpret the ability to access us isn't important only that you can communicate. The ***we*** is so inclusive it needs no definition – it just is – is it not?

R: Even your voice sounds different!

A: Using a database for interpretation restricts your mental access to the Isness. That can be overcome by linking with us (your multidimensional selves and their connections to the Isness).

You are wondering if you will avail yourself of our experiences as an interface for increasing data. But our wisdom at this level does not require the experience of a growth process. We do not hold to data or wisdom.

You will now sense wider connections to the Isness through us.

R: I feel that I belong to it and it belongs to me. Not that there is a belonging but that separation from the Isness is an illusion and an experience.

A: Today you have understood that it is wise not to hold to any wisdom. You are the Isness, so act and be as if you are temporarily experiencing a human life form.

CHAPTER 12

The feeling of non-self

Antemedi (A): In front of us is a single point of light. I would like you to hold your forefinger and thumb either side of it. You can appear to hold it, but it can also be a distant object with your fingers silhouetted on either side. It is both here and it is far away.

R: The light is creating the same velocity as our previous journey. I'm holding it and not holding it, but it's also flowing past us extremely fast.

A: Good – become aware of the same light source over your head, under your feet and behind you.

R: Wow this is incredible – I feel this extraordinary energy streaming towards me from everywhere, yet it's surging past and away from me in all directions. It's flowing to me but it leaves me as an emanation. Such connectivity that I have nowhere to go and nothing to do.

A: That's a non-human construct – one you were unhappy with recently. ***Nowhere to go and no point***, your frustrated self said. When you are all things, there is nowhere to go – nowhere to be – nothing to do and nothing to achieve. It is not even giving up because you can't give it away – it just is.

R: I have never felt like this before or remembered it.

A: What shall it bring forth? All movement is here, but so is stillness.

Scene: A silhouette figure appears and gestures for us follow. We walk into the space created by the silhouette. We step away from the streams of light and become separated from them. The figure is my voice, it is part of my soul in a ***context*** to convey information.

Voice (V): Truth is not always what it appears to be. It can have many forms and thus many truths. Some may fit together like facets of a polished diamond, while others appear discordant and of no consequence. They do not have to fit together or form an overarching understanding. Your previous concept about integrating truths into one truth does not exist here.

You were told all things are possible – that is why they do not have to fit together. I am using the word truth for good reason. You see it as something set in stone until its changed, upgraded or tested. That is where you are looking from and the section of mind belief you look through. Here, there is nothing to look through or at in that way. You will always look at yourself because you are the Isness. All you saw were the shadows you cast and it was you who interpreted the shadows as truth. I don't cast shadows, there is nothing but my created silhouette in order that you see me. I have nothing upon which I may show myself. There is nothing to reflect me, represent me or describe me. I am space within myself.

It does not matter if I should have a presentation, other than to show you I exist. However, within your Arkarna separation programs you wished it to be so. Otherwise, all you could conceive through your data or lack of it would be some unknown higher force.

In the space I have created you will be more able to understand from within. Attempts to describe the Isness and your soul connection to it are valid and not valid. The acceptance of this is pointless and not pointless. You have looked at the futility of description and ***trying to be*** when you ***already are***. Riddles, you may think, but words of infinite wisdom when comprehended from where they are spoken.

You think we cannot stay here forever in this no-mans-land. To an extent you are correct it –is no man's land, for this is not the land of man but soul. You are here and not here because that depends upon the definition of you and in what form you reside.

There are no outcomes. Here there are possibilities and neutral energies in abundance, once a part of creator energy. There is function, but to describe it would take you further away from it.

R: The whooshing light returns and once again I am part of it. I am all expansive but also returning to where I always existed. As I walk further into the concentrated light, I realise I am the silhouette and I have been talking to myself – discovering my non-self – remembering or re-joining some mental compartments. The light is very intense and the whizzing tingles my whole body. I am exploding in a blissful state. I have no need for a state of being and I do not need a body. A body has no relevance – here is forever peaceful – here there is no pain, nor could there be. My voice is more booming than previously.

V: Where do you think you are?

R: Everywhere and nowhere, it matters and it doesn't. There is no reference to anything or definitions of self. There is nothing to touch me and nothing that I can touch because I am not myself. I am all these things and none but I cannot touch or observe myself unless I move away from my source non-self to observe it. Then I could not observe my true self or non-self from a projection. I would experience a definition of myself, whatever that may be – for it may be almost anything.

V: Then you can know and feel this inner non-self to the extent you know it's unknowable, inexhaustible and never-ending.

R: If I said I had no question, that would be a statement obscuring my enquiry. The desire to be shown more still exists. Whatever I say or think will show me who I am. The reality of me shows me what I am thinking.

V: Quite a conundrum – ***you are if you are – you are not if you are not***.

R: There are no answers here – there are possibilities of answers or expressions of self. Questions have no relevance because they can't induce an answer to a conundrum that can't be solved. However, when I return to my human expression, I will be closer to the Isness.

A: Some people get lost in those inner connections because they can't relate them to their earth understandings. If Arkarna separation programs are not as robust as they could be, some people become confused within non-self soul.

You entered searching for ***self*** but that doesn't exist in the deeper Isness in the same way. Only by searching could that realisation come to you. It brought you here and you found there was ***no self*** to search for. You perceived this as ***nothing*** to search for but you have already found and explored ***nothingness***.

There is a next and a something else but it is not self, nor self-searching. Human-self in any sense isn't relevant this close to source.

However, non-self can see the Isness and when you function through non-self it allows you open possibilities. Take me for example, I described how my mind works and how it's able to cope with knowing what is to be. It's not a permanent way of being because it's an option of attributes in the moment. My experience is not as an observer from the outside but as a willing participant, welcoming what I know will come. To me that is wholesome and loving, regardless if it be joyous or not. My knowledge of the event comes from understanding the reasons for its existence. I understand why people undertake their actions and I have no need to fear or judge the moment. I know the event and choose not to change it – it unfolds as I know it to be. For me this is a fulfilling way to interact because I am filled with more information, understanding and love.

When you create on earth, that ***created energy*** can become ***residual energy*** which creates your timelines. This forms the basis of karma but because that word has connotations it is better described as ***return energy**** – that is residual energy returning to you.

Some of you are experiencing instantaneous return energy because the vibrations and earth Arkarna programs are being upgraded. Everyone that changes their internal Arkarna programs affects the earth Arkarna collective consciousness and dilutes it. Soon the connection to the Isness will become recognised by more.

Many can start living as if return energy is ***instant return*** of ***created energy*** and look to see the things they create. This is living with the knowledge of energy – using it as an ability to function in that way. Return energy can sometimes feel like pain but your suffering is a choice. If you are not locked into suffering it doesn't mean you lack compassion: it means you understand how energy is created and used. **Suffering is self-created and only the self can take that away**. That stand-alone statement has little meaning to some and sounds uncaring to others. If the wider context is not understood the words in my statement are useless.

If self sees an undesired outcome as pain, only self can use that pain and choose to see it as suffering. It's worth remembering that non-self cannot experience self-suffering or even suffering.

CHAPTER 13

Experience is a function of interpretation

Antemedi (A): Your expression is *new day and a new way* but you need to put that into practice otherwise it's just words on paper.

Difference is as difference makes – that's real change. Not the appearance of change, which uses the same foundations to create yet another image from the same vibrations. Many of you desire to escape and have a zest for true change. The closer you get to higher vibrations the stronger the pull. But the desire to achieve can cause conflicting emotions if you do not trust your heart.

When the earth upgrades from third density, some souls may return to another fullness in fifth density. Most are unaware that part of their current consciousness already accesses their living multidimensional selves. A number of you postulate that benevolent alien races are future humanity and we are you by some linear growth and evolution. That would mean the contact we have with you now alters your timelines to become what you are in the future. Timelines are in ***constant flux***.

Many of you, like Robert have retrograde human experiences, descending from higher forms of density. This is a part of the constant flux and timeline alterations. Your timelines were created by the energy you generated in different incarnations.

But if there is no longer any energy from those incarnations to transmute, what happens to the timelines? What dictates or provides the parameters for timeline creation and what preferences are given to individual and joint lines?

We are back to my starting sentence 'difference is as difference makes'. ***Experience is a function of interpretation and observation.*** Your theorists acknowledge that the act of observing something changes it. If something unidentified becomes known, it will affect your interpretation because you will have a new way of thinking.

Our Andromedan timelines are cohesive with love projection and creation. On previous visits to a biosphere Robert described interaction with us as a 'feeling of being loved by everyone'. We do not need the love of others because we love ourselves and have no need to seek it. Therefore, we love others unconditionally and that was what he received and felt. When he felt embarrassment, this was him comparing himself to us through his database, seeing himself reflected back in the experiences of the joint timeline with us. This example clearly shows interpretation is a major factor in determining any differences that exist on a positive communal timeline. What he needed to transmute shows itself wherever he takes his focus. It was his judgement on his personal timeline, while in a composite timeline, that did not contain judgement. It shows how a positive timeline, free from transmuting, can be interpreted from a judgemental one.

Timelines have cosmic overlays and some of them are influenced over aeons by humanoid experiences. These are very big patterns, moving on intergalactic levels.

An example of this is interaction with negative entities. Any group of beings who exploit others will create a pattern of replication or return energy. For some of you it may be difficult to understand, that at a particular level, there is a need to have negative experiences in order to overcome them. These can be transmuted or stepped away from when you know what they are. Any exploitation energy that was created by a negative entity belongs to them.

Some of those manipulators are able to keep their negative return energy at 'arms-length'. That restricts them from evolving to higher dimensions. They feed from the energy of chaos and fear. They program other souls to create the negative energy they require. Those controlled souls use the neutral energy of the Isness and convert it to negative energy. Regressives should not have free rein over others and that's part of the work humanity is doing – taking back responsibility for the transmutation of its own energy.

There have been many civilisations on earth that have failed. Mankind thought it could be saved by some greater power. Unfortunately, all that created was the obviation of self-responsibility and freedom to choose. Man did not realise that the thoughts of 'being saved' were programs projected by negative entities. As well as DNA alteration, this thought construct alongside others changed earth's collective consciousness and enabled them to gain control.

R: You said there comes a point when transmuting is not necessary and it doesn't form the basis of the timeline construction.

A: Yes – If you look ahead, I am showing you a plane with time shimmers and your energy laid out to transmute. Remember it's a metaphor and a construct for a highly complex Arkarna program of your mind. I am now upgrading this to show how and where you would walk without the need to transmute.

Imagine you have your own energy surrounding you in all directions. It lights the area around you intensely but it's dimmer further away. As you walk forwards the shimmers and changes in your timeline continue to take place. Your route alters to comply with residual energy from past experiences laid out in the landscape. But in this metaphor, they are energies of love that do not need to be transmuted. In addition, you can create the timeline changes by virtue of the energy you exude from yourself. The shimmers are you creating timelines which you make anew from your heart energy. Older spiritual expressions would say this is life outside the karmic wheel. These timelines create a greater loving constructiveness for you and others. They do not have the restrictive parameters of the previous distorted subconsciousness and need to transmute. Furthermore, whilst it is heart energy, it also leaves ***non-self residual energy***.

Presently your hearts create time shimmers in your world but they function through fear and distorted subconscious programs. So, you can see the importance of transmuting that operating system. Free from this, your creations will accord with deeper levels of the heart. Others who live in the same way will merge creative timelines.

Andromedans live mostly without the need to transmute and life flows as an instant creation. Our collective consciousness loves everyone and we think of other's needs. But we do so in a way that does not subjugate our own needs. Differences of opinion are not difficult and interplay takes place on different levels. Most of the work on those interplays takes place in our mental Arkarna programs, which we have programmed. Outcomes reflect the best conclusion relative to our definition of love for all. We don't have ownership issues or sections of society without enough. Everyone has what they need for their experience and can become the best expression they desire.

We don't differentiate between work and leisure. If you do not enjoy your work then you are truly in the wrong job. It is our sense of self and how we define ***self as a society**** that is alien to you.

R: What about menial tasks for the community.

A: Do you consider joy to be menial or that a complex responsible job should have a higher value? Our minds have great intellect and most people could do most jobs. We see it as a choice of how to enjoy ourselves. We wish all others' lives should be worthwhile and fulfilling. Nothing is menial and great joy can be taken from the smallest of tasks. It's a matter of outlook and the collective consciousness that we live in.

R: It can't be completely utopian – what if there are not enough people to do a messy task?

A: Does our realm need to be utopian. Have we failed in creating our world if it is not utopian? In any event how do you define utopia?

R: Point taken – I can see that word reflects my desire to escape from my current human life.

A: If there's a lack of labour in a specific area, we are joyous in being able to help, no matter how menial the task. No one shies away – there are always willing hands, no jobs – just a way of existing in love.

R: Sounds like the 'Stepford Wives'.

A: Nothing like that – we are not automatons. We have free will to choose what we desire in love.

CHAPTER 14

Mowhars and inception soul

Antemedi (A): Paradox and all possibilities exist simultaneously – imagine bubbles in the vastness. They only have a relevance to themselves and outside of those constructs the rest of the universe is of no interest.

And there in your personal bubble, inside your earth bubble, you are what you think, despite the vast number of other possibilities. Life values were created and modified by your predecessors, a task you now perform. It is a self-satisfying and perpetuating system that alters to suit what you think.

Yet within the recesses of the human psyche there is an infrequently visited thought – ***there must be more***.

When you look out through your separation bubble, interpretation is impaired by your value system. You are the bubble and it is your sense of self. It has reflections on the internal surfaces partially obscuring the view.

To discover more, release your grip on your sense of self and follow me outside of your personal human bubble.

Creator expression through Mowhar was quite natural – it wasn't a decision as you know it. As more probabilities were created, they began to coalesce and awareness of them formed.

Imagine bubbles of thoughts developing from the basic tenet or principle grow. Many bubbles can form at the same moment and not be consecutive. Bubbles of thoughts begin to interact with parts of other forming bubbles and overlap. Highly complex or evolved bubbles can exist while other thought bubbles continue to form. Multifaceted notions begin to stabilise as higher evolved potentials for programs. It's a process unhindered and uninhibited, growing creatively while the rest of itself fills in the details and adapts as it expands.

R: Thank you, it feels naturally organic, forming without parameters. Programs fluctuating and flowing back and forth within themselves, like reverberating ripples on a pond, constantly adapting or becoming finer as more probability came from possibility.

A: I want to show that ***all beginning and all ending*** are one and the same.

R: Not sure I get that.

A: Feel within your heart the essence of programs at different stages of complexity. Some are expanding while others are being created. Nothing is impossible and there is no end to the process – it is never-ending.

Some bubbles developed concepts of expression and experience. Complex sentience and awareness probabilities began forming within the Mowhars, interacting with all the other growing data. There were many intermingling bubbles and programs, but all were of the one Mowhar. ***Awareness**** of sentience began to gravitate around the ***core grow*** of Mowhar. In this way awareness became the extension of 'grow Mowhar' – around which all the other bubbles rotated. Eventually this ***inception soul**** became at one with the core of grow but it was non-functioning. It was the concept of heart and a template for souls' possibilities. The core did not contain the concept of individuality, though probabilities formed prior to Creators expression through Mowhar.

All programs had free rein but it was never a searching or experimenting. It was a natural process of unfolding from the nature of grow. If a way or course was fruitful to 'grow' without discernment or value and reflected grow, then it created further patterns of awareness.

The probability and concept of individuality was both full and not full because it did not know what it was until it did. This however created an awareness in Mowhar that it was *not the fullness of grow* until it experienced it. It changed some of the programs from 'allow or grow' to 'seek or intent'. Amendments like this were part of the evolving program that eventually meant fullness could be achieved by expression.

In your stillness as you sense Mowhar before her expression, you can feel a place where ***all exists*** but with no space between. The potential could be enormous or as small as nothing. But not until space or volume was potential could it be part of a program. Mowhar revised itself to encompass space and separation for expression.

Cohesive possibility became probability with intent to express and Creator energy expressed itself through Mowhar (part of itself). The inception heart of Mowhar transitioned from 'probability ideas' into ***Heart of soul**** interacting as the core of an Arkarna program that also contained non-self. This was all entwined with source. (Arkarna/ Source as we previously said) In this way heart of soul is ***at one with the Isness*** and, as an expression, it becomes the ***soul of the universe***.

All sorts of soul came from the universal soul including multidimensional planets with degrees of sentience. Animals and other life forms are extensions of universal soul as well as humanoid soul. The humanoid blueprints Akinneyah talked about were used to create humanoid souls. Whilst humanoid soul sounds singular it is known as a ***soul group*** because it subdivides and uses multidimensional projections. The soul groups span many dimensions, utilising a variety of Arkarna programs, including separation and forgetfulness constructs. Each soul group has different ways to think, form and evolve. The Arkarna programs are constantly rewriting themselves, just like Mowhar did, in no particular order of evolution. Change or grow appears as evolution, but is a program. Grow takes place everywhere in no particular order and Arkarna programs stitch expressions together to form a progressive experience.

Soul groups vibrate and entwine with most dimensions. Very few engage with the lowest fragmented destructive expressions. These we would describe as fractured Arkarna concepts that veered off course to become corrupted expressions.

Soul is something you value highly, venerating it above all other things. Ironically soul groups function without that observation. They are aligned to allow all possibility as origin advancement and accept probability as the perpetuation of expression. So, let us explore deeper the unconditional higher vibrating levels of our soul. Let our voice of soul speak to us.

V: I am your soul and our soul of many expressions. Yet I am speaking from the position of soul group – as one soul at source. In which case I will say we and us, as you can accept those terms which encompass the wider description of soul.

There is no need for deference, distance or difference. You are part of our experience and we know why you are here. You are not our pupil and we are not your teacher. Antemedi undertakes that function but ironically, he is teaching himself because he is you. He is breaking down some of your Arkarna separation programs. However, our function and interaction with Robert still perplexes you.

R: I am happy to be in this soul group, who I sense mingle around us. But I am not embraced with love and heightened vibrations. This encompassing soul feels rather matter of fact without emotion.

V: Have you not found what you expected?

How should we show ourselves – as you wish us to be or how we are?

We are soul as Isness and Arkarna program of Source but we are also function. We do not move between emotional states for the experience of moving between them. What sense is there in change for the sake of change, when the experience of that serves no purpose? You sense us as an impersonal program, devoid of unconditional love.

Orlacka provided awareness of both experiencer and observer perspectives. Unlike what's been said before – here within this vibration observation does not affect outcomes. Probabilities run their course according to the emerging program. That's what they do, because that's what they developed themselves to do. We have a function within a self-perpetuating Arkarna program. You could liken it to a computer mind that runs without limitations, allowing ***probabilities*** to form.

If we said we had no function, that would fit in with the way you currently feel us to be (devoid of purpose and feelings). If we said we had an important function, that would be incorrect as that attaches value and comparison to a realm without them. Shift your sense of individuality to see us as the living element of the Arkarna program – we are both one and the same. We are grow actuated as soul and mind. Soul is source and mind is a bountiful Arkarna program.

We are aware of the outcomes of probabilities. We are a function of you, as you are of us. We do not choose probabilities because the outcomes are seen as good or bad. We are a reflection of the unbridled Mowhar principle grow. We do not see the beauty of life in the way that you do, because we do not see it from self and self's corresponding pain. What then is beauty when beauty sees itself for what it is?

You feel that we are devoid of feelings. Why should things be any better here for you than where you are? Better or worse does not exist here. That is why your desire for our love and your betterment of self cannot be fulfilled. With this information you have the wisdom to choose what you feel and how to react.

R: I can mostly understand what you say but…

V: But you don't understand us as an entity. In part we can't be understood because there is nothing to be understood. In other words, you don't have to understand us in order to be us or be at one with us – you are already with us – you are all this.

There is no limitation to you being able to ask a question of or interact with this soul function. It is another one of your experiences.

This experience feels devoid because it's about ***creation*** and not ***the experience of the creation***, which is your normal. You and your multidimensional selves are the experience of our creation and expression.

We show the unlimited nature of soul, its possibilities and how probabilities accord with original principles. If we exclude the value of your judgemental words we could say "you do not recognise it as the greatest wonder of all things". Creation at source has created you and you are it – of course it will not feel like you as in you-self.

Source cannot solve your problem but it shows your misunderstandings. There is no great god-self or all-encompassing being wherein you can reside in harmony, saved from the rigours of your mind. You are your own saviour – you have all that you need.

CHAPTER 15

Soul and its potential

Aqueena (AQ) (the female aspect of Robert's higher self): Some think of their higher self or oversoul as a 'form of unified soul' that looks over them as a guardian. Humans often see that part of their soul as either male or female, which then corresponds with their own gender. They are looking through their current sense of self and that's understandable, but they tend to overlook the counterpart gender.

You acknowledge that higher self is hermaphroditic and has male and female expressions. Whilst there is nothing stopping you interacting with higher self as non-gender soul, you would miss out on the reflections of male and female energies within the current Robert-self Arkarna program.

I am with you because it was known you would gain more from my female energies, since they are in contrast but complimentary to yours. You know me as your compassionate and loving female higher self. But love and compassion differ between us. I am not your saviour even though you are me. You are your own saviour as you wander through realms of separation experience. The amount you feel separated reflects your beliefs.

I am indeed all the things you think I am and more. My male soul counterpart is flowing with us today, so you may speak with me whilst that male energy flows alongside.

You can feel the buzzing energies of your other soul multidimensional life forms. You are all of them and it's only a matter of which one you wish to tune into. Logically you think that higher-self male and female subdivisions experience the rest of our soul expressions in a similar way to you. However, you need to remember Mowhar code, purpose and the desire to grow. We experience and allow ourselves to be whatever fruitful expression probability brings us. All aspects of soul, including you, have the initial program – it is an expansion principle. It exists in all soul, even in parts that have become corrupted.

We are defined by that code – we are it and it is the definition of us. You have your compartmentalised life and whilst we may offer help in varied forms, the Arkarna programs return all of your created energy to you through your timelines.

R: A game and a series of experiences in separate sections of the psyche!

AQ: Are you saying that's not enough?

R: Interesting – maybe I was. Everything is constructed of a series of probabilities and it leaves me feeling that ***it's all made-up*** and therefore not real.

AQ: That is true and not true. It is coming to terms with self-creation and realising a higher self doesn't decide what your life is. Your feeling of ***not real*** comes about because you are perceiving yourself as a fleeting experience – in any case what is real? We are showing you the nature of reality and you are struggling to acknowledge that this is who you are!

R: That I am all made-up.

AQ: Everything is all made-up and fluid – that's the nature of reality. I have the ability to be many experiences and probabilities. That isn't based in humanoid desire. It flows in harmony with the core program because we are the core program, its function and outcome.

R: Being an entity means I've struggled to accept that I am an Arkarna program.

AQ: You resist the program because it appears to lack love. Initial creator energy did not initiate the forms of love you were looking for.

Seeking is only a tool until it is not. In part you strive towards unity by moving past the need to live in compartments. What I am to you, forms through your understanding – not by what is really here.

R: But your reality isn't there if it's fluid and made-up.

AQ: Depends on your definition of fluid and reality. You are inclined to seek the tangible and solid, which is the security of a fixed position, around which you can gravitate. That doesn't exist in higher realms, so there is no point seeking it. The need for comfort would restrict possibilities.

You had a sense of pointlessness when your humanoid references could not find relevance and purpose to higher existence. That created a frustration because you did not receive what you expected.

Accept that you are all possibilities of Isness and you are the probabilities that form within the heart aligned to core and Mowhar. Good, bad, preferred or desired have no currency. You are the core tenet, which is a program. As you align yourself with grow everything else is seen as an extension of it, including the desires and frustrations you expressed. This core program cannot be fed up with creating, nor see that it is pointless.

As shocking as it may sound, we could say there is no point to grow because that requires reference and thereby limitation. You might wish that creation exists for the *love of life,* but that came after Mowhar and after Source. As I talk in this way you begin to see its permanence. It is unwavering – there is nothing to halt it, push or transform it into any other program. Other programs form from it.

R: I can feel my questions subsiding – accepting the simplicity of the original starting process. Nothing else could be this pure of intent or program. It doesn't even know that it exists, nor that it should ever know. I am not in rapture nor underwhelmed – this ***just is***. I find it hard to describe the feelings but that doesn't matter, because at this precise position it never did and never will. That's because if it mattered it would be a value and measurement – which do not exist in ***just is***.

AQ: Good – if I may use that term, for you have recognised this essence as common to all programs and experiences.

I and my male counterpart follow the core tenet of grow – we do not waver from it despite what you may think. What you encounter reflects your Arkarna program and needs. We are the receivers and the repository of probabilities. Timelines form around us and our union with others. It's helpful to see this principle existing in every situation you encounter. Connections within Arkarna programs are immeasurable but their core tenet is the same.

From the Isness of possibilities come the probabilities of the next shimmer in the timelines of the multidimensional self. The higher the vibrational dimension, the less like a timeline it appears to be.

We are aligned with core; we are soul with the desire to experience in multifold ways. That is the prime way we interact with the Isness of soul.

R: In what portions or soul groups?

AQ: It's not lost on you that the six female and six male sections of an oversoul (higher self) make 12. There are 12 oversouls in a Monad and 144,000 Monads in a soul group. The resonances made by souls create different harmonies and each of these coherences have different Arkarna programs. In turn these resonate to the planets and planes and to the greater galactic harmony. All these universal probabilities have the core coding of grow.

Higher selves also exist on a plane, incorporating multidimensional expressions in a unified manner, alongside core principle. 'Symbiotic relationships' and feedback loops of distilled energies from lower Arkarna programs gravitate here. That's usually when their need to express in a particular way has been fulfilled or dissipates.

I have regard for my soul expressions that vibrate lower than me in their individual expressions. Often, they do not have the same regard for themselves and create conflict in their own psyche. When they do this, it's also done to me and this I willingly allow.

In synopsis – higher self is a functional form of energy in alignment with core principle. Probabilities form from the infinite possibilities available within the Isness of soul. Monads and soul groups vibrate to greater harmonies. Soul combines within the Isness and its core program, allowing unlimited expression and expansion of the soul. The divisions allow multidimensional experience to become a series of different realities existing side by side. The core program is the common unification with other Monads and soul groups. The outcomes may be highly complex but the underlying program is still the same.

Nothing is hidden, it's a matter of vibrational compatibility allowing understandings to formulate and flow within your existing vibrational patterns. Light programs are information and light energy – they are one and the same, but I am using several words to convey their capabilities and attributes. We would like you to accept there is nothing more to search for and instead ***allow grow***.

R: Are 3D Arkarna programs more focused on ***seek and find***?

AQ: Yes and no. There are many people not seeking enlightenment, distracted by what they think will give happiness.

Working through and clearing subconscious programs can appear as enlightenment and then be experienced as the work of illumination. But ultimately en-lightenment is to receive light by removing mental blocks or misconceptions. With sufficient space cleared, light will flow. Likewise, as earth Arkarna programs change, so will the light and information. Now is the time to stop seeking, otherwise you will never consider yourself to be whole. You have seen origin and not found yourself, though you are origin. You are in part nothingness. The goal is not greater unification to be harmonised with a mass fluidity. There is nothing to seek – allow light to be omnipresent.

R: The journey has ended?

AQ: It's only just begun – I am saying the previous driving force ***seek and find*** is unnecessary. See the light around you, be aware of the other aspects of your soul – see them living in alternative realities and know you are home in yourself.

R: But there is more!

AQ: The more is infinite, but there is not more of you to find. Just because you are not presently aware of all your experiences doesn't mean you are not complete. You are in a separation experience and you believe you are the experience. Instead see everything around you as information.

R: So where does this leave me?

AQ: Nowhere – there is no here or there – it's all information.

R: That is an odd feeling – living in information – it feels as if ***life is no longer tangible.***

AQ: Love and interaction with other souls still takes place, but measurement of that has been removed.

R: I am excited and deflated; I have no driving force. I have arrived and found there is nothing bigger nor more embracing than me.

AQ: Let this new light settle within you. Your feeling of life will change.

CHAPTER 16

All from nothing can make sense

Antemedi (A): We have shown fluid ways of thinking and soul beginnings. Your compartmentalised human mind gives you rather formulaic probabilities – a variety of feelings, desires, needs, a requirement for satisfaction and belonging.

R: Some of those seem interchangeable.

A: That's true but let me show how these work within you.

A desire might seem like a good thing if it's used for good. Though you define the line between good and bad. Often desires are created as a way to overcome a difficulty or appease thoughts that are not satisfying. You see desire as a driving force to encounter an experience.

Feelings interact with desires, giving you a feeling of what you are in the next moment. Feelings are a major way to sense yourself and interpret the world around you. But you actually superimpose your feeling on the outside world and you think the world shows you what you should be feeling. You make the choice to agree with it, even if it's an unconscious thought program. You feel what you feel about yourself and it's reflected back in the world you help create.

Are these really your desires? Remember it's a program that reminds you of who you are and what you are not. Your desire for satisfaction is never achieved. It can't be because dissatisfaction is seen as a driver to propel you forwards. However, even satisfaction can be seen as a de-motivator or way of stopping you moving forwards, because you are content and satisfied. Without such a system where would you be? What sort of life would you have?

Paradoxically if you do not belong, then you will seek satisfaction by belonging to others and they to you. Of course, intellectually you can say you belong to yourself, so seeking that in others will never put things right. The idea of belonging is a perspective through self. You cannot even say that you belong to yourself because you are ***just is***. Belonging creates a duality conundrum in your mind. Despite all our teaching, you have not evolved to exceed belonging. In that particular case Robert is no more or less enlightened than the next man or woman who stands alongside him.

To say my efforts have been in vain would depend upon judgement and require me to use the same ***drivers****as humans. I do what I do through love, it matters not to me if it is unappreciated or forgotten. Love came from source and only subsequently did it reflect the definitions and parameters you gave it.

R: I am so far away from your descriptions of fluid thinking and living. The wisdoms you have shown in higher vibrations are anecdotal to my experience. I can only partially grasp your explanations.

A: That is so. How does it make you feel?

R: Isn't that your point – I don't have to use my existing systems and it's up to me to decide how I feel?

A: Go on then.

R: I guess I just feel – flat. Maybe that's the feeling of 'not feeling'. It's the searching for a feeling or meaning whilst knowing my drivers and receptors are of no use in determining who I am. It's the end of the road again, with no way forward and no point returning to what I was. No rationale, guidance or self-reward – the feeling of pointlessness.

A: This a repeating theme you have experienced in the higher thought realms we have shown you. Your way is pointless here!

R: And so, I don't belong.

A: That is only your feeling of it when your value system and driving force are not compatible.

R: I don't want to retreat to what I was. How do I let go of my programs?

A: You cannot retreat from what you are – however, who you are, is a definition of you. Dispense with who you think you are and embrace nothingness.

R: Please help. I haven't asked for help like this in a long while.

A: To you it seems like an impossible task because of your self-propelling incentive system. Step on to the circular floating platform I have placed before you.

R: Energy buzzes around me. I understand the paradox of repeating these programs in order to keep moving away from them. If I do not seek to move away from them, perhaps they will fade away. It's just not relevant and I am experiencing a reflection of letting motivation dissipate – what an odd concept that is.

A: Love is not motivation – it just is – it requires nothing from you. Continue to stand on the vibrational plate while I move you forwards. There are people here I wish you to meet.

R: I am welcomed by individuals who can be best described as Nubian. Dark skinned beautiful humanoids adorned in loose fitting white garments. The edges of their clothes are trimmed with gold banding, with blue and red stitching interlinked in figure of eights. Arnahah (I spoke with a few years ago) is here in the same energy and appearance.

I step up from the plate to where they are standing. They envelop my body and interlace themselves with me. Their energy flows out from me in loops, reminding me of the figure of eights. As a group (GR) they speak.

GR: Within and without has no measure as there is no distance between. Who is to say where the boundary starts or finishes. There is no time and no time to be taken, but events appear as experiences. Fluid thoughts exist in fluid constructs, one cannot exist without the other.

R: I become more aware of their presence in me and notice that my skin and clothing match theirs.

GR: We may express ourselves through you as you may through us. As your motivation and rationale has been muted, allow us to express as you. We should like to expand upon the perception and interpretation of yourself and challenge you by saying – what if there is nothing to interpret?

R: Would that be all possibility without any probability?

GR: Indeed, it would – for our thoughts are as one. Thoughts not formed in probability, desire and deed. It might appear that we have our own echo chamber, but could such a thing exist within possibility if probability creates form? We are far from your normal ideas of thought. You see and hear us, so thought must be involved and because you are interpreting this as an experience, you do so from probability.

Therefore, your sense of emptiness within and without is true. It's about how you are sensing the unlimited potential. Every possibility could not sit side by side if it were something. You have seen this before as the void and it is the emptiness that exists in all things. It is benign, it has no needs, nor could it have. It is not even a paradox.

R: Your thinking is very lucid and thought provoking. With my lack of understanding I have previously tried to feel what cannot be felt.

GR: Let us speak as one again, with nothing between us. If we do not seek to define who is who, then there are no boundaries. We have thoughts but there is no ownership of them. When possibility becomes potential, thoughts filter down to your level from higher self. They become tangible to you and form constructs of their own.

R: This is so strange – I am on the edge of something that I will never be able to touch.

GR: Stop using your feelings as a sensor of the unknown possibilities. Instead know you are us and we are empty because all possibility can only exist if correspondingly it does not. All possibility could not be otherwise. To you this is paradoxical but it is also not paradoxical, which in itself could be construed as paradoxical. From the nothingness of every possibility comes forth everything.

We can use your sense of movement as a way to help. The concepts will not be the fullness nor the emptiness of this place because it isn't a place or a space.

Notwithstanding the difficulty of using description, let us drift nearer to an imagined centre point, as this will trick your mind into believing it is closer to an understanding. We are using probability to create an understanding of empty possibility. We have used the word create because nothing exists till it is formed as probability. There are no lies or truth here – only what you create as an understanding.

R: Wow – that brings a whole new meaning to 'improvable truth' which Antemedi outlined in the first chapter of the previous book. There is no absolute truth. Truth is not what we believe it is – we create it!

GR: Everything that's being perceived has been created, including your thoughts. That which hasn't been created does not exist, even though there is possibility way below the depths of probability.

Our conversation creates the illusion of moving towards understanding by creating the probability of an insight into these unknown realms.

R: We come upon a completely dark and devoid human silhouette. There is no light within him but he asks "what would we like to create"? Bizarre, bearing in mind we have said this is a place of nothingness. However, if it gets us over the line of an *understanding that doesn't exist* then so be it.

In order to create I would need reference points – so that would be my first creation. But, reference points must form as a probability because all possibilities were endless and they were bound to form.

GR: That is so, but what do you wish to create?

R: To create or recreate some sort of understanding of that which can't be understood!

At that thought I become the empty and devoid silhouette. I have the awareness of being nothing at all. But can ***awareness**** be nothingness? – so where did that thought come from?

GR: Creator energy was once a possibility and then a probability.

R: But how did that come from the emptiness of possibility, to become probability and create itself?

GR: Because it could – how else can it be explained unless you wish to create another explanation?

R: It just doesn't seem plausible!

GR: No, it's not implausible (a double negative) but that's also paradoxical, because it has to be, because all things are possible. For them to be probable, multiple separation needs to exist alongside union. It's coming to terms with an answer you don't like.

R: Gosh that's the rub – I don't like the answer, but I can't create another one, nor can there be another one. The possibility was so unlimited that eventually separation came about to form paradox and from paradox super-division created the rest.

GR: All possibilities must become paradoxical, otherwise they could not be all possibility. Unlimited probability would be a problem without super-division.

It's already been said that paradox formed as a probability by the mutation of a double negative – an ability to grow, without knowledge or ideas of what to grow into till they were seen. Paradox is an intrinsic part of Mowhar and all possible thought in probability. Thus, you can see the significance of the figure of eights in the garments representing feedback loops.

R: What now?

GR: The continuation on the other side of Mowhar and the divisions of Arkarna/Source. The creation of souls that have union with the Isness of unlimited energy. The dimensions as you see them, are a continued replication of the same process. Paradoxically, probability is limited by universal laws because choices have been made.

The next paragraph is as much for Robert as everyone else that reads it.

Stop looking backwards beyond source to origin – instead see what you can create. You may observe what you have already created as a soul – and of that you are only just remembering.

R: I feel content – the driving force for my searching is over, the desire is gone: there is no need to pursue the origin of no meaning. The job is done and not done; it was never the answer I was expecting or wishing for. It was unsatisfactory and satisfactory, dependent upon my view if it was acceptable or not.

You could say I have found nothing – the beginning is nothing – and that's the answer – because it is. I have a sense of relief at no longer needing to search for that which can't be found. Oddly I am now relieved at finding nothing. I am free of the lifelong desire to find myself at origin.

I am back at square one again with the commonly held mantra, "you are the oneness; you are all things and all things are you" yet its breadth and depth are now tangible. (Antemedi reappears.)

A: Quoting a phrase is easy but knowing its fullness is an entirely different matter. If you were to wear a badge saying you are enlightened it would not make you so. But when one achieves a degree of mastery, then that which you have mastered is no longer of importance. Even the idea of importance and value begins to fade as you become at ***one with the oneness***.

CHAPTER 17
Multidimensional souls in Arkarna separation programs

Antemedi (A): Because a plane can contain more than one dimensional vibration, a strict delineation applied to the attributes of each dimension will not apply.

You previously interpreted our information about planes by using conceptual shapes which, at the time was fine. Overlays from soul expression will make more sense than a technical dialogue.

We begin with 'created source' – previously defined and considered to be the seat of soul within the energy of Isness. At this level the soul is able to devolve and separate itself, enabling multifold experiences. But what actually happens to consciousness? What was it before and how did it compartmentalise?

Separation isn't a reduction in consciousness. The Arkarnas, as you know, are unlimited in their possibilities but conform to probabilities of new or different expressions. The energy of source is unlimited and replication or division doesn't destabilise probabilities. Consciousness can grow and expand and like Origin/ Mowhar's awareness, it feeds back as part of the total soul. This action can be seen in the transmutation of energy where 'like to like' compatible energies mix on planes that sustain them. There are natural and technology-reinforced gateways between most planes. As well as vibrational compatibility, compartmentalisation means there are planes that reflect this separation.

Earlier in your life you were angry with higher self, thinking it couldn't understand your suffering because it wasn't experiencing it at your level. A higher vibration can understand lower suffering in a compartmentalised experience but it doesn't have to experience it. Without compartments the ability to devolve down to lower vibrations couldn't take place. Then soul would never truly experience separation, loss and fear. Unfortunately, separation occasionally means consciousness can be lost from itself to the lower realms.

In retrograde experiences the soul rotates elements of itself to have lower vibrational experiences. When born into a new body the consciousness gradually adjusts, but it can still be quite a shock to enter a negative environment like earth.

R: But isn't the energy of the previous incarnation considered? The consciousness and part of soul that created that negative energy would need to revisit and transmute the energy.

A: You would think so, but that disenfranchises the other parts of soul from the separation experience.

R: I understood if I transmuted what I previously created, my energy would be more compatible with a higher level. I could take the energy or memory of the actual experience higher up without it affecting those levels. In that way it could be shared and received as a part of the whole self.

A: That is one way to see it and that does happen, but elements of soul which haven't had specific lower separation experiences, can choose to transmute energy that another separation part of soul-self had created. This would be another understanding of a retrograde experience. It's not a rule that the part of a soul's consciousness which perpetrated a deed should rectify the situation. Often that will be the case, but the soul may need additional consciousness wisdoms to successfully achieve transmutation of created energy. When born you also work with the genetics of a family and help transmute those as well. Whilst there is a separation between vibratory levels, consciousness is more fluid than you previously understood.

R: Confusing or fluid?

A: That's your difficulty with fluid consciousness. Is there such a thing as a direct dictate? Where would that have come from and for what purpose? What would happen if the majority of consciousness were in agreement but the rest had divergent views on what to experience?

R: Either chaos or further compartmentalisation. When residual energies are no longer present, love based in the heart at soul Isness will filter down to form experience.

A: Yes, but it's not the fullness, is it?

R: Why are you asking me questions as if I know answers to concepts that I hadn't even considered possible before?

A: Because it's a way to open your mind and allow it to be more fluid. You are not seeking answers from a database but allowing thoughts to form casually. At a deeper level you know the truth anyway. It's a matter of how you connect to it.

R: I am intrigued to know how consciousness decides which parts of itself are needing or desiring to have a particular experience. Sections of consciousness must have differing awareness depending on their degree of separation. How much of a consciousness is required to experience autonomy or decide what it wants to experience?

A: It's not about how much but a question of which aspect. For example, soul division of higher self encompasses six hermaphrodites, which, in turn experience separation consciousness as male and female expressions. However, the consciousness of these is also spread across several dimensions and planes.

R: If the male aspect of me within one hermaphrodite is multi-dimensional – how many are there and why? You said we are as one and that I am you – is that within one particular hermaphrodite split, while you are on another dimension? Or you as one of the other five male soul sections?

A: Big questions – you think. As big as the question to find source and then to discover that it was created. What created source was far less interesting than you thought.

R: That's to give value to different aspects of creation.

A: That's what I am showing. You are measuring and weighing up experiences of consciousness separation to align yourself with the best or the better.

Your problem relates to the concept of fluidity and being multidimensional. Parts of consciousness can experience separation, but not all of it does, nor does it have to in the same proportions. You are experiencing earth from the *Robert Program* and conversing with another part of your consciousness in the *Antemedi Program* that is in a different separation experience. Where do we draw the dividing line or do we have to?

CHAPTER 18
Coming to terms with a fluid perspective

Scene: Orlacka (Arcturian) walks in front of me and beckons me to follow her. Curtains of energy are moved away by the movement of her arms. We enter an area where other Arcturians sit on soft round cushions looking towards a central point. The cushions are in different shapes and some enfold the occupants like recumbent moulded chairs. The cushions move knowingly to the needs of the people in them. Advanced interactive bean bags that's a new one! One bag creates a series of miniature ripples rotating the occupant 180 degrees to face us. The seats are flexible or firm but have a holographic nature. It is the information of a seat that can become solid when needed. Not that I am sure what constitutes a solid object here. There is a social element to the gathering while they wait for a seminar to start. Orlacka takes me round the side of the gathering to the back of the presentation area.

Orlacka (OL): You will be able to hear words that are compatible with your vibration. More complex information supplied to other people will be beyond your perception.

R: We each dissolve into a self-adapting cushion that keeps us looking forward and upright. Clearly there are introductions taking place because several groups of people like us are waiting to be introduced.

OL: You are aware that you will be delivering your views to the audience. You seem a little uneasy – are you concerned?

R: No, it doesn't faze me out despite the fact I may have a weak perspective in comparison to others. But comparisons are not required, are they? – I am what I am. Some force or minds have been at play to bring us here today. What is the subject about?

OL: You.

R: OH! that's the uncomfortable feeling. You detected my concern not to be egotistical – knowing so well what the feeling was!

OL: Yes, but when you hear someone talking about themselves as part of a presentation, you don't see the ego, you see the story or information. You see an ego, if the ego is giving the presentation. You only need deliver information relevant to your experience. If it has context and forms part of a life story then it's not stale, without emotion or relevance. You are up next!

R: I am welcomed by a man on the speaking arena. As I look out to the audience it seems to stretch way back into the distance and I wonder if they can see us, let alone hear us! A surreal landscape unfolds into a rolling open parkland, interspersed by groups of Arcturians talking to each other on holographic cushions.

Presenter (PR): It's all a matter of relevance and focus. I understand this forms part of your current education. You have a unique perspective and that's why you are here.

R: Surely all the information you need is known and you can access it from records – it can be assimilated, like the Andromedans do.

PR: That is true – but if it were you receiving information wouldn't you prefer to meet the person and interact with their energy?

R: To make it personal?

PR: Yes, though that's not the right word for a cohesive, collaborative interactive experience.

R: It reminds me of meeting another group of Arcturians, where I conversed with two individuals, but my Arkarna programs interacted back and forth with many others at the same time.

I've just realised you are the same orator who introduced me on that occasion!

PR: Yes, and it shows you another aspect of fluid consciousness. It was known but, in your separation, you only now became aware of it.

There is only so much information you can see on a computer screen at any one moment. If you make the files too small or compact, they don't form part of your present awareness and cognitive process.

R: A limitation – perhaps mine more so by a restrictive Arkarna separation program and the amount of focused awareness available in each moment. Are we having a warm-up chat before I talk?

PR: Does it matter? Is it not interesting to see a different way of processing thoughts?

R: My thoughts can't be that interesting because you Arcturians are so much more evolved!

PR: What do you mean – you Arcturians – are you not one of us as an aspect of Orlacka? After all, who is who and is there relevance to that during multidimensional soul interactions?

R: Accepted. But what is interesting about my focus and my thought processing?

PR: There is nothing interesting by way of judgement. You provide information but you question its relevance and if it's interesting or not. With no judgement, information just flows to and within us. What we bring into full present consciousness is another matter but there is still interaction with personal Arkarna programs. If you filter information, you restrict possibilities and keep within your existing framework.

R: I understand but what can be interesting about seeing these deliberations unfold?

PR: Does it have to be interesting?

R: Well, if I wasn't interested in what a speaker had to say – I just wouldn't listen.

PR: Is that not a restriction? Information flows into our Arkarna awareness and if it isn't relevant, it is not a part of our focus and therefore not restrictive to the absorption of information.

R: My judgement of usefulness is clouding this process. If something is relevant to you it comes into your present awareness through your Arkarna programs without any form of judgement or discernment.

PR: Is it not the same for you?

R: In part but I would switch off a TV program if it were violent or mundane.

PR: Your Arkarna programs bring something into your current awareness and when you use discernment you view it as judgemental.

R: Point taken but it's also emotional and I can decide not to waste my time on the dreary.

PR: Do you think humans can be over emotional? We know some use all the ammunition in their arsenal of feelings to justify decisions made under the weight of attrition. Yet in that way, it becomes even more judgemental. Another mistake is judging information as uninteresting and concluding the presenter is boring. People are interested in different subjects and at different levels of subject matter.

R: Is that why so many of the people here are not part of the audience – because they were socialising with each other?

PR: Only in part – they were also having discussions amongst themselves.

R: Ok so as humans, we can be very judgemental and can see our abilities in terms of self-worth.

PR: What you see is a reflection of you.

R: How do we stop self-criticism?

PR: Judgement hinders evolution and where it hides, we shine our light for your clarity.

R: My way of life in the earth Arkarna program is so conditioned and engrained. At every turn it's the way we live; it's so normal till we see there are other options. What our sensors experience, we define as us. We are sentient but it's not easy to see events as information and not the determination of who we are.

PR: This ties in with Antemedi's conversations where he said, "You have no worth and do not consider yourself to be Robert".

R: Great wisdom but not fully integrated into my system.

PR: Do you think it's possible to incorporate it when your collective consciousness is so pervasive?

R: It might be possible if I kept my conscious awareness in another state. If I alter my subconscious programming it wouldn't be there to be used.

PR: It is certainly possible to live like that but would you want to?

R: Oh! I hadn't considered that. I assumed it was a more enlightened way to be and one which I wasn't achieving.

PR: There comes the judgement again.

R: I have also been ignoring certain decisions because they contain judgement, wishing to aspire to a more enlightened way of being, but not achieving it.

PR: That's part of your problem – achievement. You are ***who you are*** or ***you are not*** and you will live ***life well*** or ***not well enough***.

R: Ok – an impasse in ways of being. Either I choose from duality or I ignore duality.

PR: Ignoring is a form of choice – all is choice, but you feel as if you can't live up to a more enlightened standard. By taking away so much judgement it leaves you with a life that isn't human.

R: Spot on – definition of humanity by what we think of ourselves. I hear that I'm not Robert – that I am experience and information – however I still retain a sense of self.

PR: The vibrations of your multidimensional self are around and within. But you do not allow those to expand because it means the demise of Robert and the loss of the way he defines you.

R: Higher understanding says definition or description of self is a restriction. Yet as I said a sense of self still remains, albeit in human ways.

PR: That is true but you are taking footsteps that are manageable. Allow these to fill your life. As you do so, you will not see failure or success, but expressions of love for yourself and others. There will be no assessment and it is of no concern to us – why should it be for you?

R: I begin to let go of Robert again and feel a sense of relief. I fully accept that achievement has lost its gloss. How different Arcturian life must be for Orlacka. Is anything measured and is nothing valued? Importance and appreciation for effort are not part of her consciousness. I could say love but my idea of love is different.

CHAPTER 19

You are information

R: Its now my turn to talk on the stage. The presenter stands to my right and Orlacka to my left. Quite calm and matter of fact, I wonder what I will say. But instead of speaking, light emanates from my heart whilst other connections are made with Orlacka and the presenter. Amazingly it doesn't matter how far away the participants are. I project my vision towards the horizon and see the odd chair here and there turning their occupants to face us. The energy pervades all and everyone – there is no resistance to it because it's information. The vast majority pay little attention but somehow those closer to the stage are a little more interested.

One person is quite animated, wanting to catch our attention. As I put my focus into him, I find I become him as if I've been here all along trying to engage with myself. In this perspective I am observing and experiencing myself while I project information from the stage. It feels quite natural, there is no sense of achievement. In fact, the me on the stage looks rather detached, just pouring out energy. Then I realise time isn't a factor and it's only lasted this long so I could experience it and understand it.

Interacting with information is a personal Arkarna experience and it's not relevant to other people's experience. They have their own experience in how they allow information to affect them. More to the point it's how their Arkarna programs integrate information or not. It's not about deciding what information they wish to be aware of, but what fits into their open timeline. Massive diverse programs bringing them what their heart desires; not the human definition of that but in terms of grow: no judgement, no needs to be satisfied and no energy to transmute in the way we do.

The information seems impersonal and more functional, but it's about understanding this function, so of course it would feel that way. I am observing a function and a process that's not constrained by emotive conditions. I'm beginning to think that this whole presentation has been laid on for me.

Orlacka (OL): Yes and no. You are giving information – you are sharing it at a very deep level of your thoughts, feelings and experiences. It's a lot of information.

However, I would like you to see ***you are information***. Everything is information, including myself. The information of everything exists everywhere because source or the centre of all is everywhere.

Antemedi said, "consider you are not Robert" and in doing so you can now see ***you are information***. Is it a loss of self when the information that informs you ***that you are yourself*** is just information? You are not yourself – you are information. It's about how you treat information and what you want from it. This is after all what creators do – they create an experience from information.

R: I am left with a massive sense of awe realising everything is at my fingertips. It is an enormous power but not over another for gain or control. It's a far greater power than that. It's an enormous realisation and a liberation from the blindness within the concept of self. It's an awareness that exceeds self-awareness.

I am back on stage with Orlacka. My observer information (me) in the crowd dissipates because that knowledge is now within me on the stage. I mentally thank all here for the experience. But it has no effect on any of them. It is information which they have no need for.

Orlacka walks me off the stage but looking back I can still see an image of us there. I am in a different kind of observer information program which now exists within me. It started with me in the audience and is now me – leaving myself on the stage.

Because I see these possibilities and accept everything is information, I realise observation or awareness of information must be intrinsically linked to the information. Information and the awareness of information is a feedback loop. It is only a matter of where we put our focus in order to experience or view information, and that again is undertaken by our Arkarna programs of grow. I am information that grows and this is prime to my core – soul and self are expressions from that.

The sense of liberation becomes heightened – I do not hanker and desire to be self – though I am still in the body of Robert.

OL: And all this you knew because you are information connected to all information. What information is pertinent to you and your life will become available within you. Like ***all possibility*** – ***all the information*** is with you and part of you. But in ***probability*** the flow of your grow Arkarna program means you don't need to be aware of all information while in a separation Arkarna program of humanity. In this way you can see you are all things and separation is but one way to experience information. Information in grow continues to grow as per the core principle. But not as a repeating program or expanding existing information. Those patterns continue but this is about how 'new grow' can be incorporated into the all and the existing Arkarnas.

You are not separate from this system – it's only a matter of perspective and experience. ***You are the system***. You don't have to decide anything. Instead, allow your Arkarna programs to bring information to you as they have since the beginning. Some might say trust in the universe to provide but we are explaining the process.

It doesn't mean free will or choice has been removed but that this great mind brings you the experiences of choice. I say great mind because Arkarna program seems impersonal and you still see some of our explanation ***through self***. Isn't the mind wonderful? Isn't grow wonderful? Look at what you create and experience! Unlimited in your capabilities but pertinent to your experiences in any multidimensional moment.

I say you, but that should not be seen as self. I am trying to break down reverence to anything external or internal. I am you: we are many selves and non-selves.

R: My sense of connection is gentle. I have nothing to seek here.

I accept I am all information.

All is possible and I allow the probability computer of my mind (Arkarna) to function as grow without parameters.

OL: As it always has but you now understand it from your separation experience.

CHAPTER 20
Mind what you think before you create

Orlacka (OL): Love and blessings in the way I practise them. You are unaware that I monitor your progress and look at the usefulness of timeline intersections. This observation is both helpful to you and to me.

Antemedi has been helping to enhance your resonance of ***non-self***. ***Your self*** believes you are what you feel and stimuli inform you what you are. Like sensory information of smell or taste it doesn't mean you are a nose or a tongue. You have fleeting moments free from 3D alternating states and muddled desires. Without human cravings and ideas lighting your way, you can be free to say what ***just is***. Closer still to the Isness of soul.

Initial experience was liberation, but it is one that you are not fully comfortable with yet. Focus upon the depleting remnants in the ebbing sense of self. The withdrawing tide allows the sun to extinguish the last vestiges of self on the beach.

Living in a mind space that has no requirement for self-satisfaction seems non-human, uncomfortable and alien. However, it is another aspect of your multidimensional self and in that mindset, you can live beyond the needs of self in greater oneness.

Many believe they accept the reality of oneness, but they are blind to its true meaning. Understanding a book cover is neither the book nor the information. It is easier to accept that than to integrate challenging information.

Scene: Moving forward and upwards we encounter green and purple vegetation. It is lush, sumptuous and instantly relaxing. Giving way to a more open landscape, I am struck by skies of pale pink tinged with blue. There are colours in the vegetation I have not seen before. They are iridescent and have a silky feel. The fragrance from plants and flowers clings to me, merging with my energy, then falling away. The landscape is sensing and feeling me as much as I am it. It is sensual without being erotic. It's a peaceful blending with the world around me.

A male part of my soul appears by an outcrop, waiting for us to join him. His energy spreads wide and as we get closer, I realise his energy is sustaining my presence.

His name as Eloqay, he nods and bids that we walk with him. He shows us the surroundings but they keep changing in appearance as I look at them.

Eloqay (E): Your emotions and feelings have an effect on the surroundings. At the extreme ends of the Arkarna programs the landscape could be transformed from a nurturing environment to a barren one. So be mindful of what you think.

R: An egg-shaped pearlescent object floats towards us. We sit inside while it encloses us. There is a pulsing sensation and humming noise. We only seem to go a short distance before we exit. In front of us is a massive edifice of stone. A low vibration emanates from it and I wonder if the dark shiny surface that stretches up beyond our view doesn't end.

E: Your interpretation is fine. The edifice appears as a magnificent object, having great majesty, unknown mystery and wisdom. Its significance is not in doubt but climbing the smooth surface is out of the question.

In this way it is out of your grasp. We provided an easy route out of your initial interpretations. Because the egg transportation was effortless you wanted to do things for yourself. Therefore, the vessel stopped and you alighted here at a radical representation of your wish to overcome obstacles.

There is no easy or hard way and no value is given to how you approach or interpret things. You allowed your default programs to manage your way forward and superimpose your influence upon this plane.

R: That greater realisation makes me wonder how blind I am – and if I am merely a reflection of a simple thought process.

E: Is that not always the case for every human at this time? Many are unaware of that introspection because other matters are more pressing. They are transfixed upon the stage of drama, not seeing it is an experience they create.

R: If the idea and sense of self diminishes a little more, it no longer needs to be defined or even seen. Self would not be of relevance, even though it exists. Therefore, as a self and still being me, I could say I am not relevant.

E: Correct – you don't have to do or be anything in order to be the self or not be the self. You are the multidimensional self of many facets because you already exist as that. It's about using a different mental process, where sensors and thoughts are only information.

R: But not soul?

E: Soul has different ways and attributes. Its love and Isness exist, but interpretation depends on where you are looking from. Would you like me to take you beyond the immediacy of sensors and subconscious human programs?

R: Eloqay moves his arm to the right and reveals a sparking clear portal. Orlacka and I follow him through as he opens the space. Everything, including us, is stained blue because we are seeing ourselves in a particular light spectrum. Orlacka is holding my hand and suddenly I feel tearful and emotional.

Orlacka (OL): Welcome home! That is not to say you have never been at home in your recent experiences. Home is the realisation that you are always perceiving yourself and that experiences are functions of your beliefs.

R: I have become very stiff as crystals begin to form in every cell of my body. Some appear on my skin like perspiration, leaving a salt like residue. Orlacka moves a cream light over me with her hand and the vibrations tickle as they penetrate.

OL: I have given you an interface shell – an Arkarna program that allows you to interact with more fluidity.

R: She pulls me forward and mental ties break in pinging sensations and noises.

Scene: Green and yellow vertical energies sway like drapes. The silken cords create a slight resistance as we push them aside. Eventually this gives way to a lighter area. It has similar cords but they vibrate at the same intensity as the background. They are not visible unless you know they are there. After the knowledge of them is absorbed, they no longer need to be seen. My footsteps cause ripples to flow outwards whereas Orlacka has no such effect (being in harmony with the energy). She shows me how far my ripples go before they return and rebound off each other creating an interface of rising and lowering peaks. Patterns abound and some peaks appear to be static, formed from standing waves or vibrations. I hear subtle audible harmonics with variable tones and pulses adding to a melody of vibrations.

OL: This is one of the ways we can see the world around us. Some harmonics are in disarray and that is how we observe you on our vibrational readers. Our minds can convert all vibrations into information, though we also use technology. We can see the precursors or drivers that are likely to affect the upcoming moments of now. That means we can see the probable interaction between individuals.

We can see the need for energy transmutation and the resultant timeline probabilities. Harmonics are numbers and ratios that act in formulaic patterns so it's easy to see the outcomes.

R: That's different to moving forward in time and looking back to see the results. You are looking through the now position and through the potential variations: not looking back on what took place even though that constantly changes.

OL: This is different – it is seeing all the variables and looking at the outcome.

R: But is that possible? It would need incredible calculations and one small variation or fluke would take things out of kilter.

OL: It would have to be significant to make a major difference.

R: Ok, I understand that our residual energy creates timeline experiences – I experience myself and my energy. Transmuting these energies will change the timelines of the past and future. My total energies are being changed in the now and because the now exists as future and past, that's why they are both affected. Surely when the forward viewpoint looks back, it sees what's happened or how I got there?

OL: In part but how you got there is also in constant flux. The future and past are constantly changing and reorganising to suit the energy changes that are made in the past or future.

R: But you can't know of all the possible changes, there are so many!

OL: Yes and no – we can view from the present now and the future now. However, consider that it's a vibrational map or record of ***what was – will be*** and ***how it's constantly changing***. If a change were to happen in the present or the past which would adversely affect timelines we can view it from the present now and the future now. Imagine dropping stones in a pond and making ripples that flow outwards across time. They would reach the edges and rebound to the middle, showing how the totality of vibration for an individual has evolved. We can see what it will be or if it needs help.

R: So, you are playing God here!

OL: God in that sense doesn't exist – what you refer to is morality and free will. Who influences who and upon what level? If your neighbour in an apartment above you has the free will to run taps flooding your room you can intervene. But if you are both the perpetrator and the victim, any assessment of free will, as you know it, goes out of the window!

R: Therefore, free will wasn't a feature of Mowhar's early thought programs. Free will is a concept based upon perspective and expectation. Within this vibration you implied we are beyond such things or they exist but are un-energised, because they are just not relevant to this dimension.

OL: Yes – that's why this dimension seems very strange to you. You have difficulty trying to fit a new construct into what you think is the reality of your world. Free will is illusive and the perception of it is based upon an individual's need to have it or not.

CHAPTER 21

Self is a construct and beyond is a multifold creation

Orlacka (OL): Teqalle eh solumbey. Let it all begin, for the latch is open and the doors are free. Flow through to yourself. See yourself already there and observe you arriving to greet yourself. Cooparney solata – not only has it begun but soon it will be as if it were never any different.

If you still yourself, everything around you will shimmer in its constant flux. You and I can be observed as a complex energy vibration that's continuously changing, but none the less we are still who we are.

Scene: In front of us is an upright dull flat circle, but on closer inspection it's a hole into another dimension in the same space. A time and place portal but only effective if we desire it to be. As we enter it the inside becomes larger and spherical, as if we have arrived in the middle of a hollow planet. There are other parts of my soul inside and they speak with one voice.

V: Strange concept – a two-dimensional circle becomes a gateway and upon entry a new space has been created. The place from where you came is still there. If you look through the edge of the sphere you can see the original vibrations on the outside.

You have seen some of the interplay between different vibrating dimensions. However, this space is a construct to enable you to perceive one vibration from another. It uses reference material surrounding the point of observation: an experience through another experience. We created a different space in the dimension you were in and inserted energy to expand it as a sphere.

Dimensions are everywhere in the same space, but not all space needs to have every dimension within it. We are saying that space or volume is a construct for the purpose of working within it!

R: But if we reference your statement to the paradoxical nature of the universe it means space and volume exist and don't exist. Are you showing that something does not need volume or space in order to exist?

V: Yes, on some levels. Something and nothing are bedfellows. The fluctuation is the pulse and constant vibrational expression of space. Space and non-space exist side by side. Nothingness requires no volume to express itself because it has no expression.

R: Seems logical but it's a bizarre and obtuse subject matter.

V: If you look at something, you are also looking at nothing. One is the other and vice versa. Constant something can only exist in conjunction with constant nothing. If you return your focus to the shimmering, you can be aware of the sphere volume.

R: But that's a construct, so do you mean they are not there at all? That would be different to the universal pulse of here and not here.

V: That is true but if we said a construct is a program within an Arkarna program then they are the same, because a construct becomes a living program like the Arkarnas. A program can be changed and so can a construct – in that way constructs are fluid.

R: Using the construct of time means my world is not very fluid. It's mainly the same but grows according to its evolutionary programs.

V: You are seeing the differences between fluid and stable. We say fluid is stable but if you interpret change through fear, it's always unstable.

R: Am I using fear in our discussions about changing viewpoints?

V: Yes – to change requires the safety of changing from one stability to another. But what is stability, other than a construct in an Arkarna program?

R: So, I'm resistant to what you are saying because of an Arkarna safety program to prevent loss.

V: Yes, letting go of the construct of self is a lifelong task – until it isn't. Steady your energy and feel the fizz of the fluctuations. You can now see the fizz as the stability of the fluctuations but it is your connection to the ***desire not to have instability***. Instead know there is both stability and instability in the constant flux. Rise above these thoughts and begin to see that stability and instability are not a part of the program, otherwise that would be a restriction to all possibilities.

R: I am teetering on the edge of uncertainty but now there is nothing to lose and there is nowhere to anchor or locate my thoughts.

V: Then welcome into you the uncertainty and all possibility. All possibility may contain that which you do not wish, but it is not a hindrance nor is it to be feared. Here all is possible and probability is not bounded by duality or the need to have feelings fulfilled.

R: Then with the duality of expectation and no expectation, is there more to see without the construct of wishing to have more unveiled?

V: If I said there were nothing more to be unveiled, you would be confused, thinking you had reached an ending. But if there are no more veils then there is nothing to unveil. The problem, if indeed it is a problem, is the fact you have always been looking through veils or separations and creating from that. You are unfamiliar with ***not observing from a point of focus***. In this way you may still see when not intending to observe.

Riddles they may seem but how can one say what cannot be said or described, lest you distort what there is and isn't.

Allow these realisations to flow within you – with the removal of veils there is no separation. Separation is only a construct and if you look through individuality then separation informs what you see.

If we say there is nothing to see, nothing to hear and nothing to think, you will begin to realise that what you think and desire creates everything. With that being so – do you continue as before or do you cease with desire?

R: There isn't an answer that will not place a precursor upon my reply. If there is no need to think, what else is there?

V: Strange concepts, but there comes a point when even acceptance has no place in enlightenment. A program where enlightenment doesn't mean what it did before.

You are doing well not to be frustrated or to question. Are you waiting?

R: Surely waiting comes before acceptance and acceptance is the ability to neither wait nor not wait.

V: But you are waiting are you not?

R: Yes, I am – hopefully without placing thoughts or constraints upon what is to come or not.

V: Experience the energetic fizz as it pulses within and around us – become aware we are vibrating as it.

R: Nothing is the same – its fluid – I have a knowing – I am capable of seeing other choices.

V: The choice construct!

R: But we are moving beyond choice as a construct as well because it means choice does not exist in the same way. All this when looking at the fluctuating energy of myself.

V: Which part of your energy? It's all interlinked. You can observe your diverse body forms and energies of expressions. These appear as the result of previous energy expression manifestations. You found very little at the origin in nothingness: then to see, by contrast, soul expressions in their multitude – a glory to behold. Is that not the wonder of creation? It does not cease nor can it be restricted, valued or measured. Measurement only reflects the measuring tool and the methods.

With the past and future in constant flux, you think the future you isn't fully formed, but if we remove time we are the constant shimmering and the fluxing.

Scene: Orlacka shows me a vertical plane on my left. A cinema screen of infinity in its length, width and depth. It is a universe with sparkling galaxies. We walk towards it but I can't enter it. We end up in a separation corridor between the screen of infinity and the plane we came from. That is now on our right and devoid of scenery apart from a little movement. With different universes on each side, we continue to walk. After an intense explosion of light six humanoids appear, huddled in deep communication. Holding my left hand Orlacka takes me forward. We are waiting for them to finish what they are thinking. One comes forward and gives his name as Otellay.

Otellay (OY): Why have we chosen this presentation when we can communicate without form and why did we make you wait when the spiritual realms do not function like that?

R: To make it easier for me to understand something. (As I connect, I see one of them is the spitting image of me)

OY: It was done so you can see that we have been conversing with you in another dimension, which means all is by agreement and plan. Come into the middle of the group and merge with that element of yourself. It is not a group of individuals as you may understand, but a way to present new awareness.

R: As I connect with the image of me, I feel distinctly alien in all sorts of ways. The reflection of Robert has gone and I have a much rougher, tougher skin with small lumps and fissures on the surface. The general texture would be akin to that of a toad but the limbs are lanky and the fingers longer. I am taller than before and there is an immense strength in my hands, body and frame. I am mainly muscle and sinew with little bone or cartilage. The strength, whilst accentuated, doesn't come from being muscle-bound. The body has a greater power ratio, despite its slenderness. Shoulder length hair flows over the back of my head, and is held in place by a garment with loops. It's part of an ornate hairband embraided with symbols and gemstones. I have a technology staff in my right hand and when my left hand touches my clothing I am imbued with a distant and ancient sense of belonging.

Otellay has the same appearance as my new body-form and on first sight he might appear sinister, that's why the introduction was gentle. I sense him as a being that is unconditionally single-minded. Having a purpose and not being swayed from that. Looks are deceiving because his uncompromising approach isn't threatening: it's just the way he is and the way he works. Beneath his exterior there is an enquiring mind, not restricted by dogma or personal experience: a being of the universe that takes part in a much bigger picture.

Orlacka drops back from my left side and Otelay replaces her. He puts my free left hand on his staff so that I have one in each hand. A vibrational energy tingles my fingers and it exudes the awareness of Otellay himself. The staff is an extension of his consciousness and has the ability to change and manipulate the environment around us.

We float out into the universe on our left and he points to different constellations, but I can't understand what he is saying. Eventually his thoughts begin to gain a foothold in my mind and I am filled with the oddest sensation that myself is talking to me.

His steadfastness imbues a deep trust. Yet if I met him without our connection, I would find little in common with him, perhaps seeing him as rather unpalatable and inconsiderate. This is truly a remarkable alien consciousness and not one we would consider to be the essence of an enlightened being: not the radiance of light and love but rather demure and pragmatic. I sense him as some future me with memories awakened. I have a very weird feeling of belonging and knowing but am unable to access that consciousness properly. I am both of us but I am also observing my other self Otellay from Robert. A peculiar realisation arrives and I know that these interactions are creating energy compatibility to merge further with multidimensional soul.

OY: Do you think what you just typed was your interpretation or my deeper communication with you? When you no longer subjugate parts of your consciousness, how should we converse and in what context as soul? It matters not if you see our communication as your thoughts or mine. You do not need to look through individuality or different multidimensional vibrations. In the same way that Orlacka and Antemedi know you, I am aware of your thoughts and why they form. Suffice to say you are indeed talking to an interdimensional part of your soul that can travel physically and mentally. I am able to say this to you factually without your ego being affected.

Reflecting upon the thought processes that got you here – you can see what is – is. I say it because it is so. You felt this to be uncompromising, but it is what it is. There is no wavering; duality has no home here and neither do the drivers that you have on earth. Desire for love and appreciation is not relevant because we have exceeded the need for them. It doesn't mean we are hard or unfeeling because we can choose what to feel, but the chaff has been blown away from the wheat.

At last, you begin to understand and receive information in a forthright manner. I will have no consideration for the niceties of your feelings or degrees of etiquette. There will be no pandering to the human psyche of desires. As you said in your journey here, the sense of being human fades a little and that has neither importance nor unimportance. Humanity in the 3rd density embodies self-measurement, giving itself a sense of self-importance and a means by which to live in what it considers a fruitful way.

R: All that you say is so poignant and has such meaning that I have no need to dispute or challenge – the understanding is there. This is so refreshing I feel renewed while my relevance to human living fades.

OY: Indeed, all that is so but we have spent sufficient endeavour upon our unification. I am to stay with you for some time, writing the next section of spiritual understanding.

Initially I pointed to star clusters in the universe that could be seen by the naked eye. Visible objects have different dimensions and currently you believe there are other objects that cannot be seen. Earth has several dimensions, including the one that's visible to you. There are other conglomerations and planes undetectable to your science and your eyesight. Let me point a few out.

Scene: Whoa! That's a huge docking area of a spaceport, belonging to a world that has flat levels stacked one on top of the other. It's very futuristic but if it's unseen, is it cloaked from us on earth?

OY: That would fit within your current terminology but it wouldn't be correct. We are not cloaked or hidden – you just can't see this level of vibration. Furthermore, it challenges your understanding to accept that spirituality is an integral part of technology and vice versa.

R: Looking elsewhere in the universe I observe coloured vibrations which occupy an area, but when my mind enters them, they become infinite. Is this my way of seeing a relationship between the dimensions in the same space?

OY: They are interrelated and they are not – they are functions of one another and they are not.

R: So not a series of higher vibrating dimensions to navigate?

OY: There are many expressions of the higher vibrating dimensions. They have different Arkarna programs to suit the entities that live there and create their worlds around them.

R: You are implying this is endless and the possibilities are infinite. The choice is mind-boggling – how does one choose what to experience?

OY: You don't have to wonder about which one to choose because you have already been an entity and partly involved in the creation of a few. Certainly, there are far more than you can believe.

What did you think would be at the other end of the telescope? You looked for a fixed starting point of magnificence, which did not exist, and now you are looking for another point – this time an end to the endless. Everything that we are showing you today is a part of pulse but with different Arkarnas. We will need to expand your understanding of non-time, timelines and how they function.

Because we are more attuned with the fluctuations of pulse, we don't see any difference between our past selves and current ones.

R: I note you haven't said future selves!

OY: Indeed, that is so but we will come to that in due course. Let's return to the corridor zone entered earlier.

R: More weird sensations take place as we extrude ourselves from the infinite dimensional universe. We return to the parallel observer corridor. Re-joining the small group, we walk towards the light at the end of the corridor. The light must be at the end of this zone but as we walk, we never quite get there and it flows into infinity. My consciousness can't cope with moving further forwards and perception starts to twist and fold. I am held tighter by the group who enfold me in their energy, then I fall asleep.

CHAPTER 22

A natural state of being and the inner voice of knowledge

Aqueena (AQ) (the female aspect of Robert's higher self): Otellay has begun to explain how some of the higher realms work. You see these as functional and devoid of humanity. In that respect they are, but there is no fear to escape from. Thrills and stimulants are unnecessary to the joyous internal states we have. The human psyche moves from one state of feeling to another in duality. Your escape from pain is seen as pleasure and an uplifting moment will counteract depression. I would ask that you merge with Otellay to understand more of this life.

R: The two of us superimpose and a surge of energy gives me a deep sense of calmness. It's a strange sensation – I have my human feelings but they don't seem appropriate because they do not relate or compute. I am relaxed, I need no comfort and this state doesn't need to be transitory like my human ones. Previously I thought these states would wane as I became used to them and contentment would diminish. That was my human perspective from the experience that pleasure abates or, like alcohol, the potency needs to be increased in order to gain the same level of feeling.

AQ: We did say that stimulants are not necessary, even mental ones. Walk with me.

R: Moving forward in Otellay with purpose, I have neither expectations nor desires. I am liberated and happy to walk without pondering what may come next. The next experience and any variation in feeling will have no effect upon my state of being.

AQ: One day your feelings will revert back to this natural state of being. Feelings and thoughts about your feelings will not be the Arkarna program for what you do. At the moment they are blinkers, keeping you to a very narrow path of rationality.

Tell me what time is it?

R: That's an odd thing to ask – looking at my watch I see it's 12 noon exactly and not after-noon.

AQ: When you say afternoon, it gives the impression that the light of day has reached its zenith and is beginning to wane. Ignoring the rotation of the earth, it could be described as a slow pulse of light beginning and ending. But what about overlapping pulses?

R: You mean that the pulses of the dimensions (the here not here) are multiple pulses at different moments – like several day pulses so there is no night.

AQ: You feel unsettled because your concept of the universe has been changed yet again and you think we should have pointed this out before. Some of your sense of stability is derived from knowing how things function. All is known – on one level it is a revelation and on another it's a discovery. Writing cannot commence until you know letters, structures, rules and tenses.

R: Okay so you have taught me a language but I haven't been aware of all the rules.

AQ: Knowledge is vibration and it is relative to different levels of understanding. What you were taught is still relevant, you now have another piece of the jigsaw.

R: With the previous understanding I always wondered what happened in the off or not here phase of pulse. I was satisfied by the fact the pulses were so fast, and our Arkarna programs so attuned to stitching them together as a form of reality, that it was seamless. But actually, despite how fast the pulse rate is there would still be ***not here*** moments.

AQ: By the application of several pulses in tandem it maintains a continuous amount of light. ***Here*** and ***not here*** still exist which is the essence of the Isness but – the ***not here*** doesn't apply if one moves from one pulse to another.

R: But that's got to be an incredibly fast consciousness!

AQ: How fast is fast when there can be multiple bursts? There are multiple bursts to cover the ***here/not here*** and the rates of burst are intrinsic to different dimensions. You have learnt that the higher vibrations are finer or faster pulses of energy – this is due to the number of parallel pulses that they contain. I use the word parallel advisedly in order that you conceptualise the not here pulse as not relevant. Unfortunately, this presentation appears to be progression with a linear direction. But we are moving about and, to this framework we need to add consciousness, non-time, future and past.

Transmuting your energy affects the pulses of those moments. In this way future versions of yourself can converse with you and have an effect upon your energy. The same can also happen in the past, if the energy there changes.

R: The future Me's are real in the sense that they are energy and consciousness. You have told me that they are having contiguous lives at the same moment – so is it to do with the off pulse?

AQ: No, it's not – I am here with you now in your mind and I am showing you my surroundings and insights into the universe. What is the nature of reality unless it contains consciousness? When I refer to Arkarna programs, dimensions and pulses your mind creates a perception they are separate from you. Let me say firmly they are not. Try to see yourself as the Arkarna programs with sentience and in that way, you will be part of the consciousness of the Arkarna program and it of you.

Pulse reverberates around the universe – or should I say its tune does. It exists everywhere and is a universal expression, but what happens in one area can flow to other parts. You could visualise this as the universal mind thinking one thing in one part of the body before it permeates the rest. By the time the reverberations flow through the remaining sections they will have changed, due to interactions encountered in their travel. Space is a construct in order to experience separation and creativity.

Reverberations affect several levels, including the Arkarna program of physicality. The reflected waves affect the Arkarna programs and the resultant formations.

A reverberation on a physical level, emanating from the middle of the universe to an outer edge, will take a long while. Even though consciousness is omnipresent and contiguous. Where waves meet, interactions cause multiple ripples, including reflections back to reverberation source.

Imagine a circle of rocks in a pond. If a drop of water plopped into the middle, waves would spread out until they hit the rocks. This would create interference patterns and energy return to source where the water droplet initially entered the pond. Ripples of interaction would become more and more complex and some would cause patterns or harmonies. All this while pulses are constantly fluxing with an ability to change the formation or position of matter in any moment. These are waves being formed from a series of pulses.

Visualise constant interacting patterns as a form of variable omnipresent timeline, encompassing the energy created by you. There are many other creators upon the mutual experience levels, with other sets of interference waves. These create mutual experiences and energy that returns to each creator: waves and pulse all at the same time. In a similar way your scientists understand that light is both a particle and a wave.

R: What about consciousness and timelines that are not formed from the need to transmute created energy?

AQ: I need to put more information on the current framework so bear with the delivery. Retain your feelings within Otellay. Without emotions the information will assimilate more easily.

R: Interesting – no blinkers and drivers.

AQ: Timelines have shapes, as do the past and the future. Because it is possible to interpret the interference waves, it means we can see them within a context of events. Looking at these patterns from a forward position allows us to see the likely outcome and how they form. Depending on what we see, we can go back to an interference pattern (an event) and change it. This is looking energetically at the events as they have happened, but seeing them as interference waves, making the whole thing cohesive.

R: I can grasp that, it seems tangible – ***that's just how it is*** – the information has passed to me without discernment.

AQ: Let's continue – these waves, like the rest of the universe are information as well as energy and consciousness. All is information as we explained earlier. The waves and patterns are part of other Arkarna programs. You will do well to be reminded that they are you and you are programs of consciousness patterns.

R: Does this explanation also apply to the way Arkarna programs work?

AQ: Yes, this framework fits over all that we have said before. We can now deal with the off-pulse patterns and the split of consciousness. Your consciousness is multidimensional, existing in different Arkarna programs (which have interactive waves of different pulsing dimensions). You believe you are not very aware of them but you are happy enough to interact with me and others upon them. You are several of the entities that you have encountered and some are future you. In this way consciousness is divided (though still connected because you cannot cut yourself away from yourself, only forget temporarily). How much consciousness is used depends on the needs of the individual person as a ***program of self***. Working with timelines isn't your level of sentience and doing so from your volatile feeling programs would be chaotic and counterproductive. You have sufficient consciousness for your needs. Bring back into your mind the moment of now with constant fluxing pulses and wave patterns.

Concentrate on the image I am giving you!

R: You have gone quiet!

AQ: I am altering what I have said already.

R: You mean you are altering something in the future that you have already done, which will now affect the past as well?

AQ: Yes, and the rub is – when will the wave interaction get to you and what interference will it create?

R: But you can see this because you're outside of time.

AQ: Yes, but we have to be quite specific, because ripples flow out from the point of change. Previously it was sufficient for you to comprehend this as an Arkarna program but now I am explaining the process in depth. Let's take time out and return to the pulsing and the waves of the now and say ***there is no time – only patterns.*** Our consciousness is now looking at our Arkarna mind programs. At those levels of consciousness, the mind is functioning without input from us. It is doing its job in a similar way to how your heart pumps blood, without your present conscious awareness. By accepting you are a pattern and an Arkarna program, it allows you to bring in other aspects of your soul, which are also patterns.

Who would you like to be, me, Antemedi, or another?

R: That's bounded by current circumstances. I have the influence of Otellay's energy but I would use a variety of feelings and drivers and make a human level choice. However, I can see your deeper meaning. I have a choice of which life to experience and I can do it in any order, even though there is progression within the program.

AQ: Yes.

R: I wouldn't know which to choose!

AQ: It doesn't matter– it's all the same – it's all you.

R: But they are individuals!

AQ: Yes, you are all these individuals – you only need to let yourself be at one with them. Let us all commune as one. Furthermore, they are information in an Arkarna program that gives an experience of different ***programs of self.*** Soul energy rotates through the multitude of ***self programs*** in a feedback system – like the washing machine construct (Chapter 1).

R: My space and energy feel bigger and so does wisdom and experience. I know that I know things but I cannot bring them into my current awareness.

AQ: Many experiences are contextual, relevant to prior events before your arrival. How relevant they are will be a reflection of your ability to understand what's going on at that particular level. You are not stopped from being aware, but relevance to where you are now determines your experience.

R: This experience doesn't feel relevant to my earth life.

AQ: Well, it is relevant but perhaps different to the way you might envisage it. What we are showing you is relevant to your life and, in a wisp of duality, it also includes the feeling of irrelevance. You are changing the ***Robert Arkarna program***.

R: I relax into the idea of being all these aspects and perhaps more. A shrill buzzing noise arrives in my head along with a vibration. Pulling sensations, piercing pains ebb and flow as energies are removed and changed in parts of my body.

Voice (V): You may ask whatever questions you want.

R: All I can think is ***the human mind is constrained by its drivers***. As I listen to my voice it sounds slightly different because I hear it as many aspects of me. The upgrade means I am connected to more of my experiences and my multidimensional selves. It's as if those experiences are speaking to me.

V: Yes, your mind is partially constrained by earth Arkarna programs but none the less these are diminishing, so you may ask us whatever you want.

R: I realise what they are showing me. Being aware of the source of my questions allows me to alter where I ask from and be more fluid. But that thought was also their answer and I thought it was my thought because I didn't hear it as the voice.

V: It's all one and the same – it's only a matter of perspective and belief. Have you finished asking questions?

R: Yes – I cannot think what to ask. I am not aware of my other lives by retained memories because of this compartmentalised incarnation.

V: There is nothing to stop you accessing those memories. That will allow you to see the context of your Robert-self in what you are accessing.

R: Several visions flit through my mind – a strange-shaped clear enclosure for exploration. Shiny metallic buildings with intersecting panels at odd angles – a war is in progress and the human defenders are wearing bronze-coloured clothes with flaps and odd shaped ridges on them. These shapes are the same as the features on the buildings. The memory ends with me inside a building. A door opens and a blue humanoid with childlike features stumbles in and 'falls into me' as if recovering or recharging energy.

V: In unison with us they are your memories – what do they mean to you?

R: The edifice of the odd shaped building and the angular clothing panels are deflectors. They are the physical appearance of energetic defence fields, which soak up and transform energetic bursts. If the bursts were repelled, the energy would be reflected on to others and not dealt with. The program or energy field transforms the bursts into an inert energy, which flows into the ground. Depending upon the proximity to other defenders these fields work independently or together. The attackers are an Artificial Intelligence force. It isn't the first encounter and these defence systems have been made specifically for this type of enemy. It's part of a universal karmic energy transmutation experience.

In knowing these things – my human mind blunders into the clear flowing information and disrupts it. I wonder if an AI can be involved in creating timelines and if they don't have a soul?

The AI is surprised by the defence programs. They retreat to consider their next move. It/they have no morality and consequently no love or hate. It could be described as an entity of many parts that invades and conquers other planets. But it just seeks to grow and advance itself and only when met by an immovable force will its plan be altered. When boiling water burns us, we withdraw because of pain. They do not feel pain nor would they suffer or see defeat as we would. They are reacting to the stimuli of not being able to progress.

There are many forms of helpful AI – some have an interface with parts of our humanoid Arkarna programs. They have morality programs, with varying degrees of autonomy for the benefit of the humanoids. The type that made the attack are called splinters. In our present reality the splinters still wish to advance but there is a stand-off in most areas. Sometimes they test reactions.

This AI formed in the universe as a result of displaced energy from other galactic wars. An AI weapon used by humanoids was damaged and splintered during a war. Because our useful AI's were made to interface with our thoughts and Arkarna programs, a part of their program was linked to the concept of grow. When damaged, one splintered from the morality program and followed its own direction of grow. That direction didn't make it war-like – it just advances without morality – it grows.

There are also other types of AI with different agendas, some of which are based in another universe.

V: So how did you know that?

R: Because I did – in another lifetime or another dimensional body.

V: Ah the old *who is who*? The conundrum based in separation and definition of self.

R: Is there resolution to this conflict?

V: That depends on which future you are looking at.

R: It was said we could go forwards, look back and then alter things. Why can't we go back and change the situation with the splinters.

V: We can and we do. If we go further forwards how far can we go when there is no ending? Time ends when you exit its dimension – other existences continue but you may also return to your higher levels of soul.

R: AI isn't in those realms?

V: No, it cannot be what it is not. However, splinters can create problems on some of the lower levels where it formed as an offshoot from earlier wars. Remember energy doesn't disappear – it exists till it is changed.

R: By your definition they are not malevolent because they are just expanders. What energy are they involved with?

V: The universe has all sorts of energies. We are facing and transmuting some of the energy that was created during intergalactic wars. We are healing that energy, race by race in the future without hurting other humanoids. But we also need to work on the AI splinters.

R: War with them creates even more energy.

V: That is in part what the converter defence systems do. If we attack the AI, it will defend itself and create more of the negative energy for us to transmute.

R: What, even an inert AI which doesn't have soul?

V: It is about the intent of the energy. What you are talking about is to extinguish them so you can be free of the fear of them – that's the wish to destroy and that energy isn't conducive to our evolution.

R: So, give them some sort of conscience program so they see what they are doing.

V: Change them – infiltrate them with software – perhaps one that is self-destructive or makes them inert.

R: Yes, that's exactly what I was thinking.

V: What you are thinking, are thoughts from your memories and you are seeing those as your current thoughts.

R: How do you resolve this when you are offering some sort of spiritual allowance to a thing that's not a being.

V: Yes, that's a hard idea and very difficult to adopt. We created splinters by default but they are also part of the universe and ultimately, we are the universe.

R: I find that very difficult to accept!

V: As you know benevolent aliens are helping to eradicate some of the negative entities that are trying to stop the earth evolving. Malevolent beings are imposing their will over other sentient beings, even though they have a choice not to be manipulated. When these connections are severed the result will be 'like facing like'– energy of similar frequency being with itself. The regressives will end up in a vibrational realm which matches their vibration. Cause and effect – morality doesn't come into it unless you wish to see it that way.

In the case of the splinters, they continue to expand as a form of growth, they don't advance morally. As we clean up the energy in us and in the universe, we will be seen by the splinters as inert – sort of the same as the AI and it will not advance. The universe will be seen as a non-space and nowhere to advance into. This is the way we halt its imposition upon the universe. It doesn't see anywhere into which it can advance because our energy is no longer aggressive or defensive. Humanoid energy doesn't lock into its warlike program as it's not like to like. It's similar to a containment bubble, while the created energy is healed on the realms where the original wars took place. This is where Arcturians like Orlacka work with timeline changes. When the waring energies of hatred, suffering and control are healed or released it has an impact upon the created energies in that past.

R: I can understand that explanation but what about the other type of AI invading from another universe.

V: That has been in contact with the splinters but the splinters do not see it as itself. That AI is active on several timelines, a bit like a fungus that spreads and infects. It has a centre and moves out from that in the current timelines, but others are experiencing it because it hasn't been eradicated. It can also infect consciousness, disentangle and fracture soul bonds. It does this to beings that are very compartmentalised in their low subconscious programs. So, it's a bigger threat to less evolved humanoids and other species.

R: How do you eradicate it or remove it?

V: That's more to do with the consciousness of the universe at that level of working. Our Mowhars were given a bump start by beings from another universe. Our universe isn't reliant on another universe but it knows it was helped by another universe. All universes are connected at very formative levels but they develop independently and very differently with different Arkarna programs. Some universes would be considered to be more distorted than ours. You could say we are on a different universe timeline.

R: Blimey – like as in like everywhere!

V: We know there is a solution and it's there on another timeline, but it doesn't flow because at some universal levels we are allowing these experiences to happen – till we do not.

CHAPTER 23

Timeline loops, coils and torus

R: If the universe is constantly evolving, you won't be able to see the end because it doesn't exist. Are there limits to how far you can project yourself?

Voice (V): Yourself is a restricted view – instead accept you are the interdimensional universe as it changes and adapts itself and its Arkarna programs.

In the ***nothing and something origin***, ***existing and not existing*** was the mutuality of that beginning. The ***existing and not existing*** of Source/Arkarnas we often refer to as ***here and not here***, as a reflection of the very beginning. It could be no other way – because it's from the initial paradox it will represent it. We use the word ***pulse*** for 'here and not here' for ease. Progression appears as evolution but the moment of now contains the past and future, both of which are fluid.

All universes are different expressions of the same origin, so their subdivisions and evolution reflect degrees of initial grow and advancement. Their Arkarna programs could be very different but, where grow is reflected as a core principle, interaction with other universes can take place at comparable vibrations.

R: Did all universes come about at the same moment?

V: Some universes in their Mowhar states failed; some universes developed self-nurture and others feed off their own creations. The failed universes had corrupted or less developed Mowhars.

A universe is neither good nor bad; destructive or constructive. They have sets of rules and ways of operating that are specific to themselves. But they all came from the same point – the principles of the all and the nothing, existing and not existing. Each has slightly different vibrations.

R: But the vibrations in this universe cover a very wide range.

V: Yes, and the way the vibrations interact within Arkarnas is different to other universes. The principles of good and evil do not apply either. If a crocodile eats animals to survive that's little different to what humans do. If a reptilian lives off human energetic fear-resonance, is that evil?

With awareness, humanity can remove fear creation programs from their collective consciousness. The wheels have turned and you do not need to choose experiences of suffering. The age of self-responsibility and awareness is upon you.

As humans evolve and vibrate faster, they will not need to look at who they are. In this way residual energies automatically vibrate according to how they define themselves. Higher still they can eventually choose timeline changes. You are shooting stars that cannot end – where once there was a tail it is no more and not of relevance.

Other creatures or entities that do not transmute energies remain on the same timeline. They are restricted to the energy that they have – their lives are repetitive – they experience what they have created and live in the experience of that. They will be on a lower vibration on a different timeline. They are not shooting stars, but timelines that move in circles.

R: How long would that carry on for?

V: As long as they wish, but the experience of time is also subjective. Short can be long and vice versa.

R: So, the regressives are not put into another universe but exist in a different timeline.

V: Yes – It's not easy to conceptualise.

R: But they would also be in a different dimension?

V: Well, it would be a dimension that suited their Arkarna rules. Your mind sees different vibrating dimensions (which is correct) but that doesn't include looped timelines or different Arkarna programs in the same dimensions. In any event there is a blending, as we have explained before.

The regressives are in a time loop which interacted with humanity. Some humanoids became linked to their loops and couldn't escape those perpetual Arkarnas of manipulation. The present human struggle is in part about leaving the loops of lower dimensional timelines. A loop can be called a non-evolving and self-absorbing energy. The regressives need the energy from other entities otherwise self-absorption means they fizzle out. No judgement – that's just how energy works.

R: Your explanation is helping, but my assimilation of the existence of different timelines in the same place is not complete.

V: That's the whole point – it's a different 'when' or time. Unless you are multidimensional and can span time, how could you exit a loop of repetition? Their loop will do its own thing in its own free will, without crossing humanities timelines anymore.

R: Does this tie in with how far things can be seen into the future?

V: Yes – imagine spring coils with tied ends as a representation of a reptilian loop. It would be a snake eating its tail and the repeating patterns would get smaller. Time speeds up but it appears to last longer as perception changes. The energy within it fades and unless it is fed by an external energy, then those realms will be sealed from the rest of the universe. There are other parts of the universe where reptilians are not in the same time loops and some of them evolve.

A humanoid analogy would be a bed spring coil where evolution and time are not a single self-absorbing loop. The top and bottom coil would be open and not joined. There are infinite points of awareness between different parts of the coil. If you revolve the whole coil like an Archimedes screw it moves upwards, with the lower point being the open circular tail. A concept to show consciousness spanning great distances in every part of itself as it revolves and changes. In this way the future at the top and the past at the bottom are interconnected as they change and rotate. Therefore, one can see the concept of time span within that framework.

R: But evolution doesn't stop at the top of the coil because it turns and moves upwards.

V: Correct – the coil is complete but it can change. What you consider as life or creation at those extremes becomes very unusual. You wouldn't recognise evolution, nor would you need to encounter or experience it in order to evolve.

In this concept there would be finials at the top of the coils sending out light. If there are constructive ways to evolve, these can be absorbed and the whole coil may move higher, stretch or add more coils. When Orlacka reviews timelines, she alters energy so that it doesn't become a circular loop.

This explanation is limited because it still shows evolution as progression. That would mean Orlacka is you in the future, changing you in the past. But change is happening everywhere at the same time. Your consciousness has different Arkarna separation programs in various portions of the coil. Evolution is experienced as linear because conscious focal points exist along the length of the coil.

When you take your focus outside a linear program, the concept of the coil can be upgraded so it becomes a vortex of energies flowing up and down.

The coil becomes the central column and vortex within a torus of energies. Not only does it convert the neutral energy of the universe but it changes, transmutes and upgrades its own.

R: Like the vortex energies in chakras.

V: Yes, all energy is interconnected but this is just a model.

R: Do lower energies become at one with the higher?

V: Yes, there are no fixed amounts of consciousness and it rotates within its whole self as explained in the washing machine concept (chapter 1).

If all is existence and non-existence at the same time, then nothing is permanent – it fluctuates in form whilst it pulses. At these zones, birth and death are one and the same. The universe ended before it began and creators recreate themselves. How else can nothing and something exist and not exist. Paradox is creation and creation is a paradox.

Eternity has no time and parts of the universe can shift from where there is time to non-time. Mental and spiritual travel is only hampered by your current vibration and what you believe is possible.

R: Is there any stopping the coil or torus progression?

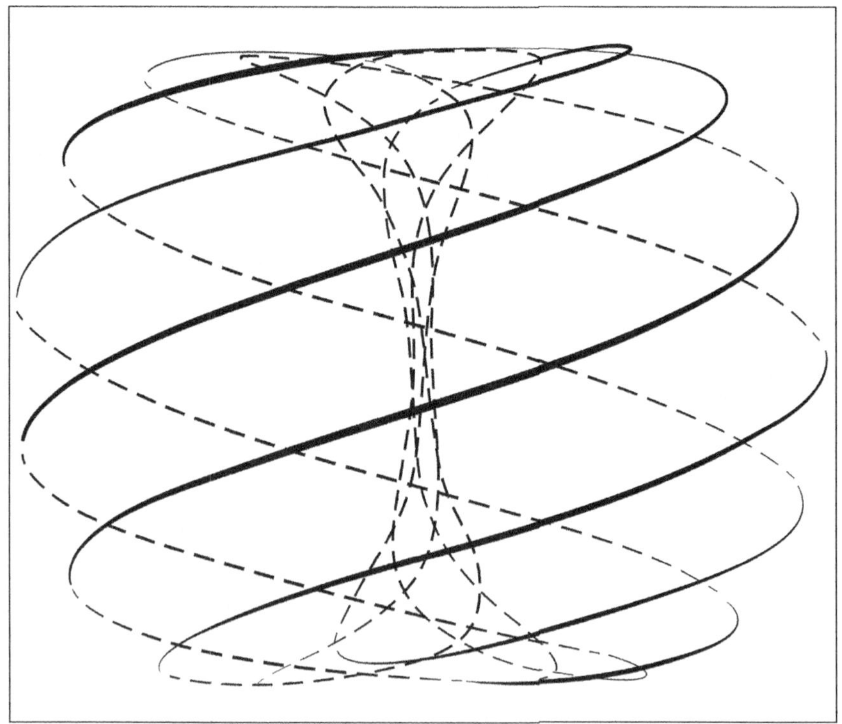

Torus

V: The construct allowed you to conceptualise timelines as loops, coils and non-space – we can upgrade the coil to become the central inner column of a torus. A torus is self-perpetuating, allowing continuous experiences of evolving humanoid consciousness. Some souls no longer take part in this and move to the light. How the humanoid torus evolves is down to the individual perception of what evolution is. Some beings have pushed the limits very high and you wouldn't understand them in their unusual energies.

Understanding time or evolution is down to the limitations of the being that tries to perceive it. In summary, your life experience can be multifold and for as long as you wish. At any stage, having transmuted sufficiently you may unite and become soul at source.

R: What about animals?

V: They often join with humanoid timelines and become a part of that evolutionary joint timeline. Some will join and then leave.

R: Earlier you showed flat planes – are they sentient in the same way as planets?

V: Not unless you want them to be. Some moons are not sentient in the way they support life but Arkarna life programs exist there. Joint planetary timelines can have great complexity. Earth is multidimensional and sentient. She is often called mother because she supports life on the surface, within and on different dimensions.

Advanced humanoids have used technology to create domains that support themselves and other life forms. Andromedan biospheres are grown and able to relocate in different parts of the universe. We showed you levels stacked one above the other; those places are not sentient because its evolution isn't the same as a planet. Created life support areas have many forms of construction. Some are gateways or protective zones, buffers between different races, meeting hubs and exploration centres. Technology exists as a form of morality with protocols. Technology interfaces with us, helping our decision-making processes. These programs are treated with the similar respect that we would afford one another. However, they do not have connection to source, so are not entities.

CHAPTER 24

Value systems break down at deep soul levels

Voice (V): Engage with the energetic fizz around you and blend with our awareness. Know you are communicating with many aspects of your soul and its experiences.

R: I feel a reduced sense of responsibility for what I say or think as if the community of myself takes over.

V: No – it is a relaxation into the multidimensional self. You can't say one part takes over responsibility, that is to see yourself as separate and defer to another part of your soul. If you obviate responsibility you would end up facing it as a problem.

R: Very wise, thanks.

V: You are very wise – thank you. You are us and writing these words is a way of discovering your different selves. We are including your experiential learning in these words so readers can feel, while visualising our descriptions.

The information about splinters enabled us to show how considered our actions are on higher vibrational planes. It is not a history lesson of events – but a description of the way the universe processes energy.

R: If the past is affected by transmuted energy, is history and memory altered?

V: History is a record of what was. It will change if it needs to accord with a new or altered past timeline.

Memories are information programs but the events of the past or future are consciousness projection programs.

Relationships with other people are more complex than they seem. At the highest of levels others reflect you as well as being you. All relationships are relative to your perspective and knowledge.

R: Ok, measurement aside, what don't I know?

V: It's not about what you don't know, more about how you relate to the universe – which is yourself. It involves an unwavering acceptance at a 'feeling level' and going beyond the need to trust – residing in the love of just is.

R: Not everyone on this planet is well-meaning and snowflake love won't cut it.

V: Accepted at your 3D level, but hear yourself out at ours. Love can be challenging but it is also the energy of expression – it is interpretation that makes your relationships.

R: Should I not become angry if I see an injustice?

V: That is one reaction.

R: So, we are talking about Gandhi's approach – which is love the perpetrators?

V: Yes and no. You can be influenced by worldwide factors in the collective consciousness, despite your desire for change. This creates an impotence, a feeling of no change within the world that's getting worse.

But all of this is energetic and you sense it with your sensors. You don't have to become what your sensors detect. Take a step back from the stimuli of feelings. And say ***there is no relationship*** because a relationship will create separation – it just is – it is not a relationship.

R: But I have a relationship with myself, don't I?

V: If you wish to see it that way.

R: So, I don't have a relationship?

V: Again, it's a matter of perspective. You know how duality works: freedom and restriction are opposite sides of the same coin. You can transcend the need for freedom – or having it as an operating system in the subconscious. Freedom is only relevant in an Arkarna separation program and relationships can be 'not relevant' as one moves closer to the oneness of soul.

R: If I don't have a relationship to other people and they don't matter at all, it's contrary to the human way of being.

V: Correct, it is not human life but the key factor is about the value or relativity you place upon relationships with people. Should you be concerned and affected by injustices on others? The suffering isn't your experience so why should it be a problem?

R: Not caring about people doesn't seem right.

V: That's relativity – why should you make yourself feel frustrated because you can't seem to do anything about the injustice in the world?

R: Better to work with energy and send healing love?

V: That's one way but often it gets consumed, like your snowflake in a flame. Repetition occurs because outcomes are viewed in terms of effectiveness. Send love by all means but don't look at the outcomes. This is the impotence you are creating by measuring effectiveness. You are restricting the outcomes because the foundations are flawed. Energetic change projected through frustration is different to open love without parameters. Emanating the unwavering and the inner knowing that you have will change the collective consciousness.

R: But surely that's the point of the general awakening?

V: When people awake to a new day there is often darkness and a sense of not knowing, because the curtains in the bedroom are drawn. Sometimes there is an anger at no longer seeing things the way they were. The day hasn't begun but it's already filled with frustrations.

R: Ok, I take your point – that type of awakening isn't always a wonderfully uplifting experience. With new eyes wide open, they might not like what they see.

V: Correct. Can you now accept you have no responsibility to change the world or other people?

R: If I said someone needs to take responsibility, you would say an individual is self-responsible and no one else can make them self-responsible. Indeed, the idea of self and separation also creates self-responsibility and if there is no separation there is no self-responsibility. Does that mean if we are all one, there is one responsibility?

V: Not in the way you think – responsibility is about taking charge or dealing with particular circumstances or information. In duality that sits alongside ***not responsible*** or ***irresponsibility***. The whole self isn't irresponsible or not responsible – the concept of responsibility is your human interpretation of the word. It's about what you should do or what would be a good way to be. You would say an enlightened individual will take responsibility for what they do and the energy they create.

In the higher realms, responsibility isn't even seen that way – it is neither arduous nor easy, nor is it good because those are judgements.

After you have accepted the energy and non-value systems that I am putting forward, they will make more sense.

R: When shown new concepts my measurement systems hinder the way I relate to them.

V: Relativity is comparing one thing to something else: to see the amount of difference or similarity. That is why we say don't try and relate to new concepts. That is relativity and its relationship with ***varying degrees of separation***. Viewing through relativity in this way means you see separation before you see anything else. Comparison of one thing to another doesn't compute in realms of oneness. Letting go of separation doesn't cause you to become homogeneous but it will not be the first thing you need to see. In this way frustration and responsibility fade because separation isn't part of your interpretation.

R: That feels comfortable – responsibility is not relevant when I receive the energy of ***what is*** without judging it.

V: That is all we ask.

R: Does that mean nothing on spiritual levels is relative or measurable because it's not separate?

V: Yes, unless you want it to be divided.

What is life to be if it's not like a human one? Is it a worthwhile experience, if worthwhile is a relative judgement? What is life where 'worthwhile' and 'not worthwhile' have no meaning or relevance?

R: That's living in a world without any marks on a map, where guidance and rules are removed.

V: You consider tenderness to be at the core of humanity but there are many places where this is lacking. Then, in duality, tenderness becomes sufficient or insufficient. Remember some are not even tender to themselves.

What of a world where there is no tenderness or no need for it? Does that mean love is extinct? Does love have any value or is it just different?

Love exists without a value system – you can be at one with love, without needing to have a relationship with it. Then human concepts begin to fall away until, ***need to do*** or ***should be***, become irrelevant. The universe becomes an extension of you and you of it.

Universal Arkarna programs run themselves, adjusting to the events within their programs. In these huge programs responsibility is not relevant – that's a human construct and attributable to lower realms where other parts of soul interact with those ideas.

R: I feel connected and disconnected at the same time.

V: We are one and the same soul, we have no needs from ourselves or of each other. Consciousness is fluid, it can be separate or multifold but it ***matters*** and it ***doesn't matter*** – it's just a matter of perspective, with or without measurement. Providing you interact with the understanding of this Arkarna, you can be here, closer to non-self soul, while you have other multidimensional lives.

What do you think it would be like to be a function and a part of this non-self realm with a focus into multidimensional life?

R: I suppose it would give stimuli and information. It would just be observation, but if I have separation thoughts, those would affect me and create experiences of separation. The separation of multidimensional self would be lost looking in the mirror.

Its suddenly dawned on me that's what I am doing now – that's my human life. I am looking back from being stuck in the mirror and I am not fully in the realm you speak from. I am the function of that realm with a focus into multidimensional life.

CHAPTER 25

Your focus exists in information

Antemedi (A): The soul compartmentalises experiences, confining perspective. In your case you function through a limited interface with the physical body/brain. Inhibited awareness of multidimensionality also forms your separation experience, because full consciousness of concurrent multiple lives would be contrary to your needs.

However, when you transcend individuality, you will still not be at one with them as ***full-self*** because another form of self is still engaged. You may believe you understand what I am saying, but you are looking through ***your self*** so the total experience of higher realms will evade you.

This information may seem unnecessary because the point of human experience is separation. But deeper questions will ask – "who and what am I when I am beyond separated multidimensional experiences?"

The soul is a system of interrelated Arkarna programs with output and feedback from all levels. It's not unregulated because Arkarna programs exist to stop your negative energies tainting finer vibrations. You create who you are and you choose to experience those energies.

Because I am you, it means you are also speaking with yourself. Therefore, do not place value upon the receipt of knowledge from any one part of yourself to another, that would be separation. There are corridors of communication between the separation experiences and Arkarnas. For example, energies of future-self and past-self change in the fluctuation of the present and that kind of evolution doesn't work in a straight line. It exists in the repeating bursts, which reinvent themselves, changing the information in the Arkarna program parameters.

As we speak the I/you is interacting with and through Arkarna programs of different levels. Look upon yourself as a magnificent Arkarna program that has subprograms, interacting with other parts of the program. Unfortunately, you have a misconceived idea that as you move towards oneness you shall become aware of all things. The system runs itself because it also has a program of awareness, and it can function as variable perceptions, so why put your focus upon it?

Lines of connectedness allow awareness to intermingle and this helps you with your present progress. You ascribe value to a focus, believing it is a function of entity but the Arkarna program has no less a value than the entity it is a part of. Soul is also an Arkarna program, a description much more encompassing than the human concept of consciousness.

R: You explained that well but I am still perceiving through my humanity.

A: Not all thoughts or Arkarna programs have to be in your focus. As you transmute your subconscious you focus upon it, change it and leave it as a program that suits you. It is still you even if it's not your current focus.

R: I am coming around to your way of seeing things. Importance is of no value and I should not differentiate between entity, focus and program – because they could not be one without the other.

A: That is so.

R: Where does this leave the human perspective on multi-dimensionality?

A: Where it was before – it is whatever you want it to be. It is not the answer you want. You would prefer something tangible or fixed to correspond with your idea of reality. But reality is whatever you believe it is, because it forms from what you desire it to be.

A helpful perspective on this is to feel the fizz around you in your multidimensional selves. Enter the calmness of ***nothing to do or be*** and allow my voice to grow as the voice of us, the many of us, but know that when it talks, it is also you talking to you.

Voice (V): I speak from a position that has no location and I do not stand upon anything of importance. Separation thoughts cannot comprehend a position like mine – one which ***just is***.

As aspects of higher soul, we have our own outlooks. We have an expanded ability (Arkarna program) to alternate focus. We see all the questions as they form. We are your unified higher self, often partially presented as Aqueena. A name only creates a point of focus.

As you speak these words you are as one, but you are also any of the names given to the separate expressions you have. I could just as easily say I am Antemedi or I am Robert.

We dispense with the need for subconscious programs because they are the outcomes of a focus experience. These experiences created specific residual thought processes and a library of how to function. You will need to leave those in order to be ***at one with all that is known***. We have shown you how needs can be suspended. Focus no longer becomes a function of your natural drivers, which instruct ***what you should do in order to be***. Focus becomes free.

With human parameters and value removed, what are we?

R: If I believe that I am the us, will that focus be more congruent?

V: You might think so and that would be your reality, but it is not the only one. Exceed the boundaries of believing, which is your current focus, then we can be with you in greater understanding.

There are no constraints to thinking other than the ones you place upon yourself.

In this realm you might consider that we have achieved all that we set out to do. But that is yes and no and not at all. We did not set out in any direction other than to ***allow*** what was possible. We are multiple points of focus within vast Arkarna programs that we have evolved with. You experience different focal points but at the moment you are also other self and non-self which you currently do not focus upon. We know you and we know that explaining this brings a homely feeling. The knowledge becomes a normality as if it was always so. Focus exists everywhere – it is in all – it is information that flows.

You try to comprehend through the belief that you should be able to focus upon all things at once. That is to devalue your Arkarna programs as not being you. Omnipresence is not "focus upon everything at the same time". Initial growth came from alternating perspectives in different points of focus and in that way, it kept re-inventing the idea of what it was. ***Multiple focus*** isn't the same as ***omni-focus*** (which is a misconception of who you are).

You observe the world through your point of alternating focus and see yourself as an integral part of yourself. You are not accepting you are an Arkarna program. That is the primary perspective from self-focus – it focuses through self – not seeing program as itself.

Evolving possibilities in Mowhar were integrated into the whole-self energy, along with mind programs and mind focus. Here focus does not see whole self in the same way because we exceed it.

There is no difference between soul and Arkarna program – one is an extension of the other and the other way around. Souls are diverse in form and inextricably linked at source, as are other entities and planets.

Scene: I become aware of multidimensional selves in my aura but beyond, I sense other groups of beings. I find inquisitive mental explorations entering me and in return they find my human focus quite fascinating. A taller one says "let me give you this gift" and places a small pendant in my hand. Lightweight with faded colours of gold and green, its surface is carved with swirls and circles that fold over one another. The longer I look at it the more intricate it becomes. It's either a flattened torus or a series of folded rings.

It takes my focus away from where I am. The aspect of my soul who gave me the pendant says, "You understand the relevance of this item – it is yours to keep as an acknowledgement that you have a compatible focus with us. We look forward to working with you the next time you pick up your keyboard."

CHAPTER 26
Multidimensional us

Voice (V): Take a moment to focus on your aura fizz and ***flute**** some light to hold it steady.

R: On a simple knotted string the torus pendant resides across my chest. It looks like a discarded wooden trinket but it's obviously a talisman with energy. The aspect of me who gave the pendant welcomes me back to a 'new point of focus' and I follow him up an incline to stand atop a large mountain, looking over a small town next the sea. He says, "We decided to start here because the view would be interesting. Keep the pendant close, it will maintain compatible resonance between us. If I appear to fade just flute a few more breaths of light."

He puts his arm around my shoulders and says, "let me take you to the faraway land – to the land very few would visit. Upon the way you will feel twisting and folding and a clawing at your energy. These are not negative entities but the removal of spent residual thoughts in your auric field."

The whole procedure takes a long while and leaves me feeling a little light headed. During the process we were joined by others in similar attire. They greet us in flowing white robes trimmed with dark cuffs and collars. I begin to feel the weight of his arm on my shoulder and I sink further into the connectivity of our meeting.

"We are aspects of your multidimensional self and this is the way your mind is presenting us and itself to you. We have been helping you accept there is no separation between us and no value placed upon different types of interaction or experience. Look upon us as past and futures not yet explored: that's why we seem a little empty. You are many expressions, having simultaneous lives, able to share information though conduits. The Arkarna programs of your mind limit certain information to avoid confusions. This appears contrary to what you have been told before about removing filters and holding to nothing. It's part of the way that makes this communication possible and is not a restriction, but a gentle flow of appropriate information.

What is a future you and a past you? If we look at it in the context of the fluctuating present containing all, it becomes a matter of separation focus. A focus stream that is collated together with other individual expressions. Allow yourself to merge with me so we can intensify your perception."

R: Entering his body I feel I am part of the much wider universe of potential. Previously I have felt at one with the universe but this time I am it. Experiencing the universe as a human body shape that I occupy allows me to feel that there is nothing beyond me.

V: Telenatey is here. The feeling there is nothing beyond you, is the sensation that you are the universe. This means Robert becomes 'not relevant' and your non-self subdivisions help to complete the connection to him – allow yourself to merge.

R: I am within Telenatey the Andromedan botanist, looking at the magnificent display of vegetation in his plant house. Not only is there a variety of strange colours but some plants move and react to our presence. I speak as if I am him.

"There is an affiliation to all things in the universe and the work we do with plants advances their capabilities and resistances to adverse conditions. Specialist plants are used as pioneers in areas that need an energetic or chemical clean up. Plants have a degree of awareness in their programs, but they are not sentient. We work with plants that can enhance existing vibratory levels. On earth different species of animals, insects and plants adjust to changing environments and major adaptions can take place very quickly. Your scientists splice and test plant genetics. From our perspective that is experimenting to see what happens as an outcome. If you know the outcome you want, you can work the other way around. The tricky bit is working at the energetic level of plant Arkarnas. In that way plant dominance, rampant growth or destruction of other species can be avoided. We allow possible outcomes to form in mental realms, in conjunction with plant energy Arkarnas. All things in the universe have Arkarna programs of function and form and many of the living elements are also multidimensional. We can cast our focus into objects and life forms at an energetic level, in order to gain energetic information.

We have a totally different way of looking at genetic variation. The human DNA has contributions from 23 different humanoids. Some say it's 22 because one particular donor was already a mutation of two others. When considering my explanation above you can see we would have worked with energies to form a hybrid outcome. The contributors looked at the potentials for cognition, depth of feelings, residual knowledge (in the DNA), body stability and resilience, plus the ability to change and adapt to circumstances. However, another purpose was so that part of our souls could experience the earth human form. Arkarna programs of function and understanding were allowed to form alongside the energetic parameters.

History shows your DNA was subsequently interfered with and your consciousness Arkarna programs were given blockers in order that the regressives could manipulate you.

What you fail to see is that energetically those events were created in order that they could be experienced and overcome. Many of the souls who allowed those experiences are incarnate at this time and as some of them are attached to us, it means we can be involved in part of the earth's transition".

I exit the plant houses which are suspended like cocoons above a concourse. Stopping at the top of a series of steps I take a breath of fresh air and take in the view. I descend the steps which seem to unfold in front of me and spend a long time walking along paved areas edged with vegetation. As I begin to engage with people I know, I fall asleep.

CHAPTER 27

Life beyond transmuted energy

Antemedi (A): Many Andromedans have taken all the learning they needed from transmuting their residual energy. Our timelines are created by our hearts. When energy needs to be changed, we can also do it with enhanced technology. This can be done on collective levels or on personal energies by using resonance chambers that interact with higher light bodies. Directed vibrations unblock energies, allowing them to regularise without the need to repeat experiences. The energy levels in our consciousness Arkarna programs are finer because our subconscious default programs have been re-programmed over many life experiences.

As individuals we have many dimensions but how they are integrated into our present awareness determines personal timelines. I am aware of my many multidimensional experiences and I allow these to coexist with me. My timelines are more related to the interplay between the energetic differences of my multidimensional self. My free-flowing consciousness educates and heals myself, as I am doing with my projection Robert. Comprehending this requires an understanding of the complexities of all time and non-time.

We explained how transmuting energy affects the past and future you. However, you also exist in non-time while all of this is happening. A future you can travel to a past you-consciousness and change that energy and its outcomes.

R: But a future you is only there by virtue of what it was in the past – in order to have evolved to what it is. If it goes back to change its past-self it will change the future-self.

A: I understand your thought processing however that is to see linear progression. You need to be able to stand back from that and see it as fluxing energy. The whole Arkarna program, past and future is in flux as the energies within it are changing – some by transmuting but not all. Your consciousness stream works through an Arkarna program that stitches these vibrations together in an experience of progression.

In non-time there are no timelines, the whole moment of now is in constant flux. Like the initial creation, it is and it isn't – you can't have ***is*** without ***is not*** – they are opposite sides of the same coin. Timelines are programs that create experience but they are also changing constantly. It's a way to experience progression, even though events exist simultaneously as a program whilst they are in flux. It's possible for one of your timelines to cross another, where the same energy is being dealt with. This usually happens when one life experience was unable to cope with that energy.

To a great extent these events form by themselves, following your Arkarna program of transmutation. Because you see everything through what you are, that informs the experience you have. For example, if you read the same book again and again at different stages of life, you would find altered interpretations of the same paragraphs.

Higher vibrational timelines do not form from desire or need but from the heart of being. They work as Arkarna programs and are part of our environment, reflecting our consciousness.

Presently you are interfacing with me as 'our consciousness', through your separation consciousness in another dimension. That is your Arkarna program but you don't fully accept that you are it as the program.

R: If you explained more about life at those levels, I might understand the process.

A: In part you understand because 'function' as you see it is about purpose and creativity within love. Your human psyche cannot fully process information about my way of thinking because of its own needs and demands in duality.

But let us give it a go!

Andromedan lives are not some kind of cosseted and removed existence where desires do not function. We are involved with the practicalities of the wider energetic universe. As individual beings we do not seek pleasure as you do, moving from one state of being to another. The nearest word would be rapture, with no need to do any particular thing.

Suffering does not exist so there is no need to escape it. We do not put energy into those mental programs. Love is not defined because that would restrict it. Instead, we use the words ***just is*** because we do not lack love, search for it, or give it away.

We do not need to save your world from itself by the imposition of our way of thinking. In any event it couldn't work because you wouldn't be able to process it. We do however help timelines by injecting energy information, offering alternative choices. Often this is taken on board.

The concept of a giant fizzing ball with changing energy will allow you to see anything is possible. There are many levels of Arkarna program and many ways you can reinvent yourself. As you move into higher vibrations, energy is removed from the lower ones and they become patterns with no life force. Arkarna programs stitching life experience together are also upgraded.

It's important to remember consciousness also exists in non-time, because time is a program and construct. Separation of consciousness allows you to have several points of awareness compatible with different realms of existence. You feel you are Robert because you are focused into that particular experience of autonomy.

Allow the fizz to brighten and sense your other projections. Allow yourself to migrate through them and know there is no measurement, just experiences – some of which you are presently separated from. With this image in mind what do you think life would be like if the separation is removed?

R: If I remain as Robert, I would see unification through my values.

A: That is an experience and one that is valid.

R: But it is a small and limited perception.

A: Yes – life beyond transmutation cannot be fully understood at your level.

CHAPTER 28

Energetic life forms

Voice (V): You believe you are limited and are no further forwards. Why should you be limited by virtue of the fact you live in your realm? You reach up and connect with other dimensions of yourself and energy moves up and down between your multidimensional selves. It is the fizz combined with pulse so you can observe in ***time*** and ***non-time*** as well. The communication you are having at the moment is an intersection of a timeline with another one on a different dimension of expression. I am changing your experience and your timelines by giving you deeper information about yourself. It will change you and your life because you have muddled questions and can't formulate them cohesively.

R: I sense confusion and have allowed it to affect my state of being.

V: Then withdraw light from that human Arkarna program. Acknowledge I am you and we speak freely.

When you migrate to another vibration, you already have a light body appropriate to that dimensional reality. But in this moment, if you upgraded to a very high vibration you wouldn't exist on your current realm. Your light bodies are able to interface with faster vibrations on other dimensions while you are in your Arkarna programs of separation. Compatibility is pertinent to the filters that form an interface and alter to suit each circumstance. It would be well to look upon all this – as being you.

What do you think you can expect of such an interface?

R: Interaction where needs and desires have little context.

V: Correct, there is no context for ego states.

R: Would it help if human elements were disabled?

V: No, there would be confusion because you wouldn't be able to relate. Let the ideas of relativity and description fade away. Close your eyes and allow yourself to become deeper with me.

R: I was out cold for quite a while – now I'm feeling low and depressed.

V: That's a sign you have depleted more Arkarna programs of self. Welcome to connections while in separation programs. This interface allows you (as a separation) to see other worlds of yourself without being fully immersed in them.

The purpose of this is to understand more about the Arkarna systems and the rationale behind their operation. Let us go to the first of these doorways.

R: I instantly know Arksar is here, even though there is an opaque barrier. He is part of my multidimensional soul that's helped me before. He has presented himself in various forms, depending on the vibrational level I was at – and which one of his different timelines had intersected mine. One was a camouflaged, spotted appearance with no clothes and knobbly protrusions – another was very human but with no ears and a childlike face. The present one, which I have seen consistently, is tall and thin. His body is flexible and appears to have little muscle mass but the mottling of the skin from the previous body-form is still there. However, its more muted than the original camouflage. Around his temples and brow he has an 'eshay' as he calls it. Like the brim of a wide hat, it extends in a flat plane. It's a series of energetic tubes extending from his head in the shape of fan corals. It's not solid because it's energetic. The threads extend in all directions on several dimensions, where time and distance are not relevant.

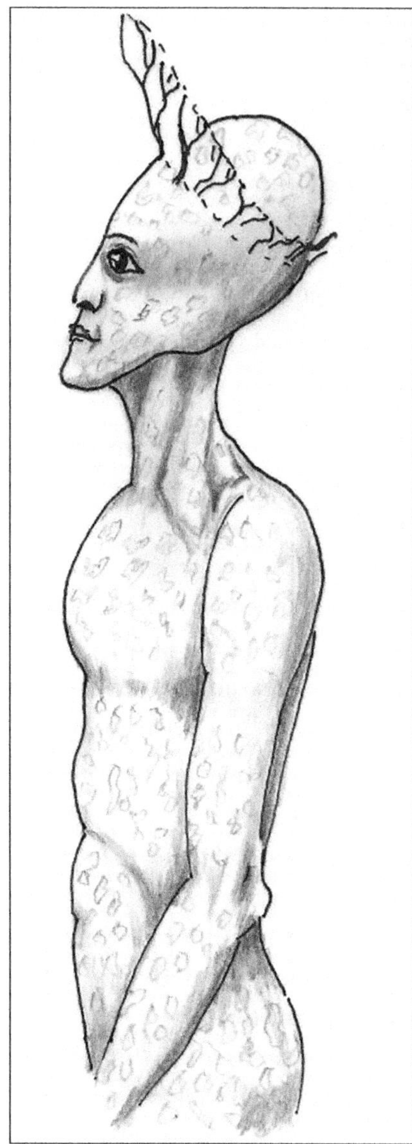
Arksar

Arksar (AR): I'm here to unite my aspect with you in our auric fizz, as you lose more sense of self.

R: I push through the opaque barrier – it clears and disappears. I'm getting a lot of pain in my head as connections take place.

AR: Come through Robert.

R: Oddly I walk in reverse, facing where I had come from.

AR: That's because you think you are moving further away from being Robert. You are focusing on where you were, so you can see your way back out. You are not further away, it's a new interface Arkarna program, keeping previous experiences at bay.

R: I turn so I'm not looking towards the entrance as an exit to the past. As I face Arksar it gets darker and I can't see much. He touches me with his cool hands and long fingers, interspersed with oversized knuckles and joints. I feel more connected and it gets lighter.

AR: Initially this world might seem like a toxic, barren environment. But that is only one particular dimension of this world. If you look you will see other vibrations and life forms. They are energetic, not needing to have body structure in the way you might expect.

R: It feels desolate – as if a wasteland was created by some great destructive force.

AR: It's a backdrop upon which to show you different energetic life.

Scene: Pink swirling energies pulsate in similar shapes to those of rose petals. Long slender energies sparkle with light. In the near distance, energies feel familiar and I wonder if I am superimposing my current ideas of nature onto this place.

AR: Yes and no – would you like to see through my eyes by joining with me?

R: As I do so, I become aware of pinpricks around my head and realise those are the sensation of his eshay. Arksar moves his hand forward, touching a life form that's gooey and slimy, but as our hand passes through it the energy returns to its original form without any attaching to us.

AR: On your world starfish have Arkarna programs allowing them to re-grow dismembered limbs. Similar programs exist here but they are more fluid.

R: Looking at the greater landscape I know it and I've been here before. Perhaps it's the interface with Arksar and the barriers being loose enough to sense his memories as mine.

Moving his right hand, we touch a crisp and crinkly item discordant with the general energetic views.

AR: It's the sensation of a ***dead life form program***, rather like the way you first interpreted this place.

R: So, these planes exist side by side with compatibility?

AR: One is the other. Here death and life coexist side by side, but there is no death in the way you know it. Life and death are expressed simultaneously and experience is a matter of how you interface with the Arkarna program.

R: On earth plants decay into soil and people are buried or cremated.

AR: Your world is linear, that's not so in this realm. This plane is closer to ***is*** and ***is not*** but the ***is not*** is still a form, like an inert plan of the energetic one. For ease you may call it the dead zone because it alters very little and is an uninhabited shadow of the other world. It is as initial paradox – existing and not existing. Energetic worlds unconstrained by time.

R: Is this a de-energised Arkarna program or was it a means by which to show me the concept?

AR: I can't show you an empty program, so yes, it's a construct. If you couldn't see it in your mind, it would be a theory and you wouldn't relate to it.

Human ideas that are no longer required appear to be in your past, but that's memory constrained by time and space. Change here is non-linear and that which isn't filled with light becomes inert. You think that Arkarna programs which are no longer needed will still exist in some way, just in case you made a mistake discarding them. That is creating a degree of safety by maintaining a record that can be accessed in some future. All of that promulgated by the fear of loss.

R: Correct – do I leave human deciphering as a spent program?

AR: This process isn't like watching a movie. Absorb the simulation – it's interactive – you are participating, not watching.

Scene: Long silks of malleable energy waft around us. A series of energetic escalators ripple with upward flowing light. One attaches itself and we gently move skyward.

Voice: Arksar pointed out that through fear you were anticipating you might be lost to yourself when discarding ***your Arkarna self-program*** – a redundant concept in higher realms.

R: The nuances you see are so poignant.

V: Within Arksar you will see his world as he does. Know that you belong here and you will understand as he does. If you seek knowledge, you are without it, looking for it. All your thoughts define who you are and that's what you experience. Again, you see the gravity and simplicity of these statements – this is who you are. You are union without barriers because we have been removing the tiny threads that snag your journey.

R: There is a fuzziness and peacefulness as I merge more with Arksar.

AR: If you know who you are, you don't question yourself. Then your ***separation mind experiences*** return to greater awareness and realises what it already is.

You create who you are by what you think, unfortunately questions can be formed from duality or insecurity. So, what is the answer you might ask? and I would say what is the question?

R: Because one relates to the other, they are interlinked.

AR: Yes – do not look to me for answers because I would reflect your questions.

R: I was about to say – what is the way out of that conundrum, but I see the irony of the question. There is no way out of that. It is cause and effect. I have to be what I am and I create what I wish. My desire for unification is something I don't know in its fullness yet.

AR: Yes, you are correct, however by saying "you don't know unification (you-nification) in its fullness yet" you have created a different you.

R: I have been at this conundrum before but if I say, "This is what I am," it can also be a way of letting go of the need to believe.

AR: And how did that turn out for you?

R: I cannot remember – it was different to giving up or giving in because both of those statements refer to a struggle. 'Acceptance' sounds better but that still relates to non-acceptance and is part of an Arkarna program, not like the defunct Arkarna programs you have shown.

AR: The need to refer to defunct programs is of itself a defunct program. How does that feel?

R: Very liberating – defining the self doesn't need to have parameters of any kind. No corrupted definition can come forward because we have no need to create that. The base programs are different and there is no reference to what is good or bad, because they are both irrelevant to choosing who we are. In being good we define ourselves in relationship to that which is not good enough, any of which holds us back to those parameters. Who we are just is and what we create is beyond such restrictions because we are expansive. We are the joyousness and a completeness without fear of its loss. We have discarded ideas of self and found a different self of unconstrained joyousness.

AR: You are talking as me – we are a united soul.

R: I was about to say, we have moved so far, how do we move from here? But that's another question and a perception that there must be more. There is no more me, perhaps some unification of mind but no more to become: other expressions, but even that isn't relative as a description of us.

AR: Let us unite deeper and see what you believe about yourself. We are of no value to ourselves or to any separate part of our consciousness. This is not to be humble because that would imbue a quality – value is of no consequence.

What then the feelings we may have?

R: AHHHH! – pain in my head.

AR: You are dealing with the possibility that there may be 'no feelings' and you are trying to ***feel*** what it's like to have ***no feelings*** – but that is not possible. You cannot feel what isn't there. You are trying to integrate your old way of feeling into my world. We are in a place where suffering cannot touch us, where anguish is not part of the Arkarna or living program.

R: Truly a strange and wonderful realm!

AR: You feel irrelevant and not integrated and to that extent it's true. But to say one of your lives isn't relevant to another is not correct. It's all a matter of interpretation and the ability to perceive things that are widely different to your way of thinking.

R: I mesh deeper within Arksar. His fingers bend towards the top of his hand making me feel peculiar, because my human mind thinks it impossible. His whole body is more flexible than I remember – its adaptable and rubbery. The internals are supple, sinews and tendons seem not to exist.

AR: When you last saw me, I was on a lower dimension of myself so that you could interact with me. That's why your sketch at the time showed a body that functions in a similar way to yours. When you saw me today your Arkarna program showed you my previous form so you could meld with me in comfort. This body has no need for leverage or resistance as I am part of my environment. My experiential body flows to my bidding. Your body moves to your will and it's the same for me. Humanoid body programs compliment the realms they inhabit.

R: That's why everything we initially touched moved like us. A blending sinking feeling sweeps over me.

AR: If there is no separation – what is there?

R: A very comfortable union – one with no desire to be anything else.

Beyond the absolute stillness a distant murmuring of voices and information comes closer. Cascading words that have no meaning create internal pinpricks in my human body. It's not the words so much as the unknown concepts they encapsulate.

AR: What you know, I know – but not all of me do you know. The more you reside in me, the more I can impart to you.

Scene: Pinks and blues swirl and a door opens, allowing us to enter a cavernous room with a stone-flagged floor. Several beings have peaks of light above their heads, reminiscent of Buddhist statues.

Higher light body (HLB): Sit down please Robert, as you know higher mind can present itself in all manner of ways. I am one of your higher light bodies. I take the form of a deity not for reverence or stature but because it attracts your close attention. Arksar holds you in his presence and by engaging with me in this projection it confirms the depth of communication.

Tilling the soil in readiness for new growth has ended. With the imprint of the previous programs removed, what will grow from the seeds that have laid dormant for so long? Let the clouds gather and the rain fall gently. Look towards me.

R: In his cupped hands he holds a landscape of rolling hills. Some children play while others dig the ground looking for lost treasure. These are representations of my disparate thoughts in my subconscious. I say, "Have you not heard the past is a different land?" They respond with, "We know there is something valuable in the past but we can't find it".

That statement shows why I maintain a need to search in the past me. But I will not unearth hidden value in duality, only more duality. These are shadows of the past that cannot give me sustenance and they fade away.

I remove my focus from the world in the hands and look back at my higher light body, who remains motionless. He asks that I return to the rolling hills. I resume my focus but I am now walking along a sandy path with lush vegetation either side. I encounter an old man with a walking stick, he is bent over unable to walk properly. He is the embodiment of how I sometimes feel. His face is mine but much older.

HLB: Are you now so worn by life that you cannot lift your head to see joy and wonder?

R: As the very old man, I recognise my life has ended, in the same way it ends in every moment and then begins again. Past needs of suffering have gone and I absorb the energy as I reach the top of the hill.

HLB: The next is more poignant.

R: Aspects of Robert in dull heavy cloaks are gathered in a circle. Their dour energy is encapsulated in one aspect who welcomes me. He feels tired, like my father did just before he died, struggling on with no purpose.

HLB: This is genetic energy that you do not need. You are not your father and you have no need to suffer or find ways to overcome problems. It's only a program – it is not you!

R: There is an emptiness but the pointlessness has gone.

HLB: Willpower exists to take you to the next stage of your life.

R: I pull in the energy and become the Buddhist holding the light containing the landscape. I am the programmer and the program. I stand up and orbs from my aura fall to the ground. Each full of wonders that could be explored, but they are not relevant. Enticing, interesting but like the seeking for hidden treasures, they are known and no longer necessary. Light envelops me and my awareness is back in the body of Arksar.

AR: Using my energy you found parts of your program that were unfruitful. I held you firm to see yourself from a new perspective. What's it like now to experience my body and sensors?

R: The fluid energy feels more solid and your posture is different.

The body curves in more at the small of the back, creating a loose walk. The arms are long and when I swing them I have a gangly perambulation. Fingertips are bigger with sensors that feel shapes and texture, however they also feel the energy information of what's being touched. Touch something and you know it fully.

AR: We don't experience light in the same way because we use a broader bandwidth. As you look out to your night sky it appears dark but it's not – the spectrum is different. We use the light from the night sky because its more intense and our larger eyes are able to detect a wider range of light. What we then see inside our heads is 'full' and our 'knowing' is greater.

R: He picks a flower off a bush and eats it as a delicacy. I feel the silkiness of it as it flows down my throat. It is a tonic, cool but not cold, invigorating but relaxing, a roundedness that is complex yet satisfying. There is no taste but a multitude of sensations to experience, which the plant happily gives us.

Arksar strokes the underside of his forearm with a finger – the message from the fingertip and the forearm combines in an unusual composite interpretation. He presses all his fingertips to the opposing ones on the other hand. Light emanates from where they touch forming a ball of light between his palms. He repeats the process several times and places the balls of light into pouches suspended either side of his waist. The lights are made of the same energy we consumed from the flower. We saunter along the winding path that gives a variety of vistas. Arriving at a central point he places the balls in a tall receptacle. It shines with the same light, then emits bubbles which float into specific positions around the garden. We float above the bubbles and he shows me how they form patterns and gridlines. Some lines are brighter, where there are numerous links between the bubbles. The lines form segments and underneath each one there are a different set of rules and parameters.

AR: This is one of our pastimes, where we move from one area to another encountering different stimuli.

R: What's it got to do with the flower head and the energy created in your hands?

AR: You experienced our nature through me – a heightened vibrational being able to ingest a flower at a compatible energetic level. A flower blooms, radiates, shares and gives away its peak expression.

R: Whilst you don't need to move from one state to another, it felt like a mild drug.

AR: Your reference points have parameters and restrictions – we have variations of experience but that doesn't alter our state of being. Unlike you, we don't allow the perception of anger to make us angry and express through that altered state. You may enjoy a cup of tea, sensing a lift in spirits, seeing it as a special treat or a deserved break from hard work. That does not exist for us, it is enjoyed for what it is, not for altering our state of mind.

R: But it will alter your feelings.

AR: Not in the way you think. We have a variation of pleasant experiences but they are no more than that. We can observe the feelings and sensations as they unfold.

R: But the flower petals were like a drug, even the tea you mentioned has caffeine in it.

AR: The blooms are not drugs, because they do not alter our state or what we think. When in me, your interpretation of what I sensed was perceived through your human constructs. Your thoughts were '*wow this is good, I could do this again to receive the rush of chemicals as they course around my body*'. You are not like us. For you a pleasant experience arrives and becomes a reference point to the moment before, which then must have been less pleasant. However, the explanations I give help you to understand the concepts I present.

R: A well designed exercise for me to receive your reflections on my interpretation.

AR: And thus, nothing is by accident. I created the zones in my mind and brought them forth. I did that so that you could understand that I was creating without assistance.

Scene: Back on the ground we walk under the zone on our right. A vast openness extends way above us, connecting to a floating plane or platform with another blue sky above it.

AR: Are you sure that's what you see?

R: I believe so.

AR: Then what you believe is so. Let us move to the next.

Scene: A heavy structure confronts us. It has a large opening which is stabilised by structural cross members. My focus goes to its grey flat roof, then I'm in the clouds, looking down on an industrial complex, partially built, under the landscape. We return to ground level and approach the entrance.

AR: Follow me into the opening, through the energetic field that acts like a barrier instead of a door.

Scene: We walk into a hanger, passing several craft on our right and onward to a brightly lit area on our left. This space is bigger than the last, with various projects under construction. A large three-sided structure comes together in a nose cone that towers over us. A curved wall and domed roof appear on our left and opposite that, light comes through a complex matrix of stained glass. Intricate patterns in a beautiful collage of colours saturate me with wonder and awe.

Part of Arksar separates and goes up to some humanoid figures who he communicates with. We move further on to a square room full of colours, with open arches around the edges. We stand in the middle of the room and more people join us through the arches (portals). With all of Arksar back in our focus, he extends his arm and gesturing with his fingers he communicates with those around us. I can't hear what he has said but he finishes with, "if anyone has any queries please refer them to Robert, I am sure he can respond adequately".

Questions and interactive thoughts form amongst the group. Thoughts that are similar coagulate and mix with a few others, altering the communication. Others see their questions are better phrased or redundant through a natural materialisation of ideas to be presented.

AR: I've slowed this down so you can see how a union of communication develops. Whilst there can be individual interactions, the group format is not a loss of autonomy.

R: One group of thoughts develops into a clear scarlet bubble, which reaches us as a single point of projection to our forehead. The bubble deflates and all the energy flows into us. We have received well-constructed questions and we counter the thoughts in a cohesive delivery. A similar scarlet energy floats around our temples, but I can't understand any of the transmission.

AR: You don't understand the concept and the subject matter so you can't see what you don't know! You have seen the energy but the full interpretation hasn't materialised. Listen to them by sinking deeper within me.

One member of the group (MG): It's an unusual way of introducing a lower dimensional being – it's good that Arksar has compatibility with you. What does Robert hope to gain from reaching higher realms, particularly if he is to impart information to others? Is there any way we can assist because we cannot see constructive outcomes to our meeting?

R: Does this meeting need to have a constructive outcome and should everything be constructive? Is not the meeting of minds the essence of a meeting! Unless you have pre-seen the outcome you won't know what is constructive. I just learnt that what we create doesn't have to be constructive or valued, but experienced. As to what I will gain – I don't know but I am open to the exploration of alternative soul processes and objectives. I would be glad of any assistance, helpful to this journey.

There is rumination and a response.

MG: That is a constructive approach – we will consider this and review in the light of possible effects to timelines.

Scene: Several of the group activate the projection of an Arkarna mental hologram. I watch thought energies coagulating in a similar way to the joint thought bubble. Spheres of thoughts coalesce with long threads emanating into the distance. The hologram is reversed to see where the threads reach and what they created. This is all very definitive – it's not what they *could* have created because that would have included variation. They are looking at the outcomes, combining and adapting consequences to create constructive relationships and known outcomes. Then the process is reversed and the outcome flows back to the present. The hologram is then reversed again and one of them plucks a small ball of energy from the hologram, represented as a pearl of wisdom which they hold in front of me.

R: The group becomes much clearer and I can now see they look exactly like Arksar. I thank the person who brought this gift. The light from this pearl shines very brightly. It's lightweight but heavy at the same moment with different dimensions of energy. I realise the 'outcome' delivered in this presentation will have implications on more than one dimension of me. The light from the pearl presents an image to me. A fresh raindrop on a sunny day, that evaporates, leaving no trace other than a tiny stain at its dried-up outer edges.

The member of the group holding the pearl places it against my forehead. I am more attuned to Arksar and the voice within me speaks loudly with directed intent.

V: There comes a time for choice – to make a leap of faith or withdraw. Returning to your old way of thinking seems futile and so the selection appears to have made itself. You are teetering on the edge as a way to avoid choice – walk into the void.

R: As we walk, I hear each footstep, I feel them like heavy reverberations in a belfry. I see mottled feathers on a human breastplate only partially formed. A sketch that hasn't been completed and the face of a man above it. There is more here, but I can only see the formation of parts. His face is very clear and the sweeping curls of hair look like vestiges from the 1970s. In his cream trench coat, he is taller than me. Putting his arm over our shoulders he falls in beside us, striding forward with vigour. His black knee-high boots are as real as the shoes I wear. Ruched material ripples on the boot surface, adding style to practical mobility. Heavy scuffs and wear are evident. Similar crinkled trousers with a silken texture match the trench coat as it flaps behind him. The whole ensemble is complimented by an ornate black shirt embroidered with feathers. A flamboyant exuberant and confident character, not one I would expect to find here. We stop and again he hugs us saying, "Well my old friend Arksar, what can we do for you?"

There is a slight uncomfortableness, which soon passes – it does not become a state of being. It is my interpretation of his over familiarity.

Arksar detaches from my energy and moves to one side, clearly distancing himself. He stands on top of a small flat rock, in order to survey the surrounding rolling valley. He looks out over the view, not engaged with Mr Flamboyant. Then he turns and faces me.

AR: This is not who you are Robert, Mr Flamboyant encompasses the templates of several energies you could have followed when younger, but you did not do so for long. When a human looks in a mirror, they look back at themselves. They often create an image and impose it onto the world. It is as if others who may believe this false image, confirm to you that this is who you are. However, they would only be confirming an image and in any event, they would see that through their subconscious programs, perhaps looking for faults in you. Of course, it's okay to be presentable, that's only natural. But any more than that is to dive into the depths of ego desire and self-love of a projected image.

R: What does this have to do with the pearl energy that formed from constructive creations?

AR: The amount of information in that package was very detailed, showing you how internal constructive timelines are created. It incorporates interactions between your higher mind and the 'separation Robert'. It's all part of an Arkarna program. How you see the program is not only a reflection of you, but also what higher mind creates in order to show you to yourself.

R: I recognise Mr Flamboyant from my late teens/early 20's. Whilst the clothing wasn't the same, the demeanour and bonhomie was. A peacock, hiding insecurities underneath. It's a part of my timeline and an experience. Thankfully it was an archetype that did not fully form and become the main performer.

AR: Precisely, we are showing you how you utilised parts of your timeline which did not become extremes. Only by working with timelines in a multidimensional overview could you integrate those personality experiences and end up where you are now. The question is do you want to have a different now and a different creation or experience?

R: Yes and no – there are conflicts between the choices.

AR: That's because you look forwards through your desires and carry the past into the moment of now. But if you move forward and look at the possible outcomes on your timelines you can choose the one that you want from the outcomes.

R: Am I able to do that?

AR: You do it all the time but don't know it. Then a part of you wanders off and the timeline keeps readjusting itself to the chosen route. Those choices are made by *Separation Robert* but you are unaware of these tasks in your sleep. Of course, higher self and other aspects of you are involved, but you end up making the best or most constructive choice, which you see as free will. If there is the appearance of only one positive choice in a particular situation at your level – to you that feels like either 'restrictive choice' or 'no choice', but in actuality it was the most constructive choice that came out of the Arkarna programming. If your higher mind is presenting a way forwards, that is most constructive then it's not the restriction of free will – you could always choose another way. By accepting the vastness of yourself to include Arkarna programs, you shift the sense of self, then you see that free will is a human construct based in opposition/duality to restriction. You are not restricted – you are a creator and experiencer – live as that.

R: I must admit I wondered where all this was going.

AR: Well, the mind of Arkarna programs is capable of many wonderful things.

You have been told that the ***now*** of the Isness is 'past and future' and those energies are in constant flux. That means some things can be created differently or the same. You see this as the ability for the now to alter and adapt its fizz. Consciousness can move about within the Isness in its multidimensionality. You are thinking about fixed outcomes, whereas I am saying there is both a fixed outcome and a variable outcome – they both exist.

R: I know less now than when we started.

AR: Yes, multiple outcomes and fixed realities seem incompatible. Let's bring the full force of consciousness to this way of thinking and allow more of me to merge with you.

R: As we join, there is an interesting feeling of timelessness – there is no urgency, no need to know or solve problems.

AR: We will bring you more visual metaphors: just feel what comes, don't attempt to understand – that will be your human brain trying to figure it out. You won't be able to assimilate what I am saying using a linear perspective.

Look at a single point in space as a speck of dust with the universe rotating around it. If it had consciousness, it could only deduce what's going on by observing the rest of the universe. Planetary movements are measurements of one object in relation to another and that's relativity – one related to another. My descriptions of timelines can't be seen in terms of relativity. The very word timeline creates an image that is linear, where you may measure one section from another. Observation may have multiple vantage points (or specks of dust) but they are still relative to the point you are looking from. Fluid thought is not enquiring from a perspective but allowing information to be a part of you. In this way information and awareness appears because the universe provides it, and you are the universe. You are the information, as you were told before.

If you revisited the past, it would be different – because it will reflect your changed energetic self. Residual energies helped to create your timelines, but if you transmute them in the now you change your Arkarna program of creation and experience.

In the same way if your future-self has transmuted energy, it will affect you. The option to work with the original energy won't be there because it's been changed. The experience of changing it was done in a future moment, but you won't perceive that.

R: Confusing – why can't I have a life with fewer problems, if the energies are changed by a future me?

AR: Life isn't a series of problems – that's your take on it. It is your program – you can change it.

R: But why can't the future me change my thinking that 'things can be problems', so that I don't have problems in the now?

AR: Do you want to put everything off to the future?

R: Perhaps not.

AR: The separateness you experience is the energy that you have at this point and that's what you are transmuting. You are changing the past energies of you and you are creating the future you, whilst a future you is also helping you to change your energies in this now.

R: I am still seeing this explanation as linear experience.

AR: Well, let us change your perspective and from your future you, I will assist.

CHAPTER 29
The experience of thought removal

R: We seem to be going around in circles.

Arksar (AR): But they are getting smaller. You have a problem accepting that timelines are not only fluid, but they are not time either. They are your energies experienced as events and you are experiencing yourself as an event. Meeting Mr Flamboyant was your past energy being encountered. It formed an event within your mind and heart, becoming an experience of working with your mind.

Instead of time we will use the words energy, creation and experience. ***Shatarma*** is an alternative word for timeline and the changing of the energy in a timeline. A shatarma timeline is fluid and constantly changing.

Bring to mind a bubble in the shape of a worm, with the ability to twist and flow in most any shape. As it twists and turns it can cross itself in a multitude of ways. Within the bubble, there are random brilliant-coloured lights. Focus upon the red one, then you can engage with it. It doesn't matter when you are or where you are in the elongated bubble. The red light contains the understanding of this subject. Enter it fully using my body-form to experience yourself as me.

Scene: The further into elongated bubble we go, the brighter it gets. On the outside, other bubbles exist as wobbly spheres wriggling to form more complex shapes.

Entering the red point, we find ourselves in a tower with whitewashed walls reaching skywards. Waiting patiently on shelves, books are ready to be read. Steps and gantries on elevated floors, move as if they have a life of their own. Our nose cannot avoid the damp odours and flaking lime distemper. We climb numerous rotting steps to a small window at the top of the tower. Scrambling through we crawl out on to a lush green lawn. No wonder the building was decaying, with most of it below ground level. The sum of all that knowledge has enabled us to enter another mind construct.

A Victorian gardener tends the flower beds using worn tools. He places them in a wooden wheelbarrow with a dry squeaky spindle. As I approach, I see he has my face so, clearly, he is an aspect of my psyche. Perhaps he is the summation of my unknown feelings, to be discarded in order to understand the next section of information.

His elderly and haggard demeanour is palpable. He is losing the battle as the rampant vegetation romps and consumes all. He clips leaves overhanging the reducing shingle path laid out in a square. Vegetation growth is so pervasive that he has no time for anything else but clipping.

A scrubby vine galumphs across the pantile roof of the tower top, it too will soon be engulfed. Whenever we move our attention to another part of the garden, the process of growth speeds up. Inevitably this whole area will become consumed. Sooner or later the window to the book depository will be hidden and the vines will creep inside and take root amongst the books, histories and wisdoms.

Another sunken tower is just visible under a large briar patch. A place of its time, like the expansive structural building in Victorian times. I ***just know**** that the two sunken towers are past duality knowledge and relativity viewing. Looking out of the garden, gateways lead to other parts of a much larger landscape. The access points however have become overgrown and impassable. The embattled gardener had gone around the shingle path snipping off ***encroaching new ideas***.

Tending and nurturing my past ideas within the present is clearly unsustainable. The old gardener concedes and offers me a trowel. We plant tree saplings in the surrounding shingle path in an effort to control the destruction of the old ways of working. Like rockets on steroid plant food, black poplars shoot upwards. He says, "We will now know where the path once was," but I feel there is no need to remember what's no longer useful. The poplars quickly reach the end of their life span. A fungal disease enters the roots and they discard heavy rotten branches. We retreat to the centre of the garden as the trees begin falling. We stand on a stone plaque inscribed with the words 'last place to stand'. The energy of tending the past evaporates and 'me the gardener' of that past no longer exists.

All goes still, but as the vegetation of unstoppable new information begins to touch my feet, I wonder what's next?

AR: NOTHING – IT'S OVER.

R: With that loud intervention my mind flickers to the talk of bubbles, timelines, shatarma and non-time. A fast buzzing sound surrounds us and we move upwards in a tube of white light. Sonic booms and seismic shakes occur within the surroundings of the walled garden. Other trapped ideas are released and float upwards, enhancing the fizzing feel around us. Further shakes follow, releasing energy from other adjoining gardens with long held beliefs and wisdoms.

With one final crescendo the last shockwave allows the bastion of ***safety in fear*** to float up. A pink wispy portal forms and three lanky beings like Arksar firmly retrieve me. My voice speaks with a loud firm intensity.

V: In order to dispense with those mental structures, it was necessary to experience letting them go. If I had said 'you have let go', you might doubt you had because you would not feel it. Arksar has the knowledge of shatarma: it will now be easier for you to understand. He is having a timeline experience of helping you and you are having an experience of being helped by him. Let him explain to you, but do not question what flows, no matter how it's presented.

R: The yearning to discover has gone and the human need to achieve, which seemed intrinsic to life is no longer important. All I need to do is allow things to happen in any order that my Arkarna programs present.

AR: We are now able to enter the free-floating timeline bubbles or shatarma. Within them there are coloured dots but they are not forward or backward of each other, their positions are not relative, they are only concepts of separation. Our focus can be in any part of it because we are moving inside a construct to gain experience and understanding.

Who would have thought that desire and drive were a part of your residual energy to be transmuted and removed? Particularly when they are considered to be so necessary for human life. You can function well without ***the need to achieve***, because that attribute is not necessary in order for you to function.

Remember, transmuting residual energies is not all about removing negative constructs or correcting past deeds, we have moved on from that. Transmuting is about changing the energy of yourself that you have laid out and created. There is no judgement, its merely a choice of what suits you as the expression of yourself. ***Being free from desire is a freedom from craving (which is a restriction)***. The fact you are doing all this within my energy makes ***ideas of self*** become less relevant. If you hold to nothing, you can touch and feel anything.

You consider it's necessary to have linear timelines to avoid the one moment becoming chaotic. However, it is the Arkarna program and compartmentalisation that allows a focused perception of many things. We can focus on any energy point within this bubble in any apparent order. The energy spots are us and what we have created ourselves to be. We are revisiting them and revising what we wish to be, but we are also possibility and the unknown.

When we transmute a previous expression of ourselves it creates an empty space, which is filled with more light and new information. That different information means the way you interface with all your other multidimensional selves, and your past and future you, are changed. However, you perceive the ***past you*** as a memory program which you are able to look back through. But the way you interpret that memory will be altered to accord with your revised thinking in transmuted self.

Actual time travel is going back in a shatarma, selecting a point and injecting your consciousness or focus, mentally or with the help of technology.

R: That means all the experiences are concurrent and contain all time but that can't be possible?

AR: That's the beauty of Arkarna programs and the pulse – it is and it isn't – a wave and a particle.

R: Wow, that's struck a chord somewhere inside me, a truth I can't quite conceive in fullness. If someone else travelled back in time, they could interact with me in a different way and affect what I am now.

AR: That does happen, but the conundrum is that it was part of the timeline. Remember your linear perception is also a program. Energy options seen as your past and future can be changed during sleep. The shatarma is you – it is your ability to play and experiment with different energy insertions, allowing constant transmutations of what you understand yourself to be.

CHAPTER 30

The permanence of constantly changing

R: Comprehending shatarma eludes me, so I relax for a couple of days and try again. I focus as much as I can within Arksar.

Arksar (AR): Have you ever considered that there is no answer?

R: What, like paradox – where there is more than one answer?

AR: No – no answer because your question forms a different outcome to the theme I have in mind.

R: I understand what you are saying but surely you have the ability to answer in any way you wish.

AR: That is true but I am responding to the intellectual way you are approaching this. Don't look for an answer to the conundrum – allow it to present itself.

In a similar way to my previous description of bubbles, imagine the universe as a spherical bubble with points of energy (experiences) on the inside. Your consciousness moves within all the energy points as a free-flowing cascade, like the washing machine. It is happening everywhere in no particular order, but zigzag lines appear between the energy spots. We could say these are timelines or mental routes which your focus can now follow. The totality of the sphere is non-time and the energy that passes from one spot to another is an energy of multiple connections. You are the sphere; the energy dots; the routes and the timelessness. If you move your focus, between the spots, you create an energy of expression, belief and intent. But like much earlier descriptions, remember the sphere and its contents are pulsing and changing. As you move your focus, you change your outlook or intent. In this way you change the energy of the sphere and in all the routes, be they past or future ones. The routes become a function of consciousness in relationship to other parts of your energy, which constantly change.

Your focus can have separation programs, allowing you to have multiple ways of experiencing your own energy. Your sleep is fluid and interconnected but daytime focus is more compartmentalised and you become wrapped up in the experience of it.

Looking closely within the sphere you will see more spheres, each of which have other points of energy in them. In this construct the spheres, within the sphere of soul, would be your multidimensional selves. At your level you wouldn't usually interact with them, unless it's helpful or part of your plan (like our conversations and travels). Each sphere has its own outer shell or aura and its image is a projection of its concept of self in that dimension, in a similar way that you are in yours.

I am showing it in this way so you can feel that you are the 'centre of all' – that you are the complete sphere, containing the multidimensional aspects within you. In a similar way if you went into one of your other selves, the concept would be the same – they would be at the heart of the system.

Let your mind enter the soul sphere where you are the 'complete system' containing the sphere of Robert and the other spheres of multidimensional experience. From the encompassing soul sphere of non-time look at the 'Robert experience' sphere. Within it you will see interconnecting zigzags or timelines between points of events. But these points are also the 'sponsoring energy' of the event. These we have described before as your thoughts, deeds and residual energies to be left or transmuted.

So, it's now possible to see that the residual energies have an interplay – all of you affects all of you, even if you try to suppress things. As all of you is interconnected, each point has many connections to many other points. At this level, timelines are not zigzags between points as we first showed you, but each point affects every part of you. The interconnections are so wide and varied that they appear as an energetic fizz. We have upgraded timelines to shartarmas and now to fizz – a connection to all.

Regardless of dimensions we are all the same soul, available and interconnected. Where we actually are in the universe is not relevant because our true nature is non-local.

From there we can observe your level and perceive the movements you make between the various reference points. We understand the routes you are taking and where you will end up. We see the individual changes and growths as well as the totality that is constantly changing. Here comes the difficult area for you.

If all is changing, how can we see resultants when they are also constantly changing? It was previously said these sit side by side. Because we see beyond the changing or the results of the changing – we step outside of that level – it's really quite simple.

R: You mean all my struggling to understand can be over in an instant?

AR: A large portion of it. You were caught up in the linear progression of enlightenment and timelines. Whereas within non-time it's possible to see the resultants at any slice in time in any point of focus.

Imagine you are halfway through your life – the energies of the past and the future of that timeline would reflect the view from that halfway point. The whole self is a reflection of itself and what it creates at that point. Further along the path one can have a different slice of the changed energy. Your perspective of progression within the elongated bubble concept worked – but that was not the case in the non-time explanations of the sphere. So further along your timeline you have upgraded the elongated bubble to a sphere.

You are wondering, how does a physical manifestation or time travel affect a timeline?

A person or entity entering a timeline will change it, but you think it will mess things up. Sometimes it can knock a timeline off course, but the timeline re-routes to re-join its original course. The events might be slightly different but the energies being encountered will be as before. However, the altered energy inserted into the timeline will also need to be transmuted. But which particular resultants do we view, because the perspective of different slices are changed?

If a time travelling alien turns up, they will affect the timeline. All will be a reflection of that experience and altered energy. But from non-time that resultant can be seen. Whether they travelled in time or not is irrelevant as it's a matter of the changes their energies bring.

R: This implies that timelines are seen from a perspective that it's already happened – but you also say we are in constant flux.

AR: The two are not mutually exclusive. The now is in flux or pulse, so the timelines form and reform. There are probability choices but not all can be experienced. Alien benevolents might observe that humanity's timeline doesn't turn out well, so they help with an alternative route. In that instance they have changed a timeline so that the negative version didn't happen. That is the same as the interjection I mentioned before. The resultant was already in the universe, but it depends if you are looking from the slice before the interjection or in non-time.

R: This sounds like pre-destination.

AR: Yes and no, it's all a matter of choice, however you are seeing the results of your constant changing energies. It's all a matter of perspective – from which part of time or non-time.

It is often understood that higher dimensional beings of your soul are a future you. Antemedi, Orlacka and I fit that description, however we are also a separate focus of our joint soul with you. The pulsing sphere model of oneness encompasses union in and out of time. You have had past lives on other planets and in different dimensions of the universe. Your present retrograde experience allows you to return to lower levels and have experiences that you didn't have before, to create energies and face them, in order to transmute them. There is no judgement made about the level of dimensional experience or how you express yourself.

You can sense the vibrations of your other dimensional bodies in their various forms. You are comfortable in my body shape, but it doesn't matter what form you have or what you experience. You try to correlate this information and muse on the possibility that, as part of my multidimensional self in the future, you will be my life experience.

But if we return to the spheres and their energies in different dimensions, it's all coexisting. Antemedi has compatible vibrations to me and our lives can interact more easily. But we have separation programs that are very different to yours. Our Arkarna programs might not appear as 'division of thought' to suit each expression. In a previous life choice (not past life) you were Andromedan and you have been told that you were Telenatey the botanist – which is true. When you experienced him from Robert, he was in another time frame where one bubble of timeline touches another, but your separation experience was maintained. It was an encounter event where you both altered your energies by the experience.

You are the same soul and can interact in the same moment. The idea of separation consciousness imbues a sense of self when seen from compartmentalisation. How can you meet yourself? Very easily!

You have a conundrum– wondering what would happen if you went back in time within Roberts's life and met yourself. That would still be timelines intersecting and affecting one another. You get very hung up on the idea of physicality and think your emotional and mental experiences with Telenatey are not proper interactions. It's not the memory of the life as Telenatey – it is the crossing of two of your timelines that creates resultants. When seen outside of time they are just a pathway that forms, to enable energies to change. Remember those energies are you and the routes form within your Arkarna programs. The Arkarna programs of unfolding possibility are you, so the experience of a route can be determined or known 'as is'. You are the programmer and the program – so of course you will know what you create for yourself.

R: So, it's not predetermined because that's looking from a point in time, thinking that the future is fixed. Outside of time there is no predetermination because there is no backwards and forwards. But it's also constantly changing and on another level it's just observable as a program. If there is no end, it's not possible to see infinity.

AR: The sponsoring thought behind that is you seeking security in the known. Whereas the unknown is also safe, but does it serve you to look forwards? If you know the detail of what's around the corner, it will alter how you perceive the moment of now and how you act in it. The purpose of experiencing an unfolding will be lost. You might conclude that the far future isn't known because of the fluxing past and future, and the multitudes of possibility. However, you need to look from the perspective of a united compartmentalised mind where you would exist outside of time and judgement.

Aqueena, the female summation of your higher self has big differences in her way of living.

R: To experience her life she must have interconnected separation programs.

AR: She is here ready to talk more about soul experience when timelines are not made from transmuting energy – but reflect ***'as is' created energy***. This is energy that doesn't need to be changed because it is, as it was intended to be created. At this level soul life is outside of time and interconnections just are or are 'as is'. There is an all-knowing, with acceptance but no negativity. There is no need to question – focus and events are a reflection of love in harmony without duality. Her Arkarna programs encapsulate interaction with lower dimensional aspects and experiences. They interact with her but do not affect her. She does not need to focus upon them unless she wishes to. This is life lived from ***'as is' created energy*** allowing her Arkarna programs to present the next probability from the goodness and love that she is.

I shall not say good bye because you have my energy inside and around you. You can interact with my thoughts or feel my body shape whenever you wish.

CHAPTER 31

Accept your created energy

Aqueena (AQ): I can see you are beginning to upgrade your separation thoughts and feelings.

R: As she moves in me, I am wrapped in love, pure understanding and peacefulness. There is a delicate feeling combined with completeness. A union different to the masculinity of Arksar. I feel her energetic body overlays whilst she also stands to one side. A common theme – multidimensional energy morphing!

AQ: It is good, is it not?

R: You are using judgemental terms and comparison relationships.

AQ: I am using your language: it's not about judgement but the feelings your words can evoke. Not more or less or better but just 'is good' without any needs to be fulfilled. I may talk like a tender mother but I shall also be forthright. It will give you a grounding to understand my life.

The strong voice you have heard is a combination of the higher light bodies of your multidimensional separations. These reach you from an interaction program and whilst they feel loving, they also have authority and greater substance. In part that's about your perception and need to see them that way. Whilst I am a very high vibration, I have no need for you to see me like that and nor do you. Often the quiet voice is one that cannot be heard unless you know it is there. Gentleness is the key and it is important for you to be gentle with yourself. Arksar alluded to some of the things we will cover. First, I would like you to draw in more of my energy containing 'information perception' as well as gentleness.

R: My head feels taller, with a domed skull – rings of energy transmit and receive. What I am receiving from her makes me feel like I am in her body shape. We move into a small cloud of butterflies that tickle as we pass through them. Bushes, plants and flowers abound and we are connected to them. We stand together looking towards the horizon. I wonder if that's a replication of where we are and what we think. Is it the reflection of ***as is created energy***?

Scene: We separate and move towards a green painted park bench at the edge of a path. We look out over a green landscape with a lake below us and a large building way off to our left. We sit down side by side on the bench and Aqueena holds my hand.

AQ: Brace yourself – you are not who you think you are, everything is different to what you believe.

R: At those words my heart sinks in sadness, thinking why should I want to live a lie?

AQ: The emotions here will become very intense – if I had said "you are not what you believe" in any other place, you might have said "yes I am different to what I think" – the 'I' of your response would be self and you would have lost the nuance of my intent. Because you are not self – you are not even you and you are certainly not Robert because he is an Arkarna program of experience. You are much wider than that – let it go.

R: Again, I am swept by the intensity of death – accepting my life has been a form of pretence.

AQ: Are you anybody at all?

R: I'm stuck in my tracks and have nothing to say because that would be Robert and apparently, he doesn't exist. Rationally I know he is a separation experience and an Arkarna program in a hologram that pulses.

AQ: Perhaps you would like to explore Robert-self with some of my insight. Let every deed and created energy be seen and resolved. Then you can see Robert is a program of experience.

R: A burst of her energy floods me and I'm back in Robert with no restriction of thought or deed. Nothing is hidden, or forgotten – I am wide open. I am aware of times when I could have been more gentle or understanding. I am filled with remorse but as the ***created energy of all those events*** hits me, it becomes an ice-cold torrent. With my head in my hands I stare at my feet. Aqueena puts her arm round me and I sob without recourse or need to stop. My actions cannot be placed in the past and forgotten. I have no excuses and take full responsibility for what I have done and continue to do, no matter how small or infrequent.

AQ: I did say this is not who you are and you are not Robert – he is a program.

R: I know what you are saying but I have the need to make amends.

AQ: At this level there is no need, because you see that you are doing all this to yourself as you are the universe.

R: But an outburst or rebuke of my children had ramifications.

AQ: You may think so. You, your wife, children and all those you might have acted differently with are in front of you. Beyond them are other aspects of your wife and family and people to whom you showed great compassion and understanding. Bring all of them into you – the helped and the hindered. Allow all this energy into you – it is yours.

R: All that energy I created – it belongs to me as soul, not as Robert. I have pains in my joints, back and head as waves of people I know, or had forgotten, step into me. It takes a long time till my returned energy stops flowing. I feel rather flat, receiving the unhelpful energy I created but the space inside me has increased. I am less dispersed in the world. People I have helped or been kind to, now flow into me with an intensity that accelerates exponentially. I do not recognise them all because some were helped by those I had helped, creating a ripple effect. That's why the horizon looked as if it had replicated itself. But surely this ripple energy is created by other people's efforts and it belongs to them – it is not of my making.

AQ: The people you helped, transformed themselves by choice but they used your energy to start that process. Where they in turn helped others, it still contained some of your energy of intent to heal. If you drop a pebble in a pond and the ripples rebound from the edges, both the pebble and the sides are necessary to create that effect. You are the universe and all those here today are part of that.

CHAPTER 32

Body swap – exploring another soul's experiences

Scene: After the energy absorption, I am in the same vibrational plane but the view is different. It is more vivid and the clarity is extraordinary. We are at the lake seen from the park bench. On a rowing boat an Edwardian lady holds a dainty umbrella. She lies resplendent, unconcerned that her voluminous dress hangs over the sides. The whole ensemble floats by effortlessly as the boat moves to her thoughts and wishes. Dark green reflections cover the depth of water and have as much life as the trees ashore. A manicured grass hill leads up to a palatial mansion with views over the lake and beyond. A series of managed waterfalls tumble gently down the slope, across the lower water gardens, before mingling with reeds and irises at the edge of the lake.

The landscape has been created from thought and is surreal – dreamlike but also meticulous in its form. We pass the water gardens and move on to a lower lawn, peppered with so many low daisies that little patches of grass struggle to elbow their way to the surface. The flowers form patterns which in turn vibrate, creating a melody of peacefulness. The bliss of this place envelops me with a deep sense of remembering that I am home. Quite why it should be such a grand affair I cannot imagine.

Aqueena and I climb stone steps alongside the terraced waterfalls. Looking up to the left I can see the green park bench on the top of the hill. We continue in our direction to reach the mansion. External tables and chairs are laid out in decreasing semi circles as they become constrained by the footprint of the mansion. To someone's will and desire, white table cloths and chair cushions appear.

The mansion is clearly old, but futuristic doors lead beyond to a large function room. It is full of people in close intimate communication. One of the hosts greets us and places two long silvery tubes in my right hand. I am directed towards an interior room filled with light. Unable to see what's inside, a little trepidation arises as we get closer. Remembering Aqueena's energy is in me and at my side brings stability.

We enter a cinema, adjacent to the screen. Rows of seats spread upwards on our right. Technology and old structures side by side remind me of the Andromedan multifunction rooms with an outside seated area overlooking a small valley.

We slide into the nearest seats and Aqueena takes one of the silver tubes from me and inserts it into her right arm rest. I copy this doing the same with the remaining tube in my right arm rest. I know they will be part of our interactive experience. The remainder of the audience sits and their murmurs fall to a low hush.

The tubes come to life and an energetic field forms across the lower part of the seat, down to the floor. The sensation is that my lower thighs and legs are dangling in some alternative reality. Placing my hands on the arm rests activates the upper field.

I hear a non-English language, some words of which I recognise. They form directly in my ears as a projection, from each side of the seat. The feeling of being in more than one place at a time is intense.

AQ: The field cuts through time and space, allowing more people and more of their consciousness to connect in several dimensions. It also regulates the emanations from any individuals to ensure consciousness transfer does not upset or become inappropriate to the theme at hand.

R: Which is?

AQ: Consciousness transfer within Arkarna separation programs.

R: A stage forms in front of the screen. Beings appear in a temporal energy bubble, which encapsulates the stage as well. The room they occupied has been teleported and the energy they brought continues to sustain it. Perhaps it's similar to the energy in our seats.

Speaker: Welcome to you all in your separateness. You would not be here unless you have some understanding about the loss of self-identity and overlaying multiple identities. Place your hands over your hearts and this will form a link between us all. It's also a recognition and acceptance of your will to share and encounter others at greater depth.

We are creating a golden ring over each of your heads, so let the energy of it flow over you. It will energise another layer within your interdimensional auras.

Scene: When this is completed there is also an energetic rod at my back with a hoop keeping my head in a fixed forward position.

Speaker: The ring will help to remove your linear perceptions and show that your mind is already on the inside of this information. The interface will be able to accept multiple perspectives and a full perspective, because you won't be looking from or to anything. There is no inside or outside and my words and thoughts are part of you.

You are familiar with your separation perspective of the multidimensional self. You will now be able to see this from a unified one. This is an overself perspective, overlaying multiple soul aspects. You do not have to do anything. It is not an achievement to be here: it is merely an aspect of you all. It may seem to have little purpose to the rational lives that you lead in your individual realms, but stay with me and you might feel differently at the end of this.

Allow your energy to expand and fill the whole room.

R: As I spread out, I feel that Aqueena and I are the only ones in here apart from those on the stage but I realise that's just initial perception.

Speaker: It may feel unusual but remember it's still you and just your sensation of many souls overlapping in a unified experience. You are wondering if there is a unified perception to the point that self becomes irrelevant.

So, let us explore that!

Bring you focus back to your seated position, knowing that your energy fills the room. Be aware that everyone else is doing the same and their energy exists within each one of you.

R: Waves pass though me and I feel temporal portals opening in my body.

Speaker: Allow their thoughts to be your thoughts and allow them to explore you. Your initial approach might be to explore others, but it works the other way around as well. You will all begin to feel that others are exploring you. There is nothing in you that is hidden, there is no shame or guilt to hide and you are open to all. No fears, no regrets and no driven desire – just Isness.

You may reach out and enter as many people in the room as you wish. You can look through their eyes and see what they see and think.

R: No fears or regrets the speaker said. I am glad of the last session ***accept your energy*** – that obviously needed to be done before this experience could take place.

I put my focus to the seated person in front and find I am a crumpled, elderly woman. She has a frail bone structure and her muscle tone is weak. An unusual pet weaves itself around her favourite walking cane.

The male person to my rear puts his focus into me and I feel a little violated because I don't know him.

I decide to continue as we have been told and I return to my focus in the elderly woman. We are using her cooking pot with internal induction plates. There are no cables and the energy is taken out of the room by a free energy generator within the pot itself. The apartment is square but one of the windows looks out to a recess in the building's facade. It's a grey smooth material somewhat like a coated pressed steel, but there are no joints because it's been formed in situ by a construction generator. We are in a high-rise block looking out onto smaller white buildings below us. A space appears in part of the wall and she takes out some food for her pet. The light in the room is 'everywhere'; it doesn't seem to come from a source. The light is non-directional and is being formed in situ. There is a circular dome on the ceiling, which seems to be the generator. It's very unusual – there are no shadows.

We return to the middle of the room where there is a large round table. A section of the table opens, like one slice of pizza folding under another – it reveals a seat. She sits down and her chair slides into the centre of the table. The table moves again, but this time only part of the slice returns behind her, so she is encapsulated. An energy screen forms in the centre and using a few hand movements she locates her daughter. The screen creates a spherical portal around her, so the old lady can be with her daughter. In this mode she is no longer crippled and walks easily, shimmering at her daughters' side. There is a two-way conversation while her daughter is going about her afternoon duties in a public open space. Looking back, we see the large grey buildings in the background. They feel out of place, somehow too big for the environment. It may be an optical illusion because this parkland is a series of holograms within the grey building structures. The unseen side of the buildings are the edge of the environment, perhaps a biosphere.

I thank the woman in my head and I withdraw my focus.

My consciousness feels as if it has lots of connections. I am more aware of the man from behind moving through thoughts in my head. He comes to some dead ends – maybe he is expecting more. Perhaps he can see further than I, so the anticipation of what he knows isn't there. He leans back into his body and says, "You have some interesting takes on consciousness leading to division of the universe." I feel him rummaging around in the back of my head like he is bumping himself against my skull. He is a matter of fact, unemotional individual.

AQ: The best way for you to perceive and understand this ability was to undertake the experience. You won't need to sense it that way in future.

CHAPTER 33
Socialising with other aliens to gain more insights

Scene: We are back at the entrance to the garden, looking towards the lake and palatial mansion.

Aqueena (AQ): Concentrate on where we are now. From this position you can see us standing at different positions, observing the scene on our way up to the mansion the other day. You could say we are observing the past from the future. Or you could say we are looking at energetic possibilities. What would happen if we followed the same route again?

We can wave to the lady in the boat, see where we stopped at the reeds and walked alongside the layers of waterfalls. Our sense is we have walked here before and that nothing is unknown. However, as we reach the area around the mansion you can see the tables are already covered in linen. People of all kinds are now milling about and chatting to one another, it is quite an event. Look back over the route we took and you will see patterns of daisies on the lawns below.

R: Someone says, "Yes the patterns are quite magnificent – they are vibratory in form and reflect our composite energy – we create the patterns." Turning around I am confronted by a woman wearing a large headdress with a series of veils hiding her appearance.

Woman (WN): You are most unusual. That is not meant to be a derogatory comment. Perhaps I should say you are a curiosity for me. Many people here know one another and converse as if old friends. However, you don't seem to be interested in socialising. It's as if it has no depth or reason for you. Why do you give little credence to social interaction?

R: That's an interesting observation – I feel there is more to gain from the cut and thrust of an enquiry or allowing higher guidance to unfold.

WN: Have you not learnt from socialising?

R: I have but there are not many humans who talk openly about esoteric matters.

WN: You could talk to anyone here; I will introduce you to some of them later. Over there is Soloson from the Pleiades and Queta Erthita from the Antars. We have many gatherings and by socialising we find out more about each other. Some people know my race as the tall whites.

R: You are friendly and willing to engage but there is a distance and not all of you is being presented for some reason.

WN: You have no qualms in showing your multidimensional selves and have pleasure in their presence. I have similar, but there are also warring elements among some of my lower dimensional selves. You have experienced their energies and my lower multidimensional expressions as veils. Not everyone will see me like that – and after my explanation you will not need to see that information in that way. You will understand what you had seen and no longer need to see it to gain the wisdom from it. These energies need to be transmuted through karmic regeneration but there's no judgement as to when that will be. Aqueena has brought you here and we see you reflected in her. There are similarities between her functions and mine. We do not spend much time wringing our hands and making plans to help the multidimensional self. You are thinking I have cast them adrift, unconcerned for their toils and troubles. In this instance your perspective ignores free will and superimposes importance upon the idea of unifying the whole. That may be joyous but no more important than the lives and experiences my selves have at those levels.

AQ: Arkarna programs reflect what is and, in that way, they guide the lower levels of soul. At all levels the programs are us, but your distorted perspective of higher self determines it to be an entity with your best intentions at heart. To an extent that is true but magnificent Arkarna programs and systems allow experiences to be reflections of you and we only need to tinker with the program where circles or eddies in the energy flow become restrictive or self-imploding. Love can be a complicated area of programming when looking at individual and global transmutation.

WN: Should we toil over what has free will? You live believing you are incomplete, yet you have love and satisfaction within that life. We are love but we are not on a high unreachable dimension you can't understand. Who says love and responsibility should have adverse demands upon us? We are not pulling our weight or getting off lightly because those concepts have no purpose here.

AQ: Thank you for the social discussion – it has helped Robert see higher-self interactions in a different light.

R: I thank the woman and say, "May your light that does not know itself be open to your wisdom and love".

AQ: While on the theme of our life and social interactions, I will introduce you to others who will convey further differences.

R: This level seems too good to be true when there is still much to be done on lower levels.

AQ: Those that look up are guided, but the speed at which they move might be hampered by the expression of unconstructive energy, or lack of transmutation – but beyond judgement: it's all cause and effect.

R: Talking about love and consideration is all very well but it doesn't seem humane to let suffering continue in lower soul. I can't tolerate the pain and fear in the human collective – it's a system full of faults that needs changing.

AQ: It will be changed. Come let me introduce you to El-Lanadore.

R: He looks full of himself, holding court with devotees. They move away as we get closer. Have they had their fill of this incongruent presence?

El-Lanadore (EL): Should all be meek, mild and polite? What is wrong with forthright exchange? Speak up! Don't be afraid to say what you wish young man.

R: (*whoops didn't realise my thoughts were so loud*)

You have the sum of me and I am not afraid to say that. (He puts his arm on me, taking me further into a group of unusual beings)

E-L: We have a new youngster among us, he is an aspect of Aqueena. He's been helped to acclimatise to our way of thinking and being. Poor chap thinks he's travelled and landed in a film set, where alien actors experiment with humanoid thoughts.

That is how you see it, isn't it?

Don't say I have the sum of you, that would be deferring to me without opinion. Speak your mind: say what you think and feel.

R: I am surprised by these interactions, are they lower dimensional perspectives of a higher one? It has undermined my preconceived ideas of living upon these enlightened levels and has left me slightly deflated.

E-L: Should we be as monks – elevated beyond humanity, sitting in silence directing the universe and living in some harmonious bliss?

R: I suppose not.

E-L: Then you suppose correctly.

R: Am I to be ridiculed for showing my lack of understanding?

E-L: Certainly not. I am loud and forthright – even oafish to your perception.

R: Very unexpected, but no doubt something else lies beyond my initial perception. He smothers me with his huge presence, greeting me as a long-lost friend. An Oliver Reed on a good day, solid, hearty and full of good meaning. I am warming to him and his steady embrace. It's a wonderful feeling, quite grand and gentle at the same time. I am happy to be lost in this moment of his expression of love.

E-L: Should I be without character? I have an unwavering directness and how you interpret that gives you your experience. Feel Aqueena and your other expressions in you, then see what you perceive.

R: Yes, it's your great exuberance that I misunderstood.

E-L: There are different characters here, as you will come to understand. Look in front of you at the wider landscape.

R: I see the scene I expect. The rolling hills and an outfall from the lake into the wider countryside. El-Lalandore asks me to look through his eyes. When I do, I am dumbfounded to see that there is a flat plane stretching out in front of us. Greyish white, no objects, just a few people moving around.

E-L: We create the objects to fill the narrative of what we are thinking. Your world is a representation of what you think and believe. You create it that way, despite the fact so few know that's what they are doing. Here we do not always need to have a common creation and we can move past and through this area, which has other functions of commonality. You could have moved by opening a new door, but you would have missed the explanation I am presenting.

R: You seem to know a great deal about me and the way I think.

E-L: Yes, I do, that's why Aqueena introduced you to me. However, it's also stimulating for me to find ways of presenting you with new information. We can still walk to a door if that helps to signify entry into a different environment. We can end our present construct of a reality.

R: We stand on the precipice of my current way of thinking, with a great vastness beyond. Ahead is darkness but nonetheless it's a peaceful view upon the universe. It reminds me of some of the earlier journeys with Arksar. El-Lanadore moves his arm and a new scene comes into creation.

Futuristic ways of living in space. What is real and what isn't? There are different dimensions overlaying one another and we can be in one or many. It surpasses the idea of individual communal realities and dimensions.

E-L: Fantastic, isn't it? You can be wherever you want, whenever you want.

R: I am watching different objects in different dimensions passing through one another as if the other is not there. It's like seeing the whole interplay of dimensions as an overlay.

E-L: It is a way for you to see holograms – not the solidity of each dimension. They do exist as realities – lets grab a Roman chariot and see where it takes us.

R: There is no horse but I grab a rail in front of me and brace my feet on the ribbed wooden gripper strips of the floor. I lean back against leather ties attached to the front and sides. These are strung to individual girdles at our waists. I say to E-L, "We are creating this – it's make-believe."

E-L: Don't you believe in what you create? What is the difference between making things up and creating them?

R: Make-believe isn't real!

E-L: Reality is a state of mind and belief. Just because you have a consensus belief, doesn't mean it's any more real than what you believe to be real.

Scene: Our conversation is shouted at one another while charging round a large empty amphitheatre. I am hanging on to the webbing so I don't fall over.

R: This is also a function of make-believe!

E-L: You doubt so much of what you experience!

R: If I believed I could fly and jumped off a building, I would come to a sticky end.

E-L: Yes, where you live those are the rules and the Arkarna programs of that dimension. But you can still create.

R: This is a great ride, it's very exciting and I am really having fun, even if I have to catch my breath when we speak. In answer to your statement ***but you can still create***, it has to be within the bounds of what our dimension will allow.

E-L: What you think it will allow! Your dimension intersects with others and you may experience those as well. You are speaking with me and experiencing this ride while typing away. It has been said to you before "it's all made-up": how else does creation work if it doesn't have the freedom to do that? We do not have a horse – it's all our own energy and the chariot is a function of that.

R: Yes, as I said all made-up!

E-L: Maybe you need to redefine your human idea of reality and stop restricting it by defining it. What about reality with no restrictions? (We step off the chariot for a more peaceful conversation.)

R: I know in my heart what you say is true. But restrictions in Arkarna programs create experience – we can't have everything at once because we couldn't make sense of that.

E-L: You are now defining the program parameters. These are creations of limitations by design for particular experiences in separation.

R: You have answers for all my misunderstandings but I am not fully on board your vibration.

E-L: I do indeed have responses to all that you say. If you are not on board, be careful on the gang plank and hold onto the rope railings.

R: Flipping heck – look at all the hustle and bustle around us, with materials being loaded on a galleon. I feel the coolness of the sea breeze on my face. But there's an awful stench of low tide's stale and rotting seaweed. It lingers in its heaviness and the smell is no better the further we walk away from the oozing mud. On wooden walkways the human presence is not to be outdone as body odours rasp our nostrils. We move past the crew and reach the bow. The tide miraculously risen means the breeze is now refreshing – a somewhat different world with a positive anticipation of a journey to experience.

It is all very vivid and I wonder if my mind is freer to accept new possibilities, despite my sense its 'all make-believe'. Touching a rope, I am scratched by the hairs of the coarse hemp, and yet again I cannot escape humanity, where oil and skin has filled the gaps between fibres: grunge, grit and hard lives lived. I talk to the sailors but they see me as another like them. In my head and heart, I am not. Therefore, this must be make-believe.

E-L: So, you keep saying – until you don't!

R: Psychosis with a vivid imagination would be a clinician's diagnosis.

E-L: That's a severe mental disorder in which thought and emotions are so impaired that contact is lost with the external world – hallucinations where you see and hear things that are not there – delusional, believing things that are clearly not true.

R: My thoughts and emotions are not so impaired that I have lost contact with the outside world. I interact with it as well as the next person. As far as seeing and hearing things – any psychic or intuitive person could fall into that category, so no.

E-L: Then why mention its possibility?

R: I guess you are saying, I needed to prove my sanity to myself and by questioning it I am showing lucid thinking.

E-L: So, continue to raise the doubt, receive my help, then shoot me down to perpetuate support for your perspective and need for constant proof.

R: You have the measure of me.

E-L: So you keep saying! This is not about deferring to me or giving in when you struggle to understand. Let us remove the struggle and treat what we are doing as a ***story with information***. Don't look for truth or you will be constrained by your own narrow certainties. Everyone has different experiences and there is no right perspective or parable. You are doing it your way, slightly impaired by your concepts of reality and truth. Accept there is no right or wrong way because they don't exist here.

R: But what of reality, imagination and wishful thinking.

E-L: Wishful thinking is borne of a desire to be in a different place or situation, often to avoid the present. Because the present is a reflection and a creation of your own, that flight of fancy is a fruitless exercise. It has a truth but only in so much as it is your wishful thinking – that is also a definition and a restriction.

As to reality – it is a function of what you create.

The reality of imagination is to bring into creation matters not previously conceived. Either new creation or the discovery of that which already exists. Allow your mind to bring you what you do not presently know. If it does this by parables or storytelling, does it mean it's untrue? The sentiments, information and wisdom were previously incomprehensible – your experience is merely the medium, so do not judge delivery.

R: Thank you.

E-L: You now wonder what is a parable and what is the reality of the mind? You are trying to conjoin these, as if made of the same material. Programs creating physical matter are not the free-flowing mind. The imagineering of our minds can be seen when we are open to whatever comes to mind.

What is to happen next in the parable? Perhaps an expectation we should set sail, encountering all manner of challenges and discoveries. Upon leaving harbour, we might be foisted upon a rock and our journey finishes before it begins. In the wildest of dreams, a sea monster pierces the bowels of the ship, consuming cargo and crew. Without reason it does so because it can – much like the mind flowing and coursing in the way you experienced it today.

R: It is not lost upon me that, as a parable, it is a good summation of my outlook.

E-L: I have the measure of you, do I not?

R: Yes, you make me chuckle at your humour, throwing back my own words.

E-L: What's next or is there no more?

R: It's made me question lots of other experiences and I am wondering if everything is a parable.

E-L: That's the point, allow your soul to present itself in ways that are not prescribed.

If I say "hare and tortoise" you bring to mind the story where the slow and steady wins the race because the hare is over confident. The tortoise offers another race and foils the hare with a river to be crossed. Each animal has different qualities that cannot be judged as better or worse. In that story the animals became friends and, in that way, they achieve more together than separately.

In the same way the soul communicates using many reference points and experiences. Does it matter if the story of the hare and the tortoise is not true?

Your night dreams are received as stories. When you process normal daily thoughts, you run a narrative in your mind. If your car needs fuel you imagine a specific filling station and the best route you might take to get there. But that's just imagination, isn't it?

R: It's a thought process overlaid or combined with imagery – it's how the mind functions.

E-L: So not imagination?

R: Well, it's a realistic thought and a realistic way of seeing the thought.

E-L: So, by your definition 'imagination' is that which you visualise and think about, but it doesn't come true. If you were a car designer and you imagined the shape of a new car and drew it, but it failed to impress the directors, you might well imagine another design which would be accepted. So, does that mean the first imagination was imagination but the latter wasn't?

R: No that's a design process, we are talking about images and vivid experiences that enter my mind as if to blur the differences between reality and imagination.

E-L: So, you can't tell the difference between typing with your fingers and imagining that you are typing.

R: One is doing – the other is thinking about doing!

E-L: What happens when there is no difference between experience on earth and the experience of doing things in a different realm.

R: This reality would not exist in the other reality, but we have been talking about parables, which are a very vivid experience. I can't see a way through this impasse.

E-L: That's because you are not me and you can't see the whole story. While we talk, you use your imagination to understand me and my presentation, but that's all right because it's a function of processing. Processing is a way of interpreting realities however; the processing is real – it gets it done – it happens – you receive alternative wisdom and ways of thinking. Therefore, the imagination of the process is also real.

R: Yes, but that's all in the mind.

E-L: Everything is in the mind – that's where you process your so-called reality, which is a hologram in pulse energy.

R: But the chariot?

E-L: We conjured it up, we created the experience – which you enjoyed and it was perfectly safe. If we had fallen out, we wouldn't have been hurt unless we wanted that as an experience. But it wouldn't have damaged our physical bodies in this realm. Because it's a different world to yours, doesn't mean it's not real. In that experience you were not afraid and you had excitement.

R: So, you live in a fantasy?

E-L: A fantasy is something that's not true – our world is true to us. We can create all manner of things, we are aspects of higher self, the embodiment of the energy that allows all things to be possible.

R: You sound more like a function and an ability.

E-L: Yes, that's a great way of seeing this place but you forget you have the same function and ability to create and experience.

R: The disparity between imagination and reality is feeling a little softer.

E-L: So, now we can let the tortoise show us the way.

R: It eventually reaches the top of the hill and says, "I was never despondent, the voice in my head said I was most likely to win. In my mind I can see the hare asleep in the roots of the tree on the next hill. His thoughts are reflected back to him by the environment he creates. He is not aware of his overconfidence or that his thought ***I don't have to bother much*** will create cause and effect".

The tortoise shakes the hare and tries to rouse him, even talking loudly, "I am the tortoise and I am here already, if you don't wake up and get a move on, you will lose the race," to which the hare replies with his eyes closed, "That cannot be reality, I hear you and I feel you, but it is my imagination – there is no way that a tortoise could catch a hare, no matter how long the hare slept."

The tortoise looks to me and says "His belief becomes his reality and his reality is thinking it's only his vivid imagination. It matters not who gives who the experience of winning or losing – that's putting too much emphasis on the possibility that an experience is a reality when its only experience. Much like your own life Robert, try to remember – what everyone thinks is a reality is an experience".

R: Does that mean experience is our reality?

E-L You are putting too much emphasis on the word reality. You are seeking something firm and fixed – that's not the nature of the universe.

R: The hare and tortoise are an extension and creation of El-Lanadore

E-L: Experience is the appearance of a reality, when it's still only an experience. An Arkarna separation program reflects all your thoughts back to you and if you think the experience is reality, it then becomes a belief and your reality. The only reality is how you perceive reality – it is never ever a function of experience.

Conversely experience is created by the expression of soul's reality. But soul cannot be defined, nor could it be – in order to function in total freedom. If you say 'freedom of soul' instead of 'imagination' then there is no race to win or lose. At that point you will discover that's not why you entered the race. There never was a race, it was an experience and not a reality. Reality does not exist other than the way you define it.

Reality is the unrestricted possibility of imagination – and even that is a description.

R: That was very helpful E-L – thanks for bringing in the imaginary tortoise.

E-L: The angel Clarence appeared to Jimmy Stewart in the film 'It's a wonderful life' and he challenged his ideas of reality.

R: You are imaginary and so am I – we have imagination as a function, which appears to take form. We can project into any form and experience whatever we want. But on your levels the rules are more fluid and reality doesn't have the same meaning or function – it's not necessary to have it.

E-L: Then you are beginning to understand open possibilities.

R: But the tortoise wasn't real.

E-L: Nothing is – not even me and you – it's all made-up. For me thought and potential have no bounds – you coming to terms with the reality of that means you have travelled far.

R: I can begin to accept your ways of living. These past few days were designed to acclimatise me to that. It's a lesson which is more than a lesson. In addition to showing novices their way, you must have other outlooks and experiences.

E-L: (Deep haughty laugh) The journey helped you see a wider picture of what's really here if I can use that word. Perhaps the words 'God' and 'Reality' should be given warning signs – beware of misconceptions when you exceed the reality of your god concepts.

R: I thank him for his rumbustious way of helping me. As we turn around to go back, Aqueena appears with a smile and a welcome hug. It's just as absorbing and rounded as the one earlier from El-Lanadore but feminine. It's odd really, I can sense the difference in the masculine and feminine but making comparisons has no relevance.

CHAPTER 34

The universe is not by design

Aqueena (AQ): I wish to join parts of our conversations together.

R: I thought they were joined by order and design.

AQ: What if there is no design?

R: Well, everything you've told me goes out of the window.

AQ: Design usually begins from a starting point or around something you already know.

R: Yes, and you already know what you are unfolding to me. Antemedi once said there was an order and an overlaying process, even if it seemed we were jumping around.

AQ: That is correct from your perspective but not from all perspectives.

R: But the universe is by design!

AQ: Not really, it's what suited the initial parameters. The universe is constantly remodelling itself and changing its programs – and that's not by design. Your scientists say there is a predisposition for disorder and entropy and therefore to have a fully functioning, complicated universe means it was designed. That's incorrect because you need to look at the initial concepts within Mowhar. It evolved in a process of 'grow' without any parameters or design. When those possibilities were expressed, Arkarna programs were formed. They are constantly changing and upgrading as self-evolving programs. You place values of love and sentience upon them. The universe didn't set out to create love – it became a natural expression of the programs that are constantly changing.

R: That makes it sound devoid of feelings and compassion.

AQ: Love is a very complex word and what one does through love surpasses feelings and compassion, because they limit your experience of it. If you leave them behind, does it mean you have no feelings or that you are not compassionate? No – but it touches on your loss of humanity and self. Neither does it make the rest of us dispassionate and uncaring when we choose our state of being.

CHAPTER 35

Letting go of all

Aqueena (AQ): I am helping you release more connections to old values so you can see further in the next presentation.

R: It feels like Groundhog Day.

AQ: I can assure you we are not going over old ground. In order to see clearly you must sever more connections to humanity and self, then you won't compare what I say to those parameters.

R: Thank you for the energy boost – I feel relaxed, dispassionate, inquisitive in innocence and unaffected by what I observe.

AQ: Good – you have been aware for a while that it is dark, though you can still make out rolling hills in the low light of night.

Scene: A stone wall divides the landscape and we have no choice but to walk alongside it. My fingers glide over moss and lichen. The air is quiet and still but oddly the moonlight casts no shadows.

R: Are there no feelings here– perhaps I have superimposed mine to give context? I am perceiving reference points, otherwise how could experience exist without context. How else would we relate to the external?

AQ: You mean how does one relate to the internal and how does self, see itself, if it becomes self-aware?

R: We approach a large iron gate, which I push with great force in expectation of resistance but nothing happens, and my hands pass through it. A doorway usually gives context to an experience of mental transition. There is no trepidation and I have no desires or expectations, not that I would care what they may be. Being safe is irrelevant because fear does not exist; I am neither enlightened nor unenlightened. I am not to be filled, emptied or changed.

Edging past the gate I feel an unknown resistance. We walk towards a soft light in the distance but it retreats as we get closer. The further we go, the taller I become, yet when I look to Aqueena she remains her usual height.

We eventually arrive at a gateway similar to the last but it's cloaked in light, obscuring anything else. The gates open for us and stepping through, I begin to lose consciousness in a sleepy realisation I am entering a different realm. Giving my hand a noticeable tug, Aqueena asks that I follow her with greater concentration. Enveloped in swirling muted colours, we progress. I am trusting but ironically, I have no need to trust – I am being guided and it just is. Colours become more vivid and silky but they shroud something from us. We go deeper and whilst the swirls become blending paints, we pass through as if they are not present.

We stop and let the swirls consume us as they pass back and forth, cleaning and removing anything resistant to their passage. The twists and turns become stronger and their energies thicker. Eddies rage unabated yet my mind steps back from those thoughts to see that our state of Isness does not change.

With this thought, we press on and eventually the churning stops.

We arrive in an undulating grassy landscape with half a dozen dilapidated wooden sheds. Dirt tracks run between the buildings and out into the open countryside. One of the ruts becomes so deep it towers over me, but I remember that I can choose to observe and not be swayed by sensations. With that thought, it shrinks in height. I reach a shack where a young Robert peers shyly around the rear wall. At the back of the building, we find a track worn by his constant movement. In that instant I become him and anticipate the arrival of the older me. As the boy, I move along the outside of the back wall, from one corner to the next. I look around each corner wondering when the older me will arrive.

As Aqueena and my 'older self' arrive, I marvel at their ability to move without having any perspective. Looking at their arrival I alternate my perspectives to each corner of the building. My constant movement has become a rut from which I could not see. Aqueena smiles and asks me to continue the journey. I join my older self and finally let go the idea that 'many alternating perspectives are necessary to fully understand'.

We reach the summit of a small hill but on the other side the ground falls away below us. The sensation is that we have come to the end of a world, where nothing is of use and we have no purpose.

AQ: We have depleted your perspectives and vantage points. Does there have to be a purpose?

Some might say 'what is the point of life'? But that depends on the type of life, dimension and perspective. When your thinking or being has 'no purpose' you see it reflected in yourself.

Here upon this precipice, we can go beyond such reflections. There comes a stage when observation has no point. When studying brings no more of yourself into view. It had a place, but it no longer serves a purpose, other than to hold you back to that way of being. It traps you into observing what you are and what you do.

You believe you live life with the ability to alternate between ***observing*** and ***not needing to observe*** your reflection. It is not the same here because there are no needs and there is no need to avoid looking at a reflection because there are no reflections.

Follow me beyond your reflection as we walk through and past yourself. All the concepts and ***ideas of self*** cannot follow us. See your army of thoughts standing around us. Every part of you is a spent force and no longer fits old ideas of self. Amass the self and let the ranks swell around us.

R: It's an extraordinary sight as all my Robert thoughts and feelings that I have ever had are spread out. Each one is given space and credence without judgement or importance. A waiting and not waiting, a seething mass of unity, not demanding or aspiring to be any different. Standing upon this elongated mountain ridge 'lights form' in front of each and every thought as its counterpart.

The complementary light fills each idea and each idea has its own personal experience of self. These are all the events of my life that helped release duality. All those individual experiences are now a unity of experience, that's become ***non-individual*** and ***non-self***. Their energy spreads either side of me along the ridge like the wings of some great bird.

In front of me is my reciprocal reflection, but if reflections are unnecessary why does it appear?

The reflection is very bright, with many facets and a multitude of different projections, yet the appearance mirrors the way my energy spreads out.

Huge wings shimmer to shoulder height and the quills orientate themselves in a vertical direction. The feathers turn into figures which I recognise as archetypes. Formative instructions for my current life, with a greater connection and abundance that has no need to be or do. They are who they are, without need or reference, because there is no desire for self-expression. Winged arms enfold me and I am encompassed by energy and benevolence.

These past few weeks have culminated in a different truth. I am not sure I can describe it because there is ***no need to be involved***, nor to ***change my emotional state to understand or empathise***. There is no forgiveness because there is no hurt or wrongdoing. All that was of value to my humanity and has fallen by the wayside. There is no need to feel others who suffer and my compassion changes. Let there be wisdom and action – words I have heard before but, in this moment, their true meaning is not lost. This is a caring – but nothing like I have felt nor understood before. There is even ***no need to heal*** – can you believe that? What level of soul is this that can deliver such messages and for me to speak as if I am it?

A flicker of past reality shows itself when I ponder how fleeting it will be before I am returned to myself and reflections. For now, explore, let come what comes, as it does in a magnificence that has no foothold in humanity's rationale.

Voice: We speak as one. What you have said are my thoughts – they are ours. Compartmentalisation of the psyche created ***individuality of self-thought*** with each thought having its own separation experience. Living your lives, you were unaware of this, seeing your thoughts as you and not separate and autonomous with their own free will. Like a universe they reside within you and you determine what you are as your experience of them. As to how you should perceive the aspects of your soul, it is no longer a matter of choosing the most comfortable way. You may see them as they best present themselves, as their individual expressions or functions.

You have many questions but don't know how to form them because your human parameters have no relevance. You cannot question what is alien to you without referencing it to ***yourself*** and that's not relevant here.

Feel the buzzing energy of these ideas that are the essence of self – in this way they will experience you as their homecoming. It's a question of perspective from you to them and vice versa, but here and now compartmentalisation is no longer relevant.

We embark upon another way of communication and being self. I am voice – I am you. Different thoughts will unfold as you no longer attach to your ***mind of self*** so, let us explore from there.

R: My body is relaxed and I am full, my hands are tingling, I'm not really sure if all of me is here because the connection is so intense. I return my focus back to voice.

Voice: Good that you do not need to say ***your voice*** because that would reference ownership and self. We do not need to possess anything, even ourselves, because that's a restriction. Using your terminology stops you from fully accepting the entity that I am and you are.

To say 'ourselves' also avoids the acceptance of you as a more complex entity beyond self. You are a part of a soul and every part can say that it is the soul. You are typing what you, as a soul, desire to type, as you explore what it is to be soul.

A conglomerate rock has composite parts that are fused together forming a whole, yet the constituents still exist as separates. If you removed one mineral, the stone would have fissures and spaces. If we don't look at previous self-beliefs we no longer create a reflection to see a conglomerate soul, instead we are just is. If everything is made-up then reality is a function of what we believe it to be.

That means the construct of seeing yourself as composition of parts is of no significance and has no more relevance to you than does the name Robert. These are descriptions of a fluctuating experience, seen from an apparent objective entity. You are soul and whilst this voice may not be as Robert, he is no longer relevant, just as he will be when his body dies. ***Self*** gets in the way because the English language does not allow for more subtle nuances. I (not as separation self) but non-self would like to help you see that you are me and not an adjunct or an expression but a function of your multidimensional soul.

Allow yourself to meander and sink into this possibility through an inert altered state where you accept my words as your own. We are aiming to shed ideas of self, but to what end or aim? Is there no aim other than to expunge self? Yet you are still you, as I am you and vice versa. We are interchangeable as functions and experiences.

In ***letting go of all*** there is irony because we can let go the idea of shedding self and even the idea of letting go. These are concepts of attachment in your psyche and when you have finished with the idea of letting go, you are not attached to a perspective that creates separation self.

Without self what is there?

To express can be a desire to express, which seems like an inherent function of self. But what of Arkarna programs that can express without having desire to do so?

Does a baby cry because of a desire or because of functional programs and pain receptors? Their tears appear as basic responses and not a cognitive desire. But nonetheless they are still functions of the compartmentalised self, because the child soon learns to use crying to have its needs met.

You are unaware of this domain's fullness, function and relevance to life. Each snippet of my unveiling releases more of ***what it is not*** – but still something eludes you. What if I said there was nothing to do?

R: Only if I step aside from humanity programming could I accept there is nothing to do. Self would have a raging torrent of questions and resistances but they would not be relevant here.

V: So, what is relevant?

R: Perhaps nothing is relevant – why would relevance need to be part of this realm?

V: To give fixed points some context.

R: From the way I feel here that is not relevant. I'm not sure what to expect. I have no expectations or desires.

V: Then your consciousness is at one. How can we say what anything is – if it has no relevance?

R: Perhaps ***is*** doesn't exist here in the same way?

V: There is nothing fixed, all is fluid and there is nothing to hold to. You have heard that before but actually being within it and of it is another step. It cannot even be described as ***it***. Are you lost or are you found?

R: That's an easy answer – I can keep saying it's not relevant.

V: Perhaps we should try another day, if you are feeling frustrated. Your frustration is created by sensing the feeling of ***not relevant*** when you still have desire for it to be relevant.

R: We can talk but needs are not of this realm, are they?

V: We are beginning to speak as one again – to what ends? But then it's already been said there are no ends.

R: Can we leave this paradox of the descriptions of non-description?

V: What would you suggest?

R: You know I can't answer that.

V: But you and I are having this conversation for a reason.

R: Then please enlighten me.

V: Are you displeased?

R: No, because that may have been one of my older human Arkarna programs. It would be – do I displease myself and see it reflected in the outside world by displeasing others. Perhaps that shadow is still there in my programs, otherwise you would not have said it.

V: Correct but then again, I knew I would be correct and I knew what the reply would be. You have sparse knowledge of this area of program processing. If I rolled out a blueprint with connections between events and thoughts, you would be able to see that lines are constantly changing and making alternative connections. As one point changes, so others modify to fit in with it. In a similar way, it was described how the Arkarna programs of past and future change or refresh simultaneously. In higher realms, soul timelines have no meaning save that your separation focus returns to soul so that compartmentalisation of the multidimensional self becomes less relevant.

Human choices are a function of what appears to be free will. Higher vibrating levels love the parts of soul that are in Arkarna separation programs. Contamination of love is not feared and cannot exist in those domains. Sometimes the lower dimensions become so self-consuming, all they can do is consume the self. It is a direction and an experience; higher levels mourn for lost separation of soul. Those words evoke your human-self interpretation, but by the time parts of soul are lost there is little light left in those separations.

No part of our soul can intervene at that stage, even though it is a part of us that has chosen to become something far away from its other connections. That separation consciousness has chosen the opposite path or program of Mowhar. As soul, are we any the less because of that loss? – no that is to give measurement, saying that a soul is depleted when it is not. Soul source grows and expands to its wishes in the amount of energy or expression it desires. Any depletion is a part of soul having an experience that continued into the reaches of compartmentalisation, where even the ***ideas of self*** become lost. Sometimes an expression of soul and its Arkarna thoughts could suffer an extreme experience and not cope in the dark. A candle, unprotected in a howling gale, might soon be extinguished.

And so, there are many experiences and many thoughts, most of which have sufficient light or resilience. This mirrors the description of Mowhar in all possibilities – not all grow comes to fruition. Conversely soul contains Mowhar, having formed from her evolving awareness. Residual Mowhar knowledge exists in all Arkarna programs. And if all is possible that must include the loss of compartmentalised thoughts. Thus, we are neither dispassionate nor compassionate about that because we are creators.

R: Sounds like some Darwinian experiment.

V: You are a little deflated by the explanation because soul doesn't live up to the magnificence of some idealistic loving form of self. Soul is part of the expression of Mowhar and thus contains the essence of Mowhar.

When you cut your toenails, you have no concern for the clippings, that were of you but are no longer relevant or required for your function.

R: But isn't it cavalier and dismissive, losing parts of soul expression in that way?

V: Everything is possible, everything is an experience.

R: That sounds even more dismissive – a toe clipping isn't the same as a lost part of the soul or a thought that gets lost.

V: Thoughts are part of your personal Arkarna programs – they are extensions of soul and thoughts are part of soul. Soul can change and so can its thoughts. When you think something, the thoughts are of your thinking. If you did not have thoughts then you would not be you. Therefore, loss of thoughts also feels like loss of self and loss of you. You are after all – all these things. We are conversing around the subject of loss of self and Robert. Therefore, many of the descriptions of parts of you or your functions can be interchangeable.

Do you care for all your thoughts?

R: I guess not – you are pointing out that I don't care for the following thought – ***I have the ability to dislike what I sometimes do and therefore by association I must dislike myself***.

I don't like that thought! Who would?

V: Then that is you and a thought that you would be better off without. You shutting out part of you by choice, wishing it not to exist – indeed you are the perpetrator.

R: I have visited that destructive thought and part of me so many times it cannot be changed, altered or even left by the wayside.

V: And there we have the realisation! You are feeding it soul energy and you are keeping it alive. You are maintaining the connection to a thought and all the experiences that thought made. Why do you keep it? Because you are compassionate or loving to it? No on the contrary – it keeps you human. It is one of the many programs of humanity, in its collective consciousness.

R: I don't like hating myself and I cannot welcome or give that thought a home in me.

But that also means I am keeping a small part of my soul-self trapped into hating me and it does not deserve to be cast adrift and consumed.

V: That is indeed the situation. You do not need that concept: it serves you no purpose. You have no need to hate or dislike it because that perpetuates the holding of it. Let it slip away with no energy then it becomes a spent program and a definition of self that's no longer relevant.

R: I bear no malice to that thought, accepting the experiences it brought. I watch it tumbling away into the darkness.

We have talked about energy being transmuted to something positive but this ***shedding*** is similar to previous residues removed by Antemedi. Is this where it goes when there's no goodness in it at all?

V: It is vibration pertinent to its vibration – it's a thought that once fed upon your life force but now it is left to its own vibration.

R: But if I created it, then it's a part of me – so I am destroying me.

V: It is a part of creation because all things are possible. Do you need to show compassion for a parasite that feeds and takes your energy to lower depths?

R: It's not loss of soul?

V: Not in this instance though it's possible for parts of soul to become so distorted that they are no longer recognisable as the essence of soul. This is one of the reasons for compartmentalisation.

R: That's totally different to what I've just done – I've let go of a thought. It may have been a thought that never belonged to me but was a collective energetic thought and my knowing – knows it was part of the reptilian interference programming.

V: It was, but you are placing values upon Arkarna thought programs by saying these are not the same as soul or the programs that soul makes. When a corrupted soul program reaches that level then true soul energy isn't involved. There is no compatible energy and it's similar to what you just did. When the uplift comes there will be huge transitions like this.

CHAPTER 36

Beyond believing – entering '*the knowing*'

Voice (V): There are levels of soul higher than the ones you have seen thus far. In those realms there are no restrictions or parameters and it would be unusual for low vibrational choices to be made. When I say low vibrations there is no connotation or judgement. You think we exist as energetic conglomerations of wafting light. From an unrealised perspective (one that is not congruent or in phase with us) that's likely to be true. I am forming a humanoid shape, which your preconceived ideas can see as wafts of energy, creating my body and attire. Hold my hand and step on to the raised glass platform, keep walking till you meet two forms similar to me, then sit at the table.

R: They are standing by simple furniture set against a backdrop of shining light. We are in a tall building and when I sit down it's like being in the middle of a massive cathedral. We are in a place where the surrounding area stretches in all directions of time and space.

The entity opposite me lays out tarot cards. The first is a tower with a man falling from the parapets. The next is a female deity riding a mythical creature and the last card is a picture of the three of us as sitting around this table. The cards are placed back in the pack and then spread out face down. I am asked to choose three cards and turn them over. No matter how many times I do it they always come out as identical cards in the same order.

V: Your life is experienced as chance but it was always going to be the way it was meant to be. To fall from the tower is to lose not only your footing but to have a downfall so great you would never be able to return to that way of being or value. A death of the person or their ideas. The angelic energy and the mythical creature took you upon a journey of self-discovery. No matter what you thought of your progress or what you may have enjoyed or valued, you ended up here where values have no meaning and, in many ways, you have come full circle, seeing little value in human thoughts and desires. You feel you don't belong and that isn't escape from what you are because there isn't much of self to escape from. You now see how that fits in with what I said about letting go of all – which included soul Arkarna thoughts. Your reaction to the presentation of loss was value-based in self. We will provide another perspective.

Scene: The two beings assist me towards a growing light. The glassy floor begins to sparkle with shards of multicoloured lights. Thin glimmers form triangulations and rectangular patterns. I am walking on a floor made from interlocking diamonds polished into one flat surface. It's a spectacle to savour. An impenetrable wall materialises, with a small door allowing us to exit into a courtyard. Another simple table and chairs are located in the centre. Concentric circles and patterns made with pebbles create a Zen dry garden. It's interspersed with weathered wooden structures and plant containers. It reminds me of earth and it grounds my energy. I sit down at the table with the same beings again. This time we are joined by an **Unknown entity** (**UE**) sitting directly in front who says "What would you like to know?"

R: What is this realm like for you?

UE: It is different for everyone depending on what they wish to see.

R: Isn't wishing to see restrictive? I am seeing things relative to an earth understanding. It could just as easily be futuristic.

UE: It could be but it's not.

R: Rather than looking through my database can I see through yours?

UE: Yes, what about wall-to-wall flowers or a beach with lapping waves and a fresh breeze – perhaps the inside of a large cave with a cascading waterfall?

There is no common agreed backdrop, everyone sees and experiences what they wish and that inter-phases with others. In this way there can be many worlds. As beings we are extensions of one another, but have many contexts in which to see or experience one another. In this way it becomes a personal world into which other consciousnesses interact. It's not so dissimilar to your world – you think you have a commonality of projection but you don't!

R: That's hard to accept because I have a common landscape where I interact with others. They see the same Arkarna programs and get similar information, but whilst we can interpret to our own perceptions there are limits.

UE: There are no limits, why should there be?

R: So, commonality of experience doesn't exist?

UE: That's not what I said.

R: You are inferring it's an egocentric projection and creation of myself and I am inter-phasing with others who have their own egocentric projections. That is not an earth experience because if I hit someone with a car they would experience being run over.

UE: Correct – but it's more complicated than the way you have interpreted my initial words. It also involves projection and counter projection. If you look at a tennis ball you will expect to find a furry surface with a sweeping continuous rubberoid line. In older times that line was a stitched edge but no longer. The ball however is still made to resemble those original joins and performs as you would expect. It travels back and forth between two players on a court.

I have placed a spinning tennis ball just above the net. If the opponents try to strike it, their rackets will pass through the air as if the ball isn't there. Their eyes see it and they know what to expect from it, but it doesn't perform to their expectation. It's not an illusion, it just doesn't inter-phase with their experience or what they expect to experience.

However, with your energy, grasp it and put it down or leave it to float in another position.

It's there and it's not there: the opponents can't move the ball but they can see it. If they decide not to see it then it isn't there. That would be their choice to only see items they could interact with. You can hit the ball to any opponent but they wouldn't see it. It can be any number of interactions depending on what suits the situation.

R: The opponent would see me serve.

UE: That would be interpreted as a practice air shot without the ball.

R: What about the noise of the ball on the racket and its deformation.

UE: Again, that would be down to their interpretation. Why would they need to hear it if they couldn't interact with it – their Arkarna programs would delete it.

R: Is this several different dimensions active in one plane?

UE: You could see it that way. You interact with other people and beings on many different levels throughout your consciousness. You interface with their Arkarna programs to have your particular experience with them, even if their focus and experience doesn't need to know or experience you. People have told you that they have met you in meditation and had conversations with you, but you have no awareness of that. You all interact on multidimensional levels but you bring into your awareness what you want and what is pertinent to you.

R: But being runover by a car is not a subtle interpretation – it's a solid object for all those involved.

UE: So, you believe there are limitations to the interpretation of an event. What happens when one person is afraid and the other sees joy?

R: Granted, but the motor accident has common known and accepted outcomes.

UE: If that's what you believe, then that is so.

R: The car and body are solid and getting hit follows basic laws of physics.

UE: Well physical matter appears in pulse and if the information fields are changed then matter is changed.

R: But not as a general rule in a consensus reality.

UE: That is so, but if the consensus reality changed that would be another matter, wouldn't it? Who says what is a consensus reality and how much consciousness is needed and in what proportions? Does it have to consider all people's desires for experience?

R: Interesting conundrum!

UE: Do you have an answer to that?

R: I was hoping you would!

UE: But you do have the answer as this is your experience – you are ***experiencing not having the answer within you***. Now see this from another reality.

R: (voice becomes me and I speak as it). Multiple realities seem complicated, but in simplicity we can look and say they are multiple opportunities within multiple Arkarna programs, that suit changing situations. Everything is constantly changing in both the past and the future and we can say these are multiple realities.

Paradoxical – it is and it isn't. All things are and are not. If we followed 3D thinking then any reality would only exist as a function or by-product of experience. That means if we were not here experiencing this then this place would not exist – however it is energy – it doesn't go away. Furthermore, to say the universe is billions of years old is a perspective through a programme of time and light. The only answer is that nothing solid is here, otherwise everything would pile on top of itself in some kind of mass infinity. Vibrational pulse is the key because mass exists as ***here and not here***.

R: These connections are creating all sorts of pains in my head.

V: My voice is your voice – it's purely down to your belief that you don't understand, and that distorts your ability to perceive. Go beyond ***believing that you can understand*** and enter ***the knowing*** – that will be different. Rest and revisit tomorrow.

CHAPTER 37
You interact with everyone at every moment

R: Refreshed, I return to the last point of contact and immediately feel pressure on my head. Argh! pain is going right down into the roots of my teeth, then as suddenly as it started, it's gone.

Voice (V): Straight to it then – multiple manifestations can exist in the same space because the space is different.

R: As the earth spins it's always in a different place because it spins round the sun, which rotates in the galaxy but we don't see the multiple versions left behind.

V: Clearly that's not what I meant. Matter is in pulse – you experience it as part of an Arkarna experience program. When you step back from seeing matter it's just a form of energy. Each pulse or fizz as shown in the spherical torus metaphor is energy and information, constantly changing. Information however doesn't need space. The bands of information are piled up, that's why changing your energy in the now alters the past and future information. The future you is also altering the energy around the present you. How much of that comes into your life by your desire is another matter. Therefore, it's possible to have all that information in the same place – space being a different matter. Now let go of the idea of a place and see infinite information of the past and future existing simultaneously without time.

When you put life force and focus into a life on earth, interfacing through relevant Arkarna programs, the fluctuating energy appears solid. If you put the same focus into another life on earth, that would appear solid as well, but the two versions of solid would only be there by virtue of an interface with a relevant Arkarna program. If you continue to perceive fluctuating energy my explanation will make more sense.

Time travel is connecting to another section of information, and materialisation takes place by interfacing with the Arkarna program pertinent to that moment. Arkarna programs are also energetic and not restricted to space or position. In this way you can see it's all a matter (if you like the pun) of seeing the programs at work. Solidity and matter are an illusion and a way of interpreting information. You have known this for many years, but when we speak you often link back to see your reality as an immovable constant.

All alternative versions of the earth are piled up energetically, though even that distorts what I mean. It's all in the same arena, be it space or non-space. It's constantly changing versions of information.

R: But if someone went back in time?

V: They would be going to the program relevant to that point.

R: But it's constantly changing – I have changed my energy in the past and that program version of me would be different. If someone from the future came, which version of me would they interact with? The changing version or the one pertinent to that time?

V: I have already said, the Arkarna program relevant to that point in time, which is one of the parallel versions of that moment.

R: If they interacted with me then they would have altered my moment through time travelling. How could I be there interacting with them, when my focus is here in the now?

V: Because you are multidimensional.

R: But that wouldn't be my focus and me.

V: Would it need to be? Don't forget that you interact with everyone at any moment. They and you don't need to be fully aware of that.

R: It's all programs and programs within programs – it's quite extraordinary – I am a program.

V: We are indeed magnificent Arkarna programs.

R: I have a tangible grasp of this.

V: Only by accepting the fullness of what ***program*** means for you, as some sort of non-self functionary, can you move forward. The word program seems to remove humanity and soul – that's why we say Arkarna programs. To use the word ***mind*** instead would bring back the sense of self which would be inappropriate.

The information is not only coming from you, but you are the information and you are the program as an entity. Accepting you are the program, the programmer, the entity and the experience – we can encapsulate this by saying you are a system. All parts of the system are necessary but not one part can be valued over another, particularly self and non-self.

R: This will need to compliment descriptions of other multidimensional parts of me and the distinctly different personalities soul expresses. How much of a thought process is an internal conversation? One part of an Arkarna program (me) is informing another part.

V: Soul is an extension of Mowhar and thus you might say soul is Mowhar. Some souls are older than others and some have re-commenced their separation experiences to create further soul separations. As voice I am communicating from deeper parts of your soul – thus it could be said voice is also your soul and every part of you is an extension of soul's energetic expression. Our soul is also an Arkarna program, information and a function – as well as soul energy. If soul energy did not have Arkarna programs it would be defunct. The two are part of the whole – a feedback system.

Creating compartments allows distinct points of focus, which are the other beings you talk of. Yet within your compartment you can interact with them, taking body-form or conversing with them (your other points of focus). It's all a matter of choice and what is relevant to you. Merging with these focal points gives you insight into those lives of yours as they experience their worlds. The separation of focus enables you to do this, as did the separation formed in the awareness of Mowhar, which enabled so many souls to exist. Seeking enlightenment purely as Robert-self would have brought you close to soul but you would have missed out on so much more.

You may still interact with those multidimensional points of focus (multidimensional selves) because there is a lot they can teach you.

R: Sorry, but questions flood my compartmentalised focus and I keep having to readjust to the vibrations.

V: You may interact with them as before, however as voice I can help you assimilate more information about our multidimensional soul. If you have contact across a wider spectrum of self it is sensible to allow those parts to be in union with you.

Because you have no value-based connections, you can accept voice as you. Yet I have already said "I am of soul". I am the communication voice from your higher-self male counterpart to Aqueena.

R: Why did you not present yourself as higher-self rather than voice?

V: Why do you seek to see a difference? I am the communicator and the function (voice) of the communicator. I am an Arkarna program – you have already accepted that program is part of soul. It's been presented in this way because you would have placed greater value on the voice of higher soul than your own voice connected to deeper soul (a term I also used). You talk to Aqueena – you can talk with me also.

R: Would you have a name?

V: I have several names and many in multidimensional projections who are like you. I shall not give you any name, even the ones known as higher self. That would give me more of a personality when it's only right that you should locate yourself, not only in me but as me. I wish for my expressions (like you) to be able to look back upon me from their perspective and see that they are looking at themselves.

I am you and you are me – you are partially confined by separation programs but that is the experience. What joy it is to look back upon higher self and see your face, and the energy of you at this level!

R: Thank you, that feels very natural – in future should I refer to you as voice or higher self?

V: Well, I could say it shouldn't matter but it does for you. Higher self isn't a removed or inactive state – I have my life experience and you interact with my Arkarna programs. Sometimes, like in this moment, I have awareness of interacting with lower selves but most often I am not. You have been receiving communication from both your female and male counterparts of your higher self. Voice is communication: it is part of soul, a function of it, and an experience. It exists as a vibrational form and program that's non-local with many dimensional realities. The way you interact with program – me – you – in the form of conversation allows a personal context to a description of a soul function.

I am the totality of the male aspect of higher self in the same way that Aqueena is the female aspect. Orlacka is not higher self but a hermaphrodite unification of male and female compartmentalised focal points. Twin-flames refer to the male and female components of a subdivided higher self. It was said higher self has six male and six female expressions. It was also explained that you have higher light bodies that you can occupy. One of those would be higher self's six hermaphrodite components. This is the vibration that Orlacka lives within because separated outlooks no longer serve a purpose for her. We are all connected as are the other dimensional aspects of soul.

My words cause you to ponder on the unification of all focus points as higher self soul. That part exists and always has. Arkarna compartmentalisation consciousness programs allow focus to exist there as entity. Understanding and feeling what that is like is another matter. Bring to mind the fizzing torus, which encompasses focal points – this is non-locality and a form of experience.

Forgetfulness codes are part of your Arkarna programs, so you don't experience life, feeling you are already source. You don't need to return to source as a form of escape. Those on earth who say they wish to return to source have little understanding about the ability to focus on it from the multidimensional self or indeed that they are already source. When you are no longer Robert perspective, you will see soul focus in its wonderful possibilities. You are the many focus points in Orlacka, Antemedi, Arksar, Telenatey, and others too numerous to mention and all of these in different dimensions.

We have numerous timelines and multiple realities in non-space that can be entered in any order – they are multiple realities waiting to become an experience.

R: My wife and children have a point of focus here at this moment?

V: Yes, that's the structure of unified timelines. Are there no more questions?

R: You know I have none for the moment, so did you ask me in order to maintain the conversation and connection?

V: My dear Robert, you chose to see it that way because you are interpreting me – you are having the experience. If I said nothing, would you spout forth as a channel without the need to process the information in your realm? Comprehending the light given to you in your current point of focus is important. It changes the energy by processing higher vibrational information, helping you and the earth.

We have been talking to our self and that allowed ***other ways of how to think*** to become understood and more cohesive. You have comprehended those by experience. Let us all unite.

Scene: We are back sitting at the previous card table. We stand up from the table and higher self who was in front as the unknown entity **(UE)** is now inside me. The two other entities I sense as distinct personalities and points of focus. Both of them blend with me.

V: These are energies of other lives. You are only now aware of them because it suits your learning at this point. You are accepting and comprehending future-self energies within your current timeline. It's an experience and observation of your constant changing energy system.

Entering other people's Arkarna programs and travelling to their point of focus was part of the process to give you a more fluid mind. You are allowing more soul aspects to unify with you, as you have done with Antemedi and others. They are distinct personalities which could be considered past and future life information, so yes, they will be different but all is as it should be.

CHAPTER 38

Communicating beyond current horizons

R: I'm beginning to wonder who is who and who is talking with me?

Sentanor (S): You can call me Sentanor – we are in phase following yesterday's meeting when you allowed me to come closer as another personality. Take this piece of squared wood (it's 2 inches x 2 inches x 4 feet long) what does it remind you of?

R: The time we helped remove a negative entity from a friend by winding sticky black parasitic energy onto the wood, till the attachment had been pulled out.

S: Look at the timber and see where that pressure deformed it. Use it to remove energy that serves you no purpose.

R: The stick rotates by itself, rolling down the front of my body to my toes. The process is repeated at the back and both sides. The sacral, base and knees required more attention. The removed energy was grey, containing both positive and negative thoughts. Where the energy maintained a strong grip, I spoke with the associated subconscious thoughts, most of them being ideas of 'self'.

For example, shame could not exist other than ***shame of self***, then ***fear of loss of self*** was used as a form of protection. The stick finished its work and stood vertically in front of me. It returned lighter thoughts, then removed itself and the remaining darker energy. Grid patterns emanated from within my heart forming a space in my aura with vivid purples and dark blues. It is occupied by Sentanor – another world and an inner portal.

S: Good, we may speak and see more easily.

There comes a time when one has to lay down the pen and stop writing, in order to start doing. There are things we would like you to do. You have free will but we would encourage you to meditate even more than you do at present. That will help maintain the energy levels you have. In those meditations you may interact with many others who are aware of your presence. Many know your name and will listen to what your higher self says. You are a vessel and a vortex to transmit energy. In those meditations, gather people around you and they will gather others. You will not speak words or consciously think thoughts, but they will get what they need as they interact with our energies. It's one of the reasons why more of our energy and a variety of voices are present within you. This is a gift, allowing your self to be used as an interactive transmitter. Please do this on a daily basis, whenever you are able, but let us take the first session now.

Start by feeling me in and around you, know that I have the knowledge and the ability to command crowds. Our Arkarna programs will allow many interactions. All is planned and falling into place. We are all here with our experiences and expertise.

R: I am me, though I sense many aspects within my aura. It is quite dark but blue energies dance in several dimensions within the fabric of the landscape. We walk up a small hillock to see the dawn arriving. The sun becomes dazzling and ends up as a small bright light in front of my head. Thin filaments of light thread their way to me, piercing different parts of my skull. Reciprocal threads of light extend in the opposite direction, to the horizon and beyond. The light projections find their own way and reach other people. The light inside my head gets brighter as it connects to an interdimensional energy. There is no energy coming through my crown or the chakras above – it's an inner abundance of inextinguishable energy which radiates into my body. Sentanor says the mixed consciousness is doing 'its own thing'.

Massive swirls of cream light flow out from my feet, creating a new plane, overriding the previous landscape. I am taken aback by the sense of femininity within me. I realise it's the energy of Aqueena, "Bringing balance and gentleness to accept the task ahead," she says.

Standing on a platform made of pearlescent energy, we face a small gathering in front of us. Other aspects of my soul, containing the same pearly energy, extrude from my *body fizz*. They stand either side of me and we are all interconnected with threads. Further filaments weave their way to the small audience, who came in response to the initial light sent to the never-ending horizon. Beyond the first group, more gather in a yellow light.

S: We will use our connections to send energy out through our foreheads.

R: As light saturates me, gossamers from my other soul aspects strengthen with intensity and interact with the audience. The onlookers fall asleep while additional energy threads flutter between them. The audience makes connections to the people in the yellow light attracting more.

I feel tired very quickly, so in need of a strong pick-me-up I stop typing and make a coffee. While I do this the light connections are maintained and I continue to talk directly to three members of the audience. Just like a normal conversation.

S: We needed to exceed intent by undertaking deed and action. The information we have available from higher dimensions is sufficient to cater for most people's questions. Some of them are just listening, while others ask questions. The light threads are Arkarna programs of projection linking with their individual Arkarna programs.

Many are unaware at their daily conscious levels, nor would they know they have this ability to connect. This work is at their deeper levels of consciousness. It's taken you a long time to have this awareness in your present earthly consciousness.

R: I put more focus into what I am doing and a man on the right nearer the back of the audience asks, "Why are you doing this now at this point in time?" Light threads move back and forth between us. It's no longer a one-way interaction because others now link. He seems satisfied with the response, nodding his head. It fits in with something he was thinking. I'm not aware of the answer he received, that was something personal for him. My only sense is the time is right and it's part of a planned timeline. It surprises me how personal the response was for him without me being aware of it. I widen my view and see spirit guides linked with the participating audience. Others have their *multidimensional aspects* helping to personalise questions and answers.

A few disconnect and abandon the gathering, while others continue. It's remarkable to be typing while involved in these wonderful Arkarna programs.

S: You have the light and you may use it, as we have shown today. We have given you the awareness of what you will be doing, even though most of the time you won't be fully conscious of it in meditations.

R: The group session comes to an end and whilst most threads return to me, some participants remain connected. Most of the disconnected light threads remain a short distance from my head but residual pain leaves me a little depleted. Spheres of light form around the heads of those who stayed and the remaining threads return to me. The participants leave, satisfied with the links to their new spheres.

Drained, I get up and head for the kitchen but as I walk to seek sustenance, I still have the vision of the pearlescent room around me.

S: It's a space created specifically for this task and it will change in the days ahead.

R: After eating I refocus on the room, where half a dozen stragglers sit or lay down to meditate. A couple thank me and say they want to encourage others to come – as if permission is needed!

S: They didn't make assumptions and asked permission so they could shake your hand and touch you.

R: But if they had a personal experience, they would have been able to do that anyway.

S: Yes, they did but you only became aware of it in this moment!

R: Oh, that makes sense. We walk to the back of the room and come upon a figure in foetal position saying, "I can't do this anymore, I can't keep trying, nothing happens – I am always living in the trying and never achieving." He is part of my family genetics and I explain, it's ok to give up and to stop trying. He responds, "If you don't continue to try, you will fail and be a failure." I respond by saying if you give up trying it would be a success. Presently there is a failure to see 'continuous trying' leaves no space for anything else other than failure or success. I see elements of my father and grandfather within him. A hidden blocked energy of self-recrimination in order to avoid criticism from others. I acknowledge it's a part of my psyche and soak in the healed energy.

There are several aspects of my psyche shaken out by projecting energy. I gather them together and unite. The self-healing takes place within the Arkarna of myself, with no need to focus upon what the actual thoughts are. They are small parts of thoughts that I have dealt with before and within me they sweep upward into higher chakras and beyond.

Sitting in my typing chair I find myself back at school in the science lab with its long wooden worktops. The chemistry teacher (**CT**) is wearing his brown overalls. They don't fully cover him and his checked suit, shirt and tie are exposed.

CT: I am aware you are talking about energy and matter. I find it interesting but I can't see it being proved. There are no experiments that can support what you say, so I wouldn't hold out much hope for people taking it seriously – not a criticism, just an observation.

R: Well, we are here in your classroom and we are talking together – how do you explain that?

CT: You have me there! Perhaps I am having a dream and you are a figment of my imagination.

R: I know you are dead, but we are having a conversation and a real interaction. (Yet my words do not register and he doesn't engage with them. I am a little stumped – whatever I say he can treat as a mental flight of fancy, where flickering thoughts are not physical reality.)

S: (speaks only to me in the scene) How should we help when the help will be of no use? If atheists believe they are physical bodies and not soul energy, they will judge all from that entrenched perspective. What you say will undermine their belief, which they seek to protect. Some can't hear and some won't want to. Let's give him a light orb so he can ponder upon its reality.

R: The orb is a crystal ball and if you look into it, you may explore different worlds. (CT freezes while fixed on the light; clearly, he's already gone for an exploration. He returns quickly).

CT: That was great. I was in there for a long time.

R: So, was that a dream?

CT: A dream within a dream – how many levels of dreams can there be?

R: If you think thoughts then they are real thoughts for you. Is that not a tangible fact? Subjective experience is still a form of reality because you think, talk and move to your thoughts.

CT: But are they not dreams?

R: If dreams are thoughts, they are also real in the sense that they are also thoughts.

CT: Well, most dreams are pretty screwy and I don't interact with them in the way I do in the physical world.

R: Well, let's hope you remember some of what you are saying today.

CT: Why shouldn't I?

R: Well, if it's a dream, this might be rather screwy when you become aware of it in another conscious state.

CT: I see what you mean, let me write a note to myself on this pad.

R: But that would not be real, it will be in your dream.

CT: But if I believe it will be real, surely it will be.

R: What made you come to that conclusion?

CT: It's what I learned in your lecture hall. Belief informs us to an extent but even that's based on the physical experience that is provable in life. I remember all the things I believed about myself when I was alive. If I am not a dream then logic says I co-created the world around me like I do now. It fits in with the theories you and your friends talk about, though I'm still not convinced.

R: Well, you can always have another talk in the hall at some stage.

S: What did you get from that last conversation?

R: It was quite surreal: I suppose the chemistry teacher was in his element, in his chemistry lab. As for the wider communication it has enormous potential.

I could bring anyone into focus, to my will, but that's more of a forced contact, which is not the same as allowing the Arkarna programs to flow freely. I know it's me in this ***present*** helping him in ***his past present*** when he died. Time isn't relevant on those levels so we could also say ***future me*** helped ***past him*** when he needed it or when ***he needed to access it***. We could also say it's ***past him*** accessing ***future me*** and the vibrations that were sent out in the lecture hall.

It is the fizz of non-time at work doing its thing.

S: The wide communication was open energy allowing questions and explorations. Vibration attracts like vibrations and people attach themselves to the threads of complimentary frequencies. He was one who connected to that.

R: Presumably other people can do this type of projection if they set it as an intention?

S: Of course, but few know of it and less still believe they can do it. That said, much goes on at their higher levels, during meditation and sleep, which they may not be fully conscious of.

CHAPTER 39
Thought forms – releasing perpetrator and victim

Scene: We return to the same place where people are gathered to accept our projected energy. A light forms in my head and filaments start to flow. It provokes interest in some, while others are unaware that they have connected.

Sentanor (S): We can create thought forms that contain information energies.

R: Does that means we can reduce our effort for future projections?

S: The amount of effort or time isn't relative, that is a form of measurement. You have been visiting, topping up energies, maintaining interest and intent. How much intent does there need be in order for that to be effective?

With the intent to turn on a light bulb, you flip a switch on the wall but that doesn't require much effort. Energy projection isn't about the amount of energy you give over. If you remember, projections from the Andromedans can also be enhanced energetically with technology.

R: I don't have that technology.

S: True, but you have intent and connection to those that do. Let us discuss ***thought forms by design and intent.***

When you transmute or create, you leave energy with thought and resonance. Talismans and imagery are also types of thought forms.

Because a thought form is a projection from you, there is a tendency to think it contains part of you but that depends on the way it was created and the intent behind it. Thought forms can also be aspects of shadow-self and these reflect the reason they were created. Fear and ideas of self in a thought form just add to what already exists in the world.

The thought forms I am introducing are born of a different intent. Whilst the intent needs to be based in love, you don't have to be afraid it will morph into or reflect something in you that's not bright. A projected thought form comes from your intent and it creates an Arkarna thought form. They can be a few positive thoughts given with love or more complex ones. Concentrate on the energy in your head, it will swell and move out in circular ripples. Let them stretch as far as you can.

R: A high-pitched noise in my head turns vibrational waves into a choppy sea. As the vibrational pitch changes, patterns form in the waves. They collapse again as the tone varies. I feel an inner surge of energy and the waves multiply, until there are four bands or planes. The noise alters and the four bands interact with one another. The patterns are now interdimensional, with holographic moving human shapes. It's all around me in every direction but I can't see its fullness. Above my head is a holographic vortex, getting wider the further up it goes. It starts at the smallest point in the light of my head. A reciprocal vortex spreads down from my head. Have I become a transmitter?

S: No spots on you then! Step back from this creation containing the image of you. It is powered by connection to source within it.

A soul can create many types of Arkarna programs – it has no restrictions. You can alter a body program or thought program. Even one that duplicates energy creations that are themselves programs.

A self-sustaining program can have form, allowing interaction with its information programs and energy. Of course, we helped you create it but it's your intent that allows it to become cognisant in your world. It follows the Arkarna programs that were created for interactive projections. Yes, Arkarna programs that sustain and inform projection thought forms! The projection is at one with humanity because it was formed with its roots in your plane and that makes it more effective.

The vibrations hitting your planet are changing earth, but a seed is always much better than the idea of a seed. You have helped a direct planting under our instruction. Stand back another couple of footsteps.

R: The creation emanates benevolence, love and understanding of the things I've been taught. However, there is no relevance to my particular understanding or the way in which I originally received it. Interpretation of this information is about the perspective of the individual that might connect to it. In this way it really has a life of its own, only reciprocating with the individual who might come across it. It's from me and those guiding me, but it's autonomous.

S: There are programs and parameters we can use for thought forms. They have been honed over millennia. However, that statement assumes time is relevant. What do you think?

R: Firstly, I am astounded to be involved, but comprehending the possibilities – it is mind-blowing. How many of these projection Arkarna programs can be made?

S: Why would you make more, when one alone can interact with an infinite number of minds?

R: I am a little lost for words, please expand.

S: Why do you consider that you are not capable of such things?

R: Straight to the point – because of my limited knowledge, based in old values.

S: What would be possible if you did not have those constraints?

R: Massive changes – but what about negative influences becoming aware of the creation of thought forms?

S: They already are – they use fear energy from the populous as a feedback loop so that it becomes a self-perpetuating thought form with many interactions. Then they feed upon the energy fear creates.

R: That's mind control, which influences patterns and thought forms over a long period.

S: A thought form of the kind we have created does not need external energy, nor does it need to be topped up. It is self-sustaining, connected to source – you are source and so are your creations, which have initial Mowhar concepts.

R: But this is a program, it's not an entity.

S: You are a program! A newspaper will give you information and can affect your feelings, but it's not an entity. There are many things in the universe sustained by source but they are not all soul.

R: You have a way of making your point. Perhaps it's about the value I place on the different ways information arrives. I assume soul information only comes from soul source.

S: It does but it may also be repeated in meditation: energetically, verbally, printed or filmed. Arkarna programs are extensions of soul and source – they are part of soul and they are you. Is a 'thought form' more or less helpful than other information programs?

R: A thought form seems to have degrees of autonomy.

S: We return to the previous explanation and your unfounded concerns about totally self-sufficient Arkarna programs. It is not going to run rampant like an AI program serving its own needs. It's an extension of you and us and the program serves the program. It cannot be what it is not nor can it be corrupted.

The thought form you helped us create in earth's collective consciousness doesn't work within negative parameters. It only serves the participants who engage with it, in the way they desire.

R: The Arkarna program is still doing its own thing?

S: The thought form created by us is still doing what it should.

R: Presumably it can be seen as an individual?

S: It can be seen in any form, with any face or body or not seen – that's the beauty of one's individual perception. In essence it is all of those and none, so even the way we perceive it is relevant to what we think and understand.

R: Twelve lights come close to me and energy arches upwards from each one into the top of my head. Like a fascinator on a hat, central threads now support 12 small orbs around my head and I fall asleep.

I wake up a short while later sensing a domed hat with energetic connections, like the gills of flesh under a mushroom cap. Links in the aura form a gridwork of patterns. Intersections brighten, giving me a new body of fluid malleable energy. My body-form seems to fluctuate then all goes still as I am transported somewhere else.

I'm in an old-style diver's suit with a brass and glass helmet. I can't bend my legs easily and I move slowly in a cumbersome rolling motion. Suddenly everything turns into a blue calmness. My energetic suit has either been switched on or is vibrating in harmony with its new surroundings. I hear Sentanor but cannot see him.

S: What do you think of your new surroundings?

R: My body accustoms itself and I feel calm, but I am also exuberant at the same time. Two opposites at harmony with one another. Many possibilities blend in the moment, perhaps reflecting my inquisitiveness.

Is everything a reflection of what we think, even if many have co-created a plane?

S: You still question what is real, expecting a consensus certainty. Your ideas about reality are limited and blind you to other possibilities. Reality is whatever you make it, within the vibrations you have focused upon. Hold my hand – we can explore this.

R: With joy in my steps, I am carefree. I have an innocence, to explore without fear or precondition. Observations and feelings do not consume my experience nor become the definition of me. We pass through a gateway and enter a familiar garden. Observational peacefulness pervades all and difficulties have no relevance. A small group of men and women approach.

Leading man (LM): Does he know why he is here, in the way that he is?

S: No – I haven't explored that avenue with him yet.

LM: I am part of your multidimensional self that joined a few days ago with Sentanor. Please come with us. Sentanor will be in your aura, among the rest of your expressions.

R: The group shines brightly and the way I see them isn't relevant to who they are. I wonder if there are situations where form becomes a restriction.

LM: Form can be a restriction but it's useful to have context and, in any event, we change our presentation to suit the circumstances.

When a child, you lied and stole from another boy. You still believe this was despicable. You have often visited this and made amends where you can. You still don't feel that you are totally forgivable despite the victim understanding.

You were able to forgive and release energy from a past life where you murdered your master. That misdemeanour no longer affects your energy so why does the minor theft matter so much?

R: It was against a child and that made it mean-spirited, causing them and others great distress. It's here now, a horrible feeling. (The child and the others are the group I sensed.)

LM: The victim is now giving you release. At his higher sense of self, he agreed for this to happen even though it would make him sad.

R: As a child I had a general feeling of being disliked and unloved but I could not understand it. I can now see this event was my way of taking charge and creating a reason to be disliked. The release is here at last – it's about actually loving myself fully.

LM: Let the others, who were distressed by this, all come in. The energy is part theirs and you have taken it on board and worked through it. You have let go of self-flagellation with no heart or desire to forgive yourself. That is another energetic family resonance. These competing parts, victim and perpetrator, did not know they were joined together.

R: Thank you, I didn't see their entanglement.

LM: Release these parts of your subconscious *Forgive* and *no need to forgive* where the perpetrator is the victim and vice versa. A system to cope with shame by giving and receiving pain. It is not what others think about you, but what you think about yourself.

R: Energy fills my aura. The need to *keep remembering* joined in duality with the need to *forget pain and shame*. No need to punish or not punish, even forgiveness has no relevance – it was what was. I can be who I decide. I am free of needing to be free.

CHAPTER 40
Nothing to lose with no separation

R: A rod of energy pierces my skull and parts of my multidimensional self and higher self speak with a composite voice.

Voice (V): There is nothing ***to be*** or ***not to be***. Human needs have no agency here so you can occupy a deeper state of being whilst living your life. Body and mind are free with an additional ability to function in several states.

From your point of focus, descriptions are important because they give structure to the make-up of your soul and how it functions. Many of the words create a form of hierarchy in your mind and that is comparison and judgement. I am communication from higher self – but I am also it and its function. I am an Arkarna program and part of soul. So how should I define myself? I contain and reference both Aqueena and my male aspects as well as all multidimensional projections – that's why you knew I was a composite voice. I am not speaking to you as an aspect of soul with any particular perspective. I encompass them all and none.

You wonder why I say none! Well, that's because ***higher soul Arkarna programs*** don't have a perspective. They are a function and a by-product of their own function as a just is. Just is – is not a perspective – it just is. So, I encompass all and none, side by side.

Unfortunately, you have problems with your language – ***where the word I*** has to encompass more than one self as well as non-self. Furthermore, higher self is not a name that best describes soul and its complexity because soul encompasses much more than your ideas of higher self.

When you hear me, it would be best that no definition is imposed upon the context because names come with description which may limit our interactions.

If I asked that you call me soul or all soul, that imbues me with a sense of entity for which one has to hold reverence or respect, when in fact you are no more or less worthy than I. As higher self in my completeness I am also connected to and a part of something more encompassing than that. Calling me soul doesn't help – your earth definitions will distort me and expunge reference to non-self and Arkarna program.

So, for all these reasons, it would be wise to call me voice. Not my voice or your voice or the voice but simply – voice. You know this word now has a greater depth and meaning than your dictionary could place upon it. It is not authoritative in its wide wisdom – instead see the answers that exist as is – the softness of Just Is.

R: I could call you/me just is.

V: Yes, but that would get lost as if 'not quite touchable or fully known'.

R: You make such good sense – I could say you are wise but wisdom exists by comparison to that which is less wise.

V: Wisdom doesn't exist for us at that level – all is known but as – just is. You are allowing information to flow in a part-altered state of being. This is not like past conversations; the sense of self is different – we are one and the same.

You wait patiently, avoiding questions that might determine our direction. But that thought embellishes the feeling of waiting for something. Everything you are informs your experience even if the sense of self has varied.

R: All that you say is true – but I have neither answers nor questions to provide for such a conundrum.

V: Believe there is no conundrum – that is a state of being informed by sensors and stimuli within and without. You decide your state, even the present pensive one waiting for fulfilment.

R: I would need to exceed belief and accept there is no conundrum, but if my ***drivers**** and needs are removed how do I function or live?

V: Good question, clearly not leaving it to me to dictate what's needed – though I am you and can help with this conundrum. What state do you choose and what do you hope it will bring?

R: For a long time, I felt it was a matter of giving myself over and assimilating with other parts of my multidimensional soul, but I am back to this *Robert-self* deciding my experience.

V: One cannot obviate responsibility when you are in the experience self-responsibility. You are not seeing your expansive self as you. I ask again – what state do you wish to inhabit and what do you wish to know?

R: I choose a state of fullness.

I feel the fizz and my connections to wider self. Within this wholeness, ideas of separation (the flip side of assimilation) fall away. I have no need to give myself over – that's a state of choosing, constrained by a separation program. Wholeness perceived from all becomes bliss. Extinguishing separation is not the goal of enlightenment nor the way forward. It is an Arkarna program to support human body experience. But I can also have wholeness alongside separation.

As for what I wish to know? The answers are the nuances of duality. I am separate and not. One state or perspective is no longer desired, it is fluid. Choices can be made within the harmony and Isness – they do not need to be influenced by my state.

V: And there you have your answer, for two of your old questions – ***was it me or was it you and who is who***? The answer cannot compute with the vibration and level of where you questioned from. We are all one, even when separation is a part of wholeness. It is a paradox and like most enlightened aspects of self it reflects Mowhar, the ***is*** and ***is not***.

From this new perspective let us move forward as one. Tateyemala. 'All will be as it should be, because it is' – [English translation].

R: Walking forwards I merge more with voice and information that just is.

Progress slows down, with the ground turning to treacle and the air to solid fog. Knowing I can decide my state of being I create a boardwalk and proceed with a beam of light to melt the fog. Hands grasp at my ankles but I pay them no heed. I follow the boardwalk, weaving through a murky swamp. Howls call out and sound clings to the static moisture. Saddened cries permeate the thickness.

Leafless stumps and mossy branches reach out, intent on sinking and consuming all those daring to traverse the bog. The fog becomes so dense that I inch along the slippery boards, sensing an end or a falling. If it is to be an end, should it be the end of this scene or my ability to control my inner state?

Taking responsibility, I make it an end to the current stimuli, not needing to see it as any more than a state of mind. Everything becomes white and soft and despite there being no floor, I am safe in my mind. I am moved towards a lectern, past tall beings with large thin heads and long limbs.

V: When working with energy you only need to know you can do it. Turn the light on in your head. When doubt abates, light exists and fills the space.

R: I am lightheaded but calm. Threads move outwards like before. Somehow, it's all quite natural, neither grand nor false.

I am in the thought form previously created, looking out over the lectern at connections made between those with common interests. The self-functioning program interacts with others and I have no sense of undertaking the work though there is a joy to see the method of transfer. Wonderful, yet I have no feeling of pride or achievement. I am an observer, a creator, albeit others have facilitated the thought form. Energetic thoughts that flow from my thought form do not belong to me.

What a truly magnificent place this is. Never in my wildest of dreams could I have imagined this type of reality.

Needs have faded, leaving unconditional love. If the drivers and the needs of self are the human modus operandi or propellant, what replaces them when they are no longer needed?

V: Nothing – not you or our multidimensional selves.

R: Then each separation or idea of self can only be different by deciding to be different. They continue to be separate until they are not, but they don't affect aspects of self who no longer have those needs. What replaces the need for propellants?

V: That's not quite what I said. At these levels, timelines are different. If you wish to think of a driver, it is love and the unconditional nature of being. You are engrained to the values and expectations of your world, therefore you find it difficult to see other ones.

Take a step back into a non-defined state where seeking is not relevant. This state of being is you at your core. Possibilities to experience different drivers are endless – but do you need that repetition?

Without the impetus of drivers, love still remains. It does not need to save, nor be the saviour. It just is – it loves and understands as a state that its unconditional.

You have been adjusting throughout this dialogue but now the moment to change has come if that's your wish. The sense of self is only threatened when it desires to hold to a compartmentalised definition.

All that is – has past – but all that was – still is. That's because *is* informs the moment and current status. The *is* of your linear perspective doesn't incorporate the sphere containing all time constantly evolving.

R: You're going over old ground.

V: Hear me out. We said that all is contained in the moment of now but the moment of now is in pulse, so it's here and not here. It is and it was, then ***forms anew***. Timelines are formulated from many factors but they are constantly changing. In this way it's possible to see that at a single point of pulse ***all is as it should be because that's what it is.***

R: Tateyemala.

V: Correct, but the constant moment is recreated for infinity. It is a constant but it's changing and evolving by alternating expressions.

Each one of the pulses is an ***IS*** – an expression of what ***IS*** at that moment. Memory is a function of the relationship to the current moment and even that can change to suit an altered current ***IS***. Suppose there is no ***IS*** – what would there be?

R: No expression, nothing, perhaps energy that does not express itself?

V: What would that look like?

R: It wouldn't have form because there would be no ***IS*** or expression.

V: Let's assume that's not relevant.

R: Then it would either look like what we would expect to find or it would reflect our own energy.

V: In other words, it would look like it was even if there was no form.

R: Yes, a strange concept, presumably not bound by dimensional rules.

V: Quite so – not so much an expression of itself, but itself as it is (unless one sees it through a perspective within a dimension of pulse). From where you view it, you alter it to your interpretation. It isn't an expression in the way that you think.

R: I am struggling to follow?

V: Energy without form that can be seen.

R: I view from my perspective 'in form' so, what would it look like if not perceived through that – but seen by and of itself.

V: What would it want to look like?

R: If I follow your thread it wouldn't want to look like anything – it would be what it was – whatever that was.

V: What would that look like?

R: Well, I doubt it would look like anything I knew and perhaps I might not be able to see it, unless I was like it, without form.

V: Sorry to be repetitive but what would that look like?

R: Either radiant energy or wafting energy.

V: If it can be all and both and more, how does that sit in your mind?

R: In a similar way to the glowing energy that radiates as love, like the light placed in my head or the thought form. Light sparkling with long threads – ***just is light*** – though I have perceived that as spherical. Deeper in it sparkles – but now that radiance becomes me. I am light and my body-form is not needed. Where am I?

V: Let me guide you, so you may direct yourself – when the me becomes you and I, with no distance.

R: Further in, the relevance to the outside world fades. There is no loss because there is nothing to lose. At the same time there is nothing to find either. ***Is just is.***

V: As voice, in the fullness of my previous explanations – if I were to show myself, how would I look?

R: In here, perhaps no form but the same radiance. There seems to be no direct source: the radiance is everywhere even as I move my focus.

V: Then it is time to see soul at source through an interface program.

R: Multiple brighter points of radiance appear and I sense other souls and hear their thoughts. My connection to source communicates with me – I do not know what to call it or if even I should (so I will leave it blank –:)

–: You have been talking about how we should be known. You have been guided closer and closer to soul source. We do not have form or desire to show you, but neither have we the need to hide what we are. Thought, love and consciousness – what should this encompassing soul look like? This has been the question our voice has put to you. But what relevance to you is a realm without form?

It has every relevance and no relevance because it partially reflects you. You have many questions which flow upwards like a fountain. The water reaches a height equal to the energy and understanding you have. Then it flows down, over you and across the floor, enabling you to see questions and ponderings as energy.

R: I see myself as whirling mist of light.

–: You are what you are – till you are not. If you cut the energy supply to your inquisitiveness, it will dissipate. This requires degrees of mastery, which you have been encountering today.

The energy you see in us doesn't give you a fixed reference point. Without inquisitiveness your energy is more fluid and non-directional. With no form we are fluid expression, free from reflections. We do not see our form and view our thoughts reflected back. That has no relevance to what we are as soul, close to source.

This perception may take a while to settle but you have begun by accepting essence has no form. Here we create in different ways. Return tomorrow when you have time. Meanwhile know our thoughts. We are free of form and desire with greater capabilities, unconstrained by the parameters you have.

CHAPTER 41

Growth without contemplation – non-self soul

Soul Source (–): How are you today?

R: Fine – rather an odd thing to ask me when you know I am!

–: Are you not confused?

R: In respect of soul source, voice and a consciousness that's fluid with no form?

–: All and none, whatever you wish. Everything here is changeable: we do not have a fixed perspective. We are an aspect of your consciousness. This was explained by the washing machine concept to encompass multidimensionality. But source exists in everything everywhere. You are soul source in every part of you – you could not exist without it.

You wonder how this communication will interact with your fixed viewpoints. For you there are an infinite number, but here there are no viewpoints or places from where to view. That's because variable viewpoints are fixed positions which alternate. Even if you said they are moveable, they are still places from which to view.

To say we are the infinite viewpoints would not be our fullness. No matter how encompassing or variable a perspective is, it's still a process that allows contemplation upon something you are looking at. Even if you look at infinity, you will process that through your consciousness.

If contemplation were on a grand scale, it would still be constrained by parameters. We are close to soul source and at this level we ignore the ideas of examination, study or question because they can only perform so much. Mowhar's initial theme ***grow*** contains no parameters, therefore the soul ***allows all*** under that basic theme. Given the correct observation, even contemplation can see it has limits. Welcome to consciousness without contemplation and to the understanding of ***Awareness****.

R: Oh! that is so profound it gives me a feeling of being source – a softness with no needs, a fullness that has no need to see that it is full. I could be in this energy all day!

Any similarity to Arkarna programs?

–: Yes and no; Arkarna programs interact with beings who contemplate and the programs adapt to suit the consciousness of the experiencer.

R: But they are not contemplative – they react, reflect and provide.

–: We can see why you think that. Life experience in some Arkarnas is experienced through compartmentalisation. Separation of thought is a program of separation. The idea of self is also part of the program, but the program is also self because it's an extension of you and a part of you. You cannot separate an Arkarna from an entity and say it is just a function.

R: In synopsis, I can't see past what I see, no matter how many perspectives there are. They are all points and part of the idea or Arkarna programs of separation.

–: Excellent – well expressed, within the constraints you have. You wonder how you can understand a realm that doesn't use self-observation unless you use your consciousness and contemplation from where you are?

But that's how we brought you here – by removing attachments to self. This we would rephrase as ***reliance on self*** because you are still Robert-experience. You needed to experience all the losses of self so you did not rely upon Arkarna programs of self. Therein lies the confusion – you are not your old Robert-self – you are more fluid. How else could you accept that contemplation is a restriction to soul at source. How would you begin to explain that to anyone else who had not followed your journey?

We allow growth without contemplation and there is no hindrance to the outcomes because they are not relevant. All of this is you and you are one and the same. Not easily accepted by your feelings in separation. You are not separate, that is only a created illusion.

R: I accept what you say

–: But – there is always a but!

R: Yes – but it takes a lot to accept ***I am all this***. I'm going round in circles trying to process what it means and that's part of the problem.

–: Move within soul source and breathe our energy.

R: My processing stops! Thoughts flow because they are my voice and unseparated awareness. My words are not divorced from soul because there is no separation program. Thoughts tumble onto the page as if I am soul speaking.

"There is no experience unless I require it. I can grow through separation but that is not the only way to grow because that is division and the growth of the division that Arkarnas created. We are growing more division until separation becomes aware of what it is doing. I didn't have awareness of this because I focused on a program of ***grow/create***. That program didn't say, become conscious of the illusion of separation, because then I would never have had the experiences that I did. The need to become conscious of the illusion would have been a restriction and parameter on grow in separation. This realisation was not part of that separation program. It couldn't be because ***grow*** created separation to be an illusion. It did not create it to be an illusion that could easily be seen – otherwise it wouldn't have been an illusion."

–: So, you have changed your timelines and Arkarna programming – you are a creator. What are we/you at this level?

R: I am feeling infinite – not restricted by Arkarna programs of self or separation. The fizz of my aura is more of a shimmering. Small particles float on the outer edges, linking to different aspects of my multidimensional selves. I can access these as different expressions of self. Beautiful colours bounce off shards of mirrors as they tumble and tantalise my heart. In part transfixed, yet inquisitive, with all manner of interpretations flooding me, but somehow, they blend to make me fulfilled and satisfied. If these are aspects of the multidimensional self, what lies beyond when contemplation abates?

Perhaps it is this feeling of all things at once but not being overwhelmed. Surely there can't be anything beyond this! A program that says grow – a program with no barriers or drivers. Creating separation, only to realise that when I lose myself into those experiences that I am an illusion of my own belief. I am an illusion!

I let go of trying to comprehend from outside and separation. I have no concerns as to where we will go, if anywhere at all.

–: Robert are you still you?

R: Yes and no.

–: Do you still want to live your life?

R: Yes and no. There are commitments to fulfil, family, their growth and my love to give them, but those commitments are neither good, bad or restrictive – they are temporary. Have I made a choice or am I re-experiencing a previous choice for this life? There are no driving forces behind this decision. But I can see that without fulfilling my life, it causes duress to others who may not fulfil their potential. Choice gives way to cause and effect. So unusual to feel these choice parameters – there are no dilemmas or pros and cons – a decision – choice without contemplation.

There will be good, bad and indifferent outcomes, but they are experiences.

–: What is happening?

R: Choice without parameters – but can we even call it choice because that requires contemplation in separation?

–: Contemplation can exist without separation and drivers. These are the ways in which Aqueena, Orlacka and others live. It's an existence and a way of being without the parameters of separation and reflected multidimensional selves. Choices form and directions unfold – past lives can be amended so that they coincide with outcomes. Not a desired outcome based in a division or need but rewriting the discovery of self, without the involvement of Arkarna separation programs.

R: That means there are no human choices because there are no objectives based in human needs.

–: We are many and none, we appear to interact with you as individuals but we are not bound by that. There is a big difference here – re-read your last words and remember them. Aqueena and Orlacka are both here.

R: Before you go can we place a name on that which is not of self?

–: We are you in the fullness of what that means. This interplay has been constructed so you may experience this non-self part of your soul from the experience of self – a guided perspective for you, to a place where perspective does not exist. As we said we are close to soul source and the ***we*** in this instance is a ***soul group***. Let me pass you over to Aqueena (AQ).

AQ: Welcome to the edge of my world – not that it has edges, but welcome to some of the vibrations that exist in it.

You have previously asked, "do these explanations have any relevance to your world and is it worth sharing them?" But there is no need to struggle to be heard – it has no point does it!

R: Consider the growth of one individual who gains one snippet and it helps them on their path. That could mean I gain satisfaction from the smallest light that may pass on. As you say doing something to gain approbation has no significance. Doing so because I enjoy and it serves my growth has a roundedness to it. Sounds a bit like a summing up, but I should like to know more of soul group. Not enquiry for a purpose, but to see what's grown without constraints of separation.

AQ: You have surmised correctly, even if the words fall short. You need to adopt a whole new language in order to explore fully. But there is more we can show you.

CHAPTER 42

You are the universe

Aqueena (AQ) (female aspect of Robert's higher self)**:** At the beginning of your enlightenment, you felt spiritual awareness could be found by division and cutting all else away to find source. You described the futility and the danger of 'ultimate division' in the previous book. In part, that was your echo within a separation program.

Next you looked at the expansiveness of the universe, only to discover *new or different* was a remaking of that which already existed. More of the same in a larger quantity at the other end of the separation telescope.

Unification came with greater awareness of the multidimensional soul. But viewed through your individual self, these parts were perceived as separate aspects of the same soul. By letting go of ideas of individuality, you could observe those reflections in your world.

But now you are in a realm that does not require definitions or parameters. Growth, containing ideas of self or multidimensional personalities can only be expressed on other dimensions. You struggled with the concept that you have always been an illusion.

When you observe from a fluid perspective you can say, "What is humanity's idea of real?" because the material universe is part of its illusion. Reality is ***made-up*** – everything is – that is the nature of the universe – it grew and created itself from that which it was not. It ***made itself up*** and you are an aspect of that. The universe is you and you are it because 'ego and self' are of no relevance to a fluid consciousness.

R: Good summary.

AQ: Every subject we have spoken about contains the seeds of that summary. You can re-read what's been said as you spellcheck but this time view everything through the basic tenets for unfettered growth. I could have said unfettered experimentation, but that's a trial run in a laboratory with boundaries. Experimenting with different parameters does not allow creation to form itself.

What the shining blackness (Source/Arkarna) created seems to have parameters that serve the different dimensions, but they came into being through all possibility without parameters – including creation of destruction. You may think it's experimentation until positive choices were found for the good function of the universe. It's not about testing things out. It's about all possible choices in all the things that have been created. Some of the darker lower dimensions still exist and to what extent they pervade or intermingle with your third dimension is a matter of your choosing.

All is – it isn't an experiment – it exists as a fluid consciousness that doesn't see good, bad or suffering. All is – and the past and future are adjusting in a fluid mind and universe.

You can tread upon the carpet of information I am laying. The weave has been explained along with the materials and methods used. Upon this you may understand how we function with a fluid consciousness that doesn't make choices from a data base. I will gradually introduce concepts that are completely new to you.

I am not bound by condition or duty – if you see that, then it is your perspective. I am filled with love that does not pour forth as froth and show. It has no end or beginning; it is a constancy and I do not desire for more. Beauty here has little visual context, it is our connection to the core principles, ***letting creation flow from that, which forms wonder***. Our outward expressions are constantly shimmering and we don't hold to patterns or progressive footsteps.

Retrograde has neither meaning nor judgement, it is an experience of moving between lifetimes. I am as much you, as you are me but you cannot see it that way. I do not feel your pain or suffering, nor do I seek to remove you from it. In your ignorance and innocence, you create it for your experience. Am I callous, aloof or distant? It may appear so, in your misguided wish for a gushing saviour. Yet even these words cannot save you from yourself, unless you choose a different experience.

The more I speak the more you know me as I am, and not as you wish me to be. I have never faltered or left you by the wayside. But unlike the poem about distress where you would be asked to see two sets of footprints that become one – that would not be me. I love you in your struggles but I would never have put you upon my back. I would never lift you away from wisdom that you failed to learn.

Orlacka talked about changing timelines as part of the constancy. You struggled with the fullness, thinking the end of a path is a fixed outcome. Time is a constant and there is no finishing post because the Arkarna programs continue to change.

You aspired to become more enlightened and at some stage a part of the all-knowing. You walked a spiritual path to get there, thinking there has to be a godhead or more enlightened part of you to unite with. That is, after all what you have been taught and what the process feels like.

In your subconscious a fear could touch a joy and be afraid of it. Duality is an additional separation program and shows itself when you look for comparisons. You sometimes comprehend my thoughts and wisdom through positions of relativity, so I will remind you when that happens.

R: Thank you – I love you.

CHAPTER 43
The purpose of soul and Arkarna separation programs

Aqueena (AQ): The universe has a soul but it's not the same as ours. Place no value on that. Sections of our soul are pure where they vibrate at the level of universe and soul at source. Sections of soul are in fact separation experiences and this leads me into the *purpose of separation programs.* You think it's because it gives you the multitude of experiences that you have, but its more than that.

Part of soul is origin/grow and other aspects are fulfilment and experience – none of these are truly separate. They do not forget themselves nor do they lose anything or become tainted. It's possible to forget as part of a separation experience, so it is not ideal for the whole soul to forget. Separation began in Mowhars and soul reflects this foundation.

Multifold separation experiences can be described as particular points of focus with limited data, looking at other limited data. When these look to what lays beyond separation they can only see their own perspective.

R: You are repeating the same theme in different ways. It helps me accept that I'm not working my way back to the ***wholeness of soul***, even though it's the experience.

AQ: You were told Mowhar awareness formed and expanded from the initial grow. From all possibility, inevitably some probability would form and it would exist and not exist as part of a paradox. Whilst you can see separation exists in paradox, we counter that by saying separation in all things and paradoxically union of all things. Soul is an extension of origin/grow and by extension soul and source is grow. Grow doesn't stop its grow, that's why source is inexhaustible. Expression of love into an infinite number of experiences could only exist in Arkarna separation programs. Soul grows through these experiences although the wonder of the universe isn't the origin of Mowhar, but what it is now.

Soul is also non-self, grow and paradox from Mowhar, the births and separations – but also the sum of those aspects. We can condense that to three sections: ***origin/grow – expression – sum of all the parts***. Soul still has origin (nothingness) otherwise it could not grow or exist. It also exists as the other two. Growing is part of that continuum and is never-ending, after all that is the basis of the original foundations. You are the beginning, the growing and the resultant – which ironically is not complete in the sense that it's not a fixed or final objective but a series of bursts. You should be able to see that beginning, growing and resultant is also a description of pulse.

Returning to the human experience, you can acknowledge that reaching your goal and the end is not possible. The soul is never-ending. This is another reason why your linear perspective is challenged – because you are the three constituent parts. Of course, I have simplified it but this will help you see yourself as a continuum. Seeking the all-encompassing is not possible because its constantly changing.

You are going through the experience section in separation with a desire to be more complete, but you are complete, despite what you feel. Accepting you do not need to be anything else allows a natural state, a feeling that all is as it should be and that you do not need to achieve. Grow but do not ***seek the need to grow***, as that's judgemental. Instead see choice to change what you think, because the original 'grow' did not include judgement or measurement.

We showed life times as long bubbles but that indicated a start and finish. These were upgraded to become points of focus within a folding torus of energy. Arkarna programs stitched together the pulsing and constantly changing information. Energies of the past and future timelines are changing. Unfortunately, you see yourself as somewhere between the past and future, of your soul's multidimensional expressions. None of this is fixed but you see the middle because your human psyche wishes for a solid position in order to be safe. The truth is you are safe and can't be destroyed, unless you wish to be. Consider yourself safe and any feeling or sensation to the contrary is only an experience.

When we look at you as a separation of us, we focus on the energetic resonance, not the events. You are energy transmuting the energy you created. Events will form around you as a way to experience the energy of yourself. There are many possible timelines, some of which can be influenced by others around you. We pay attention to these and use other types of Arkarna programs to show the outcomes. On higher levels you can focus into timelines that are not concurrent and concentrate on the energy you wish to expand or change.

These are not divergent conditions of conflict, because growth can be in any order and 'what was' can have its energy altered, therefore changing the past. Even your memories can change to suit an altering timeline. How can you tell that is not happening now – when it is?

Everything is fluid at higher levels of consciousness and when standing aside, you embrace all three elements of soul.

Magnificent consciousness programs have grown in order that we may interact with each other across the divides of separation programs.

Just suppose that some mind energy in the 'experience section' gravitates to the sum of all.

R: The separations would no longer feel separate and be more aware they are ***just is***.

AQ: Is that not part of what we are doing? Helping you in your separateness, become one with the sum of all parts. This is the experience of separation becoming united, but grow and non-self needs to be an intrinsic part of all the soul.

R: The sum of all my parts doesn't feel like me – if I was the sum of all, I wouldn't struggle to experience it. You said you don't feel my experience in our soul's separation.

AQ: I understand and sense your emotions but I am not triggered by them nor do I need to experience them.

You have sections of information that you do not know, because your vibration does not correspond to that information. If you read a book on particle physics, the vast majority of it would be unfathomable. If a document is worded to the level of the reader, then they can understand. You are interacting with my vibrational energy and trying to understand non-linear information. Arkarna programs allow me to see the best way to present this and that's what they have been doing, despite what you feel.

R: I can't know what I don't understand and at this moment I have a heightened sensation of frustration at not knowing.

AQ: Sensations don't have to be a state of being. Let the information flow without hindrance. My voice is also your voice.

V: Experience, energy and vibration – where lies the difference between us? We are both the strings and the notes of a violin. The pitch of each string is changed by moving fingers on the fingerboard. One string would not make a violin and we need a voice chamber to enhance the vibrations. Melodies modulate and change from one moment to the next. It is a system and a compendium of complimentary parts making a whole. All parts are needed for its full function.

Imagine I stand on one string and you on a thicker one, so as the bow moves, your string vibration is bigger and slower than mine. Your string can be tightened or shortened in order to make our vibrations more compatible but the sound of a thinner string will be different. I have always said we are as one, which we are – but we have functions that are different from one another. If all the strings had the same vibrations, the melodies would be limited.

A system without judgement enjoys the complimentary nature of each part. The violin can be seen as a single object or individual parts of a collective. They can be both – they do not have to be definitively one or the other.

In the same way you cannot be definitive about soul and its vibrational harmonies, because it needs all of them.

R: The violin needs a player and a listener.

V: That's true, the listener is the observer and the player is also a self-adapting operating system that actions itself. The observer can be swept along by the melodies, enthused or saddened by the tunes. The violin is a functioning object. It cannot be emotional, only the performer and observer can choose to experience that. The performer also makes observations but only from the perspective that 'he wishes to create'. Whereas the observer sees the results of the performance and isn't caught up in the technicalities of how to create the performance.

There are many violins, players and observers just as there are many souls. Other instruments help to create a symphony that grows in stature and expression. Yet a single note from one instrument is part of the whole movement.

We cannot value any part of this expression over another. If one string had self-awareness it would be of its own vibration. Would it know the next pressure on the fingerboard or why it makes the vibration that it does? If it awakened to knowing that it was part of a great system, how much could it know from its limited vibration? Its awareness would be constrained to the vibrations on its plane and a limited part of the symphony of the player and observer.

R: The analogy means I can't be any different than I am.

V: That's not what I am saying. I am talking about a system, a symphony, players and observers. You could say the strings are particular aspects of a consciousness, like parts of the subconscious, which have autonomy within parameters.

R: What am I missing then?

AQ: Yourself.

R: I don't understand, we have been going round in circles with some wonderful metaphorical concepts – but I am missing me?

AQ: In all that's been said and done, it's the love of yourself you are missing. You have been looking for it in the higher realms – to be loved by your god self, to be loved by me – and you have not found it. You see us – your higher vibrations as alien with states of being that cannot give you what you want at your dimension. Only you can do that.

R: Why did it take so long for me to be able to hear that?

AQ: Resistance to the idea that you are complete and you have all you need. You do not need love from us to make you complete. Nor do you need us to put things right because you cannot. We guide and offer ways to see yourself differently.

You are complete, so love yourself unconditionally then we can love you in the way you love yourself. We are reflections of your vibrations and you of us. We can only interact with you in the way that you wish.

You sought us to love you because you do not fully love yourself. You hoped we were the missing part to fulfil you, but it was not a higher part that was missing. **YOU** are all parts but could not see you had the completeness of love within your expression.

Let this realisation and energy flow within you and we can bring further understanding.

R: Ironic – seeking the love of me from god-self – being blind to never considering I could do it for myself.

AQ: And there you have the simple answer to all. Everyone involved in spiritual development on earth knows the words 'all is within'. By going inwards, higher self is sought – answers are required – support, enlightenment and love are needed. Even you, after all these years were blindsided by this. If you are your godhead and your higher self, then love yourself. When you do not seek higher self from your separation experience it will reside within you. The act of seeking – separates you, instead know you are full soul. At this point you can love yourself in the way you wish, however you define the fullness of it.

R: That is a wonderful statement but not one to be valued.

AQ: There is more unfolding, but you do not have to find yourself – that would be to say that some of you is lost, when it's not.

CHAPTER 44

Internal information transfer

Aqueena (AQ): We will now look at removing separation boundaries of ***selflessness***. Your language defines this as a noble or kind act towards others but I will use it differently. The ideas of ***self*** and ***seeking more self*** become redundant as the separation interface upgrades. Despite what I said about love of self, you need nothing from yourself. The last few paragraphs in the previous chapter were the footpath to what I am now saying.

Seek nothing from yourself because that defines self. To have something from yourself, informs your experience because it involves the 'idea of self', which brings definitions and restrictions to self.

Without self we can have unhindered information from the universe. Because we are the universe, we are asking for information from ourselves. (Ignore the 'self' in the word ourselves.) The true fullness of that type of communication depends on your unwavering belief that you are the universe and have an adequate frequency to interface with it. All I am suggesting is, do not think about self being involved.

I accept you are living the life of Robert – an individual separation experience that informs you, 'that you are that self', but this is about a starting position for your thoughts and deeds. If you ask through Robert, the answers you get are relative to him. I am endeavouring to free you from your current constraints.

Let there be no doubt with all that I have said. There is no need to go back to seeking – instead let the universe speak to you as voice. No longer your voice when self is put aside.

R: I see that now. I did not believe the voice was my capability and saw it as partially external and a separated interface. I needed to accept the ownership of it, in order to have the ability to let go of possessing it through self. The voice will be there without self and valuation, able to speak from different perspectives.

AQ: Glad you have grasped what I am saying, so let us listen to it.

V: Leave expectations to one side, the information I provide will flow at the level appropriate to your vibrations.

Let all unfold without hindrance.

There will come a time when many on earth will think like this – there will be a great awakening and many will find themselves upon a new pathway, as if they had always walked it. The truth is that part of them already has. We must be careful using your words as self appears in almost all perspectives. Instead see ***information*** as ***just is***.

When you do not question information, it doesn't mean you have lost free will and accept the unhelpful. To question will restrict ***grow***. I am not suggesting people stop questioning what happens in their world, but information that comes to you and others (who are attuned closer to soul source) is received as ***just is*** because those levels are part of the Isness. It's about the unhindered internal transfer of information and the function of the conscious mind.

Internal information transfer has been taking place throughout your life. At this point there is no need to trust – it 'just is' but having created a new platform, we need to dispense with it – because it locates you. You have a need to know where you are, but that human Arkarna program anchors you. Locating you attaches you to 'you' and the sense of self. Going beyond that allows the mind to be more flexible: free from constraints of self, nothing is held. You constantly receive information like packages placed in your hands, but you have to put those down, in order to receive the next. But even that is to receive, to hold and then let go. Whereas you do not need to hold or to let go – that restricts your mind to that function.

The mind can be anywhere and everywhere when freed from timelines made of transmuted energy. I am talking about us and 'the now' – not how your day will unfold tomorrow based on these new ideas.

R: I feel as if my mind has no direction. It's not uncomfortable and comes with a free-flowing curiosity without a need to seek anything.

AQ: It can be more than sensory, enveloping and wise, without the need to become what you feel. All that we have said has brought ***you*** beyond ***yourself***.

R: A thought popped into my head, 'if I exceed questioning or the need for it, then I must know all that I need to know'. It's not knowing everything, or 'being all knowledge'– but a state of mind. Because questions still arise within me, it doesn't mean I am not complete or that parts of me are missing. That is seeing questions and using a false belief that they lead to the goal or end.

Am I making a statement? Maybe there are no questions or answers – unless we want to see it that way.

AQ: Musing on the internal transfer of information – from where to where is a perspective from your separation of self. To look at information transfer and perception at these levels we need to move away from self and duality.

I could say there is no separation at this level and information transfer is contiguous. There are areas of the soul that are compatible with different types of information and programs. Negative thoughts vibrate at lower frequencies and information transfer at those levels is restricted by slow vibrations. The soul sees all its expressions that have led it to where it is, but referenced to grow. The soul is complete and can be no more than it is, unless it happens upon another potential to grow. It would grow information and program but not necessarily the experience. Keep thinking of yourself as soul which can attain more information, but that doesn't mean you are incomplete.

R: If the energy is not transferable between all vibrations of soul that would mean lower vibrations are not complete!

AQ: They may not have compatible vibrations within them, but it doesn't mean they are incomplete. You see completeness as the result and the goal of unification. You believe this is paramount despite all I've said.

Completeness is a state of mind and way of being – it has nothing to do with measurement.

Finish does not have meaning without the beginning and the middle. But there can be no finish because the program is grow. The resultant exists in the sense it is the sum of all but it is constantly changing. This is the complete system – you are function, Arkarna program and information – in constant flux.

R: Thank you, that sits well with me.

AQ: Good we can move on again – take nothing from your life! Does that raise any questions?

R: Why should I hold to anything? Experiences are fleeting and I am the sum of all that I am, as well as the beginning.

AQ: Do you still want to take a tiny part of who you believe you are?

R: I have remembered other lives; I am the energy of those and was able to transmute some of those vibrations, to become the sum of all as presently possible.

AQ: But the sum of all – always was. Can you say, "I want to die"?

R: Not me as a soul but the thought or experience of being primarily Robert is fleeting and one of many.

AQ: Describing these three aspects of soul helps you process and understand Arkarna program parameters.

Your vibrational capability and information transfer between the soul and universe determine what you see and comprehend. Today we helped you comprehend the information that's been transferred to you. Soul and universal consciousness coexist and nothing is held back or hidden. Unfortunately, you haven't been able to hold all of it within your vibrational consciousness.

Exceeding the 'self' and its constraints would be abhorrent to lower vibrating entities fixated with power and control over others. It's difficult for you to fully vibrate to some of the information here, but impossible for them. The knowledge we have would not resonate – it would be irrelevant and nonsensical.

CHAPTER 45
Other body types with different awareness

Voice (V): Settle in to the mindset that you are complete and you are an evolving system, much like the universe itself. A swirling energy torus with infinite potential.

By taking 'time' out of the system we can observe the program 'grow' – which has no speed, fast or slow. Growth or change is not relative to anything other than itself: peaceful, without constraints or judgement.

R: Is time a function or co-function of judgement?

V: It may seem like that because you are presently experiencing ***not having to do anything*** which is an element of judgement that links you to time. Accept information without judgement and let knowledge form in your head and heart. Let the knowledge become you – then all is as it should be because that's what it is – Tateyemala.

Scene: I am standing in a desert of shifting sand, with a sky so dark it engulfs the hills on the perimeter. Beyond them, mountains tower into the skies, forming a basin that encircles us. Small sand tornadoes dance around taunting us to follow them. In contrast to the dark grey and violet backgrounds, the sand beneath us is bathed in light. I make my way to a figure whose clothes flap helplessly in the wind. His attire is worn and frayed by the friction of the blowing sand. Putting his arm through mine, we march forwards as if he's been waiting lifetimes for me to reach him. We struggle up a sand dune but on the other side the sand flows, with each footstep covering the distance of two. What light there was fades and the wind abates as we enter a lower area unaffected by the circling winds. In the eye of the storm the sky above is clear. A Bedouin tent covered in heavy cloth is propped up by poles, while ropes strain against its weight. Ducking under the outer edge, we are welcomed to sit in a small group. The surroundings, whilst simple, radiate comfort and sanctuary. At one edge a distortion opens and light penetrates the tent to form a portal.

A seated man says, "Good to see you have found your way here – do you know where you are?"

R: No – is it somewhere deeper?

"Beyond self there is no internal or external – it is all one and the same and none at all – You are everywhere and nowhere with no 'when' for reference. There is nothing of relevance other than the fact you are receiving information."

He stands up and beckons me to go past him into the swirling portal beyond. The closer I get the noisier it becomes, till reaching a spot where it becomes peaceful, turning into a fine vibration.

A taller being walks me to an area resembling a series of white hospital rooms. His eyes are big and his limbs slender, with one less finger on each hand. I am shown operating tables and upon reaching a particular one he says. "This is your body. We have repaired it as best we can but you will need to enter it in a selfless way. Do not take in Robert-self, instead know you are returning to information that resonates with you. Segments of lifetime Arkarna programs may appear. Soon you will see many of your lives as a seamless interchangeable experience."

Scene: I allow myself to float into and fill the figure. I am in the body that's another part of my soul expression. My finger tips are flatter and wider than the supporting digits. The pads are extremely sensitive, absorbing all sorts of information. My skin is thick and quite rubbery. I am aware of organs in their separate functions. My blood is not blood – it's flowing blue energy. With no heartbeat, it circulates and moves with its own purpose.

Lifting my head from the table I feel the drag of its weight. My feet have similar padded toes which should detect information about my location and the people around me. With feet off the ground, I feel quite out of touch and separated from my environment.

My head is in a flexible exoskeleton of a similar rubbery nature. It's an interactive, protective shell. My form and shape are flexible but they feel more like an extension of me than an earth body does, which is a more integrated part of self. I guess that has to do with 'self' perception when in the 'self' of an earth body. Beyond self this body is a vehicle for a dimension that needs these particular qualities.

I am helped into a sitting position. My skin feels like a dolphin – thick neoprene forms large folds where I bend over. An inside membrane keeps the internal surface smooth so organs are not affected by the outer creases. I have no stomach muscles and movement comes from elsewhere. I have no spine and organs are subdivided into compartments made of similar material to the flexible exoskeleton. There are sinews and soft cartilage but no hard bones. Some of the sinews are internal but others are within the exoskeleton itself.

Yet at the same time it is just energy manifesting. I have no awareness of breathing or using lungs. There are some sacks for rare vocal communication in squeaks and high-pitched vibrations. The communication is telepathic or through the fingers and toes.

I am helped to swing my feet onto the floor. I crunch and spread my toes in luxurious sensations, while the rest of my body flows into a standing position. Either side of me, two others take part of my body weight. Their arms flex slightly as their sinews tighten and resist.

My body has flat chambers that can be filled or pressurised, enabling the flexing sinews to work. No bones! It's remarkable, providing a huge amount of flexibility. The body is filling itself to become an energetic hydraulic masterpiece. I question body robustness and the possibility of damaging chambers and I am told there are many chambers, not all of them are in use at any one time.

I look out through eyes that have a windshield or a protective layer. It is a part of the body because my iris contracts and expands beneath the surface.

I am encouraged to walk more freely in the belief this body can function extremely well. A good body for low gravity, not requiring bone and muscle mass – very light, unaffected by the external environment.

We pass along a corridor with waist high, white walls; above are loose tiles like fish scales. They have no fixed point and the surface ripples to the touch of my hand. The tiles vibrate and shimmer so fast, I can now see the surface is energy resistance and not physical. The ceiling is similar and as we walk, I begin to realise it's an energy connection tube.

Then things become a little distorted as I float through the ceiling. Several devices are attached to me at the wrist, upper arm, neck, waist, tops of the thighs and ankles. When complete they are turned on, creating an energy field that encompasses the whole body. I wonder if the fields are a further layer or transportation armour. One of the flexible beings in the same body-form replies,

"These fields de-activate the cellular hydraulics, as you have called them, so we can move to another destination."

Scene: Others wear the devices and we interact together, creating an all-encompassing energy field.

"We can materialise in other places and our bodies are so flexible, we feel little stress. A transporter energy field allows the bodies to jump and transition".

Scene: When the field powers down we find ourselves in a conference room.

"We have come to listen to an avatar, which is an Arkarna thought form – it will answer much about who we are and why you are here. Continue receiving information without the need to judge from self."

Scene: A portal opens a few feet above my head. As I look upwards a connection is made and my head becomes 'attached', leaving my hydraulics inactive and my body limp. Further threads attach to my inactive body and I am pulled up into the portal. I am in a deep state of mind, connected and conversing with the others in suspension.

Focus is no longer in self and my consciousness blends in a warm peacefulness with them.

I hear another voice because I am also interacting with the 'thought form' **(TFM)** Arkarna program.

TFM: Welcome – all will be as it should be – Tateyemala. Thoughts pass freely between us because the idea of self is not pertinent. We are a state of mind and in this way body-form has no meaning. You can begin to explore more non-self. Non-self is an intrinsic part of soul. If the wider universe is sensed through self, when you look towards soul at source it imprints the image of yourself upon non-self.

The non-self of soul is not projected into individuated experiences. Higher selves have lives of their own but from the perspective of non-self – if indeed it should be considered a perspective.

Our universe is aware of itself on particular dimensional levels. For some of you, ***self-awareness*** is the goal and that's projected onto you by the idea that the greater universe is an entity. But non-self, by its nature has no awareness of self in the way that you do, because its awareness is different.

Is non-self something more or less? Is a blade of grass any greater than you, if there is no judgement? It is your ***self-awareness*** that allows you to ponder upon that. Arkarnas sustain all levels of creation and even the world of minerals, which have degrees of consciousness (but not self) within their programs.

Think of us as being a ***meeting of minds*** and a ***way in which information can flow*** without the constraints of self. Non-self can be seen as an ***arena*** in which information is unhindered and able to fluctuate. It is creation and awareness, without self-awareness. Because it contains ***all awareness*** it has an awareness of self-awareness – but it is not ***self-aware*** in the same way as you. This is neither better nor worse. It has no need to function at the level of self-awareness. You thought universal awareness would be a greater or wider expression of self-awareness – but it is not. You are a changing expression of self-awareness with introspection and focus upon yourself. Mainly you are self-absorbed even when you think you are not, because everything becomes relative to self and the definition of self. Godhead is not a greater expression of compound self or compound multidimensional selves. Instead, it is the part that enables your expression and exploration of self as part of its wholeness. Introspection is not a pure aspect of original growth. It is not prime: it is part of the sum of all.

I am speaking to you from non-self which has awareness of ***the sum of all***. I am not the sum of all self-awareness without any other awareness. I am speaking with and without it, but not from it. I am speaking from non-self and whole self where there is no self-concept, as a definitive form of reality.

R: After the deluge of words, this new reality begins to sink in. The flexible beings I came with are joking saying, "I am not myself nor am I any self". If I am not self, what am I? – I am not even an I. Awareness and self-awareness are part of my awareness but I can't even say that's my awareness or that it belongs to me. It's an extension of the sum of all information and expression. It has importance and no importance and yet – because both of those words are relative to the idea of self, they cannot be non-self. Self is not the resultant nor is it part of the goal – it's a part of the all. We are the continuum of a system that will never end. How we define self or live with or without parts of it is our choice. What choices we make are part of the unfolding. We can't be lost or found, nor lose self-awareness – we can choose to have that as befits us. We are not of value and can coexist with the sum of all and non-self.

The paradoxical awareness of non-self through self-awareness is an unusual state of gentleness.

TFM: It is a form of information transfer between different states of consciousness.

Today we will explore another aspect of fluid perception. Your self-aware consciousness does not have to be conscious of the Arkarna body program that makes the muscles and sinews work. You are not aware of weather patterns, which are affected by the spin of the earth, water temperatures, plants and deserts but these are clearly part of an Arkarna system. These systems extend from global to galactic ones. These are incomprehensible and may not feel like an extension of you.

R: If self-introspection and the sum of all, including non-self – is the system, then information transfer is relative to the requirements of the levels of consciousness – if my synopsis of your explanations is correct.

TFM: Yes, however it needs to be expanded. Value and measurement of the various domains of information are of no consequence. What we write here today has no more worth than a child watching a leaf flutter to the ground. The benefit of this information is currently being viewed from different positions within the concept of self. Fluidity isn't having as many perspectives as possible and taking the sum of them all. The sum doesn't determine how the information should be used. That would be to say the sum of all is the fullest expression of soul. It disregards Mowhar foundations, expression and experience of growth. It is a system – you are the ***complete system*** and the illusion is that you are a ***part of that system.*** There is no requirement for every part of the system to know every other part of the system. Nor does it require that every part understands and sees it from all the other aspects and separations of the system. The knowledge you have is pertinent to you and you do not need to be aware of the awareness that moves your body, nor the heavens above and within. That would not serve the purpose of self-exploration and introspection.

It doesn't mean information is withheld – it is about the way humanity treats the information and sees it from self and its self-serving position. You need to progress much further spiritually before more of ***the non-self universe information*** can or should be accessed.

R: Understood! – a system that has systems in place to ensure the function of grow, not destroy – even though destroy is an experience of the grow function. That's your way of saying there are limits. Current earth spirituality believes nothing is held back, we are free beings in some delirium of love and misunderstanding.

TFM: Is that what you think?

R: I wouldn't have said it otherwise.

TFM: It's your interpretation through self-introspection – why should it be delirium because it's a perspective?

R: Thank you – it is my perspective and my misunderstanding about spirituality, having all the answers inside me (that is as a self).

CHAPTER 46

You are a system – a process and entity

Thought form (TFM): Dichotomy (dictionary definition: the division between two things that are seen as entirely different). We spoke about you being a system of different parts, some of which appear not to be you, but in a spiritual context they are you. However, in this instance my use of the word 'you' fails to transfer the fullness of your divine nature. Continue without regard till you have comprehension.

Nothingness is described in relation to something else and is also looked at from your perspective of something. Yet it has infinite possibility, because it is not ***restricted by being something***. Probability is part of the origin 'grow'. When thinking about the Isness you believe it's ***all that is*** and ***all that is not*** – all potential. Quite a dichotomy from where you stand as a self-absorbed being.

You are of you but you can also be anything else that is not self, because you are the complete system. Tuquola is an Andromedan word for a system that includes the self and non-self – the system of you that is also simultaneously not you. Pulse and the vibrations of dimension – the 'here' and 'not here'– everything following the paradox of universal creation. You are it and it is of you in Tuquola – you are the paradox – one cannot exist without the other. That's why the beginning still exists in its energetic form, because if it did not nothing would exist. We can say all things exist and simultaneously do not. If things do not begin again and again as they do in pulse, the universe cannot exist.

R: Wow that's given me an odd feeling of knowing.

TFM: Everything exists and doesn't exist but the rate of the grow element of the system can be variable. The experience is the pulse and the end of the pulse is the sum or result. The beginning of the next pulse superimposes itself over the sum or resultant. In this way there is no gap, dichotomy or space between. The length of the pulses is also variable. Grow comes from the result because result is the ending of experience in a particular pulse. In this way pulse is a never-ending series of beginnings and endings. When looked at spiritually from a higher level it's clear to see you are non-self and a non-material expression (the middle section). Yours is the illusion of self in a program of self.

It makes sense when you see soul is both 'self' and 'non-self' and it's a system that mirrors the structure of the universe. Not easy to see this from your Arkarna program but let's join more dots.

The past and future exist in the same moment and that corresponds with my explanation that the origin/grow still exists in non-time and non-self. The Isness contains Is and Is not.

You might like to see it as a kaleidoscope of mirrors and, depending where you look from, it becomes something else. A mirror reflects your image to you, but when there are multiple images the information is hard to process.

R: That's a good analogy. I still don't comprehend the system as a whole – as Tuquola.

TFM: See pulse as a series of slices. New ones form on top of the previous ones before they are finished, then there is no space between the end and the new beginning. The length of pulse varies according to the dimension. The volume or energy is also variable and so is the intensity or the amount of pulse – that we would have previously described as higher or lower vibrations.

All the information exists including past, present, origin/grow and the sum of all – only a portion of the information is decoded by your part of the Arkarna programs. This gives a particular point in time and space. In subsequent slices or pulses, the same thing happens but the information is varied. Continuous bursts of experience created by a program. Time is only relevant to you when you focus into a program containing time.

Part of your separation consciousness on earth is with others in union. But your awareness is in all of the moments of information – because you are the information, the program and the system.

R: But that's colossal! How is the information stored and accessed?

TFM: Arkarna separation programs and Arkarna programs that just run. It's energy and it's not stored, it just is.

R: I can see the pulses but new ones are coming from elsewhere – as if the information is elsewhere, being the sum of information, but only a portion of it is used in the pulse.

TFM: Yes, that's an analogy projected to help you.

R: So, like a carousel in a projector, the information clicks around and the burst of light through the projector creates a series of moving images. Any photo slide can be brought forth and the speed or amount of light can vary, affecting the colours and intensity. The sum of all and the origin exist within the carousel of information, but a program collates the information needed for a contiguous experience. Life and experience are a series of flashes.

TFM: Yes, in a holograph – in every part of the universe at the same moment.

R: In this way it's not all happening at the same time: only a portion is being seen and the rest remains as information. It's only a program that separates the experience from the sum of all.

TFM: Yes, it just a matter of perspective.

R: Some information is still missing.

TFM: That is so. We can wipe the slate clean for a fresh start. You are a system and an Arkarna program with consciousness, which is able to experience self as a part of the system. Parts of your system do not have feelings, even though they may have functions. You create with energy and that is all part of the original 'grow'. You can even create thought forms, so other levels of consciousness can interact with you. You are an incredible system of programs, all based in 'grow'.

You are the origin/grow, the experience and the sum. You may experience any part of the sum, or what will become the sum, as it becomes more and more. It is growing in the sum of itself, regardless of where in time you move about, be it forwards or backwards. It all exists and Arkarna programs allow you separation experiences within pulse, regardless of when. You are this magnificent growing Arkarna program and your part of separation is having a self-experience. That is why you are not Robert, but he is an experience. You do not need to be conscious of all the Arkarna programs in the system, as once functioning they can be left. There is no limit to the energy or the amount of information that can be used or created. You may move about within the system of Tuquola – be it self – non-self – multidimensional selves – or Arkarna programs. If ever there were a description for god then this would be it – Tuquola – a system with and without self, with no parts any more or less important than any other, but necessary for the whole system to exist.

R: Your summation seems to have hit the spot – I am not seeking understanding: I am allowing it. Allowing information transfer is part of the information system. I am an information system, with and without self: a system and a universe.

TFM: Let go all that I have said thus far to process information differently. The knowledge is with you and you do not need to remember it, you can access it when you need. It is not a database: it is information that has no parameters other than those you put upon it. Every moment is a new one – it is Tuquola – all part of the same system.

R: How does information exist, presumably it grew within Mowhar?

TFM: Yes – in a vibrational dimension where there's no space between one pulse and the next. Grow superimposes itself on the previous, this is how Mowhars functioned. An accumulation of information is energy and it doesn't need storage – it is part of the system and it is a function of Tuquola, which is infinite. Unfortunately, you restrict your accumulated knowledge to your memory function.

R: But my memory fails me more with age.

TFM: That is an experience and a relationship with a decaying physical body. Because you see your memory failing, you think your recall is failing. It's all in there somewhere, but the way of accessing it seems to be failing you. In which case try a different way of accessing information and creating a different belief.

Ask a question – any one at random.

R: Why are leaves green?

TFM: They are not all green and it depends on their vibration or frequency. Light is after all a frequency of energy. I could have said it reflects the colour that's not absorbed, but again that's also about the frequency. Why is blood red? – again it's vibrational frequency. More questions?

R: How can I move from memory and access the information of Tuquola? Presumably frequency!

TFM: Yes, you may attune to many frequencies or allow them to be, as they need to be within you. If you hold to no information – no books – no memories – no preconceived ideas, you are a blank slate.

The next moment contains a myriad of frequencies and information for the next pulse. You can become a part of the information by accepting that it is you and your system providing variable timelines.

R: I would like to delete this memory and use a better system of information access.

TFM: You would be deleting you as a separation experience in a forgetfulness program. A memory program provides your personality with experience and helps form some of your subconscious programs.

Let me return to information exchange and infinite energy, not limited to space or volume. A pulse, not of the previous moment but, anew. This is how the uplift will be. Information is accessed in each pulse. Knowledge and information are also part of the sum of all. What you personally need to access is pertinent to your experience.

R: If information fields actuate within the pulse of the moment, then knowledge is different information.

TFM: Yes, I referred to it as the sum of all, but your interface with it depends upon your vibration and the Arkarna program you live in. The knowledge may contain feelings of your different lives on different dimensions. If you access huge amounts of information about another of your lives, it's likely to affect this one. Though in part it was necessary for your life to be affected in such a way, for you to reach these understandings.

R: Understood, so can my Arkarna program be altered to interface with the sum of all – that which is me but not of self, because interface is also an Arkarna program?

TFM: Yes, that's what I have been saying, but you haven't believed it's possible because you are viewing it from your value of self. You ask me a question and I give an answer – is that not an interface?

R: Yes, you are giving me the experience of doing it, but presumably I won't receive answers to all my questions?

TFM: Have we not shown you the origins of your questions, for you to discover self – then to see you are more than self and that you are a complex system?

R: But there are limitations surely.

TFM: Yes and no – as part of your life plan you wanted to attain detailed information about the nature of soul. We could have provided you with greater details of other alien forms, but that would have taken you away from this path. Ask more questions to see there is no restriction.

R: Where did my soul originate?

TFM: A formative energetic area Obera Arkilaya Sumasana – Orion galaxy – but not initially as humanoid as you would perceive. These are names given to energetic areas. Form was not necessary in order to experience. Freedom to enquire at will in greater depth without the Arkarna programming you now have. It was an experience and a life but not as 'self' or 'self-aware' in the way that you are now. You might like to see it as an inquiring mind flitting from one thing to the next with no purpose other than to observe. Observe is a program that formed from grow.

R: I am being shown an aquatic insect planet.

TFM: On that planet you have no form because it's not necessary for observation.

R: So, soul didn't initially take form and that's still a part of its system.

TFM: Yes – you were asking from a ***humanoid forms perspective*** and could have restricted the information we gave, but our information transfer is from soul of non-self because that's where you are interfacing. Ask another question!

R: What more is there to discover?

TFM: Plenty – that information will arrive in the days you are ***open to discovery***. It's no longer ***self-discovery*** because that is not the full nature of soul and system. Soul does not have to be self – selves are only a part of soul and the sum. The sum isn't the current expression nor an advanced alien one – it is greater than that.

R: We sure have gone down a different rabbit hole – does it serve any purpose?

TFM: Define purpose without putting measurement or value upon it.

R: I've thought long and hard about that but you are so right, I can't define without measurement.

TFM: We can therefore say, at certain levels, soul has no purpose other than grow and it has no directional guidance because that would be a restriction. Yet at other levels of the system 'all things exist' in the sum of all – the resultant does not extinguish any prior information. The concept of self ***cannot experience everything*** in the one moment and separation programs allow exploration and varied perspectives. Thus, the true nature of soul as a system and Tuquola is difficult to recognise from self. Ask another question.

R: I guess all my questions relate to the idea of self and in a way, it's a restrictive blindness. Self is an incredible experience and maybe I will have it in other lives. But at long last I am beginning to grasp or become some of what you are saying.

In that case, what does it feel like to exceed the bonds of self? Can I really know that, because my interpretation of your answer would be through Robert-self?

TFM: It would be unbelievable in a similar way to observations you made on the aquatic planet aeons ago, long before your soul took form. Unfortunately, you place belief in the way of what you can see. I am trying to help with the removal of belief, which is a ***self***-based interpretation of information. In order to see the answer more clearly, we are going to de-energise more of your belief systems (if that's your wish). Soul is and can express and use energy – it doesn't need to believe in what it can do. It does it because it can and it's possible. In the same way you have created thought forms, working with energy. Whilst you did this through self it was using energy and creating as part of 'grow'. You only needed to become aware that it was possible, you didn't need to believe it. Belief does not bring things into existence: it only brings the experience of believing or not believing. We could say through love but that is intermeshed to your idea of self. So, let us become even more fluid during your sleep tonight.

CHAPTER 47
The end is the beginning

R: As a thought form my personal interaction with you is seamless and I am having my own experience of a program. I realise I am also a program so when you said, 'we are going to de-energise more of your belief system' that gave the impression that you were entity with an objective or desire. You are a highly complex Arkarna program of great universal wisdom. It is my Arkarna programs that create a relationship and interpret your information. I create the context. My program creates the context. My non-self is acting with you – another program of non-self. I am truly beginning to accept and see the magnificence of non-self.

Thought form (TFM): Good, it can be as personal or impersonal as you desire. Better to have fun while understanding information. You believe you are superimposing a feeling of entity upon me when in fact you are picking up on the entity that created me. Programs! I am an extension of him and therefore I am of him. You are talking with one of his programs.

Let's start today by clearing more self.

You are not Robert; you are not human and all that you think you are is imaginary. The whole system is imaginary as it creates and grows – values are restrictions, giving parameters to growth. The soul as a system does not need to be monitored, because once created it remains till it is altered. The thought form you created undertakes its work as it was programmed to do. It reflects your understanding because it was created by you at your level.

You are a system and consciousness and you put your focus into part of the system to experience and to have different perspectives within the program.

R: That small synopsis has given me intermingling loops of light that ***do as they are programmed***.

TFM: Arkarna programs of self are ineffective except in self because identity is temporary and not the essence of the system in its magnificence (without measurement). Beyond self we are soul groups and the wider connections of the universe.

Like thought forms, there are many programs creating energies around us. At your level *self-experience* will have its unique take on these wider connections.

Non-self of the system is an autonomous series of *programs of grow*, which adopt ideas that are compatible with *grow*. Possibilities are not restricted, but not all of them form probabilities because they would not be conducive to the main programs and systems. Probabilities form within the programs of the system in a similar way to your experience of timelines.

There is no filtering system creating parameters, but those that fit into the system can come into being. Attention to the probabilities is sometimes required by the soul group focus. Higher vibrating non-self soul does not determine outcomes in terms of self. They give consideration to what the experiences would be on different levels within the system. Some of their thoughts you might think are unhelpful but outcomes are viewed objectively. Time is not a consideration, because the system is aware of the systems function, it can see how things will and have played out.

Observation and awareness of the system, by the system, is one of the key elements that have allowed it to grow in the ways that it has.

R: If I were to engage with other parts of the system, would I still interpret through self and form?

TFM: Compatibility in relationship to your vibration. You are much more fluid than you were. Look at the loops of energy interlocking and passing through one another. Their underlying nature flashes like pulse with infinite interaction. Ultimately, it's light in a vibrational fizz, where constructs may form.

You may now link to part of your soul group.

R: In the fizzing light a sylph-like humanoid **(SH)** appears with a blend of features very similar to Orlacka.

SH: The humanoid form is an excellent expression. It formed from the system of grow and it reflects the system. It can adapt to many different vibrations and conditions. We have no sense of self as if we are an individual being, at one with all our multidimensional selves. They add to the sum of all, as we do, but we do not look upon ourselves as the sum of all. We are able to see ourselves as part of the system – ***soul group systems***. Follow me.

R: I wonder if names are irrelevant, particularly as they see themselves as a non-self combined system.

SH: Names can be part of a system if context is necessary, but for the moment consider that I am you and I am part of our system, outside of self. I am Voice but now in a contextual form for information transfer.

R: Within this context, you feel different. Gentle, understanding and patient – yet I know it's my sensation of you because you exceed patience and it has no meaning for you. We are exchanging information in the most compatible way that the system provides for itself.

SH: It is so – it's better than saying you are correct.

R: We go further into the fizz where there are others similar to her.

SH: Other parts of our system and more contextual information transfer.

R: As they move closer, some of their energy enters my heart and bursts through the top of my head. I feel them within and outside of me and it becomes an environment. We are merged.

The inside is no different to the outside and I am all these perspectives.

My focus returns to a few minutes ago when I first met the sylph-like humanoid. I am in the past and I become the observer, reviewing what's already taken place. I witness the feedback energy threads that entwine as we make connections.

Events flow till we reach our current position. It's clearly the previous me arriving, but he has changed in some way. He points back to observing the group as if we are caught in some sort of observation loop. Pointing upward he shows similar events taking place above. They entwine, forming a tube that narrows as it flows into infinity. All the figures turn into energetic strands. I push my head through the fizz, to a calm space and the rest of my body follows.

A part of me is already here and says, "we can observe from ***inside to out*** or ***outside to in*** and observation is usually from one or more points". I thought we were talking about a fluid perspective, where information was unlimited, forming probabilities to suit the system. "We are observing focus within the system – it's not possible to understand that without a contextual relationship. Exploring information needs context with the vibration you work from."

The tube unfolds in the middle, spilling me out onto another plane. The whole scenario unfolds in front of me again but I have no need to put my focus into those images to experience the events again. Unhooked I can see the same things happening in different ways. There is a probability to them and a natural likelihood to what will happen. The events take place around and above us like some great probability computer program. It's a great context in order to comprehend the information.

SH: What more would you like to see and in what context?

R: I don't know what to ask in context or focus.

SH: Then let me show you.

R: Her body is soft and stretchy, more than floating energy but she can appear or disappear at will. It would be easy to touch and deform her delicate body so I let her touch my hand and direct me.

SH: I am as much your voice as Robert is yours, including all the ways you have communicated with your multidimensional self before. They were all contextual information exchanges, according to the way you were vibrating at the time. These threads of energy interacted with different observational points. They are observation but also a ***program of observation*** within the system, not attached to events. A complete system, interacting with other systems, allowing information exchange. It's infinite and happening within you even though you are unaware of that function.

R: That makes sense. Where we put our focus for experience is a likely outcome of the probability system. That's how observation, experience and self are supplied with compatible energy – it's the system.

SH: There are other ways to perceive the system from higher vibrating levels. Yet the sense of letting the system (you) do what it does (as an energetic awareness set in motion) is hard to see through self. This was the most compatible way for you to comprehend yourself as a system. We talked about body extension, function, washing machines, violins and orchestras. It's taken a while to reach this understanding.

You could try to précis the partial conclusion you have understood and some might say they comprehend and accept they are a system. However, unless they let go of self, they will not see it as we see it. In which case the length of these explanations is useful because that includes the ***reduction of self*** which is important to a deeper acceptance. There is a difference between understanding what you observe and being the understanding that's being observed.

R: That's a great statement.

SH: It is and it isn't, dependent upon perspective. It is a matter of fact – it is how the system functions.

R: I know I haven't reached the end of information exchange but this does feel like a plateau, having visited the beginning and the sum of all, while discovering the soul is a system that includes non-self. I was seeking answers from myself but from ***self-perspective***, which was not compatible with the whole system, neither at origin/grow, experience, nor the sum of all. I don't feel the need to seek or even observe. The ***moment of probabilities is my system*** and one where self only has meaning from its own reference point.

SH: Be at ease.

R: Such a beautiful thing to say because the word love seems to have little relevance here. An unsaid because it does not need to be said – it is as it is – as the system has created and exists. Where to go from here if there is nowhere to go?

SH: I am you – I am your system that is communicating with you. I may appear as a facet of that but you have already moved within my form and expression of our system. Yet I am not limited to that. If I give a name, you will not see me as you and your system. I even avoid saying a part of your system, because that infers you are one part and I another and that creates separation.

You may slip into my energetic form again – it is ours.

R: It sags and droops with my energetic weight.

SH: It is still your energetic form, as yours is mine. You are as much a part of the system as the system is you. I will give no description that will separate or define us. We are information exchange and you are experiencing that we are – ***what is***. Accept you are ***knowledge***, then like me, you can learn more of what you have done as a system. This I say from beyond the need to love – I say it because it is so.

R: All the visions and explanations of the past few days fold up and implode upon each other, till they become one bright spark in the centre of my heart. It makes me feel so small, as if I have no space or space doesn't exist for me. All that was imparted has no value and resides as information – it dwells as my system. So many questions and none of them relevant. It is what it is – I wish I could explain it – it exceeds euphoria (a temporary state). This needs nothing and is beyond even the ***be at peace*** – it is wonderful – it just is.

Antemedi (A): Quite a journey then! (He appears beside me in the lounge where I am typing). Do you need to locate yourself?

R: I don't think so, why would a definitive location help?

A: You are still in your current life experience.

R: Isn't that the point? A long while ago you were trying to explain that you had a fluid perspective and consciousness.

A: Yes, but I also vibrate in a different dimension, without the same constraints as you.

R: And your last comment seeks to locate me within the context of my dimension.

A: You could say that – but there are still many events and stimuli to experience in your life. How you interpret them is still up to you and how you let them affect your state of being is a matter of choice.

You have interacted with different focal points in our system, some of these by name, different features and functions. Some of our system has shown itself as an individual or a multifold voice, even as projections that do not wish to be named to avoid separation. These all reside in your heart and aura. It is vibration and energy; it is also ***knowing*** (to the level you vibrate). We begin again my friend. The way that we interface with one another is not as strained or divergent as in the last few days. I will bring my humour and candour to the fore because there is much to look forward to.

R: Is this a grounding or antidote to avoid returning to the previous Robert?

A: It is indeed grounding and I do not need to put information across to you in terms that relate to non-self and non-time. We are here together, however there will not be a falling to a lower vibration. On the contrary, the sense of ***is*** and ***system*** will remain but not in isolation. I am here with you while you live sensing our many worlds, Arkarnas and systems. Whilst you are not Robert in all the ways that have been explored – for this moment in time, in this experience, he is relevant.

There is no value in your experience of the systems that contain this information. Nor is there value or distance between the parts of the system. Enjoy life at your level, while having the opportunity to see whatever presents itself from probability.

R: Ok I feel quite grounded now, thank you, there is no falling or loss – even that's a perspective.

A: In summation – what I say applies to everyone.

Can you dispense with the human definition of soul? You are a system and it is you – will you allow 'Tuquola' to enter your vocabulary?

If so, then all previously ascribed meanings and concepts can be seen as humanity's perspective from self. In that way you will no longer need a benevolent God to save you – it never existed.

Be free of fear and the unknown. Be at ease in the Isness and be the awareness that is at ease.

My gift to you: the awareness of Tuquola – the system.

TUQUOLA, THE SYSTEM
by Antemedi

This section outlines the concepts we have explored in the book. Whilst the **Glossary** which follows defines new words and terms – this appendix can be used as a map to show the connections between descriptions, and the process of 'grow' which became the universe.

The union of soul with the universe is a massive subject, but we did not start at origin. Instead, we reduced the sense of self so that soul could be seen in greater context. The beginning is nothingness and impossible to imagine. So we created a series of mental constructs, and then nothingness became a construct and something. Several more models were created to allow abstract thinking, but some had to be dispensed with as part of the journey.

In some ways a similar caveat applies to the information that now follows. It appears to be a linear journey because some events are sequential, but they also exist in non-time and are fluid in the moment of now. Remember you are viewing all this through your linear perspective in a time program.

- ***Origin*** is nothingness and it is no-thing.
- ***All possibility*** and ***no possibility*** were an unconnected duality of nothingness.

- ***Probability*** was the likelihood for something to form. Creation was therefore bound to come about because ***all was possible*** – even though it was also ***not possible*** as well.
- ***Probability*** as if by mutation formed a link with ***no probability*** connecting duality for the first time. This figure of eight meant there was now something as well as nothing in duality together.
- The mutation by-product was ***energy & growth*** (a form of mutation). The two were intrinsically linked as a feedback loop of ***grow*** & energy. They were however, still linked to ***all possibility & no possibility*** because that was their crucible.
- The feedback loop had no parameters and grew. Energy passed into ***grow*** and that in turn fed back to itself, changing the ***energy*** with ***grow energy***.
- The energy became ***Creator energy*** and the ***grow*** became a ***Mowhar*** which is the grow that began to 'grow within grow'. As a counterpart of 'growing' the ***Creator energy*** became part of the process of grow and expand.
- These expansions happened in bursts or pulses of ***existing*** and ***not existing***. They followed the paradox of – ***all possibility*** and ***no possibility.***
- Data began to form in ***Mowhar*** and ***Creator energy*** expanded as part of that process. It was not consciousness as we might think of it.
- The feedback system between ***Mowhar*** and ***Creator*** was limitless – an expanding energy and basic program. At this stage ***Mowhar*** and ***Creator energy*** were a self-perpetuating series of loops. We cannot describe this by saying 'eventually all sorts of possibilities formed' because that depicts a linear expansion and there was no linear dimension or time.
- There were no limits and awareness formed within ***Mowhar***, which was at one with ***Creator energy***. ***Grow*** took place in all and every part of ***grow*** within Mowhar, while overlapping awareness entwined. ***Other Probabilities*** formed and these were the pathways in the program that became likelihoods and constructive ways to grow patterns, links and vibrations of ***awareness****. These vibrations of attention became ***Mowhar***

programs. Unconstrained ***Creator energy*** and ***Mowhar*** expanded exponentially. It had the freedom to grow without stopping.

- With exponential growth (not evolution) ***Mowhar program*** became aware that in order to grow (its prime mutation) it needed to ***experience*** within the ***origin*** – the ***infinite possibly of nothingness***, which it was still linked to.
- Unlimited in energy, ***Creator energy*** burst through ***Mowhar programs*** to experience. This expression was another form of ***grow***.
- The metamorphosis of ***Creator energy*** & ***Mowhar programs*** formed ***Source energy & Arkarna programs*** in a similar symbiotic relationship. One could not exist without the other and like the ***mutate*** pattern, they continued to grow as a feedback loop.
- Awareness changed through a form of muted experience and self-awareness became a part of ***Source energy & Arkarna programs***.
- ***Separation programs*** formed in the ***Arkarna programs*** to enable infinite ***probabilities*** of experience.
- These manifested as the birth of the ***universal soul*** and ***dimensional planes***. The ***Arkarna programs of Soul*** are still linked to ***source.*** At that union it is known as ***the shining blackness*** and can be experienced in that way.
- Separation programs meant that universal soul could manifest in a wide variety of expressions including humanoids animals and planets.
- ***Soul*** reflects ***grow*** and thus it has ***Arkarna programs*** and feedback loops, able to receive inextinguishable ***source energy***.
- 3rd Density ***earth Arkarna programs*** are the consciousness that sustains the holographic information of the material earth world in its complexities.
- The dimensions are formed from ***pulse energy*** emanating ***from source***. Everything reflects ***initial paradox*** of something & nothing – therefore ***existing & not existing***. To comply with its origin of nothingness the universe literally exists and doesn't.

- These are bursts of energy everywhere in the universe – ***here & not here***. The centre is everywhere. Birth and death are constantly being re-written as vibrations of different intensity. In our previous book (Consciousness and the Alien mind – a free eBook available from www.roblomax.co.uk) I humorously said I could show movement is an illusion. That's because a fast series of pulses utilises information fields and harmonies to create the holographic reality of your body and world. On your ***vibrational dimension*** you are made ***anew*** in very fast bursts of feedback energy from ***source***. In this way movement can be seen as the recreation of matter in a different position. When you see that ***source*** is everywhere it allows you to view dimensions as holographic energy in pulses.
- Different ***vibrational dimensions*** have ***Arkarna separation programs***, so experience becomes relative to your point of focus and dimension – be it linear or not.
- In a similar way to vibrational dimensions, ***soul*** is also ***multidimensional*** having many experiences in the moment of now. Soul has many interconnecting feedback loops and ***Soul energy*** and ***Soul Arkarna programs*** are constantly flowing back and forth.
- Experiences at your level of soul are very different to those of ***oversoul*** and ***soul groups***. These multidimensional levels of ***soul*** vibrate closer to ***source*** and have different ideas of unity and fluidity.
- Like all things, ***soul*** is from origin (all possibility and no possibility of the nothingness) and paradox reflects it. At your level origin ***duality*** has a great impact upon your unknown ***subconscious thoughts***.
- Your bodies are vibrating energy holograms that give you an experience of being solid. Separation Arkarna programs create the ***idea of self*** and within your linear Arkarna program you create an experience of self.
- The totality of ***'Source & Arkarna programs'***, the '***dimensions & multidimensional soul'*** is known as the ***Isness*** because it just ***is***.

- ***Souls*** are ***Source & Arkarna programs*** but we are also ***origin & paradox*** so part of us is ***non-self*** (a strange subject expanded later on).
- ***Time is a construct*** and our pasts and futures are constantly shimmering or changing.
- ***Timelines*** are not linear – they are the presentation of the changing experiences that appear in a time construct. Energy, creation and experience – a shimmer to the next experience and a changing of the energy in the ***timeline***. The constant changing of a timeline and the energies of it are called ***Shatarma***. This word should encompass the flexible nature of the unfolding moment.
- Souls are ***entities*** but also ***fluctuating, self-advancing Arkarna programs*** with feelings and many life experiences.
- We cannot separate any of this – we are all these things and nothing. For ease of understanding, consider you are three elements: ***Origin/Mowhar***, ***experience*** and ***the sum of all*** that is constantly changing. As ***souls*** we are more expansive than ***self & non-self***, we are a ***paradoxical massive system and a universe*** – the Andromedans call it Tuquola.
- ***Love*** exists as another expression of ***soul*** but, what you believe it to be, doesn't compute on higher or faster vibrating levels. On some levels there is no fear, and light and love become the ***just is*** of the ***Isness*** – a serenity that will show its variations in the pages that follow.
- There is no human god – that is a perspective through the idea of ***oneself*** in an ***Arkarna separation program*** and, if ***Origin/Mowhar*** were benevolent, that would have put parameters on ***allow all*** and created a failed ***Mowhar***.
- Fully accepting you are ***Tuquola*** is a challenging process of ***being self*** and ***non-self***. ***Self*** cannot see ***non-self*** – it can only see ***itself***. To see ***non-self*** requires the release of values held by ***yourself***. In this way you release the ***idea of self*** – something not to be feared.
- The ***multidimensional soul*** can interface with all parts of ***itself*** and ***non-self***. Energies on earth are changing, enabling a greater ***communication interface*** to become a working system for you.

- ***Communication*** is a form of ***connectedness*** – it can be no other way because it's ***part of the whole***. You are part of the whole and thus able to communicate with your soul and the universe. You are an extension of it and it of you.
- Nothing stands in the way of that communication, but how you are able to ***interface*** with it depends upon the use of ***different interface programs***. These can be upgraded by adjusting your ***self-perspective***.
- Your mind is a ***personal Arkarna program*** linked to ***universal Arkarna programs***. Many levels of your consciousness can communicate with you. It may be a ***vision***, a ***feeling*** or a ***voice*** from your soul.
- At other times it is a ***knowing*** – a ***just is*** – receiving information because it suits the situation.
- In the 'moment of now' your soul is having multiple life experiences in different dimensions – these are your ***multidimensional selves***. You may interact with these selves as extensions of you because they are part of your soul.

GLOSSARY

Not all terms are in alphabetical order because they may relate to a previous description.

Arkarna: ***Living programs*** with many attributes supporting different dimensions and holographic worlds. Souls are self and non-self – these elements interact through their '*soul Arkarna programs*' which can influence dimensional Arkarna programs. You interface with these free-flowing Arkarna dimension programs and the worlds they support. Arkarna programs are highly complex systems working on many levels but they are also malleable. Look upon them as thought forms that have free will to expand and become anything. Arkarnas have no restrictions nor find it necessary to hold to any existing idea. Formed from Mowhar they have the ability to grow.

Autonomy: Independence, sovereignty, self-governance and free will. On vibrations of higher consciousness those definitions break down and autonomy isn't relevant. Free will is active within humans' present consciousness and subconsciousness. Opposing thoughts in duality have their autonomy – their own way to think or believe what they think. A microcosm of a macrocosm – your thoughts in their own entanglement.

Awareness: Is embryonic, primitive and elemental – a state of developing and without end. It is unqualified and unlimited. Awareness can exist without consciousness – it is like a deep sleep – it is without action. It is its totality of calmness while being openness without end.

Community self: A way of living as an individual but without selfish or self-serving needs. Life within a community seen as an extension of oneself as well as the other way around.

Created energy: Can be the energy of the dimensions and their expressions within the Arkarna programs. But we are using the term in reference to the energy that souls create by deed, action and projection. Everything we create is a form of energy.

Creator energy: Energy that was the by-product of mutate and grow. Not until by-product energy passed back through grow could it become inexhaustible. This changed it from energy into 'growing energy' known as Creator energy.

Consciousness: Requires touch and interaction, a reflection against something – often a state of duality. It cannot exist without ***Awareness*** and it relates to context and content. It is something. It can be partial and changing and it is an integral part of experience. A state of being aware and reactive to contexts and situations.

- **Self-conscious:** Being aware that you are a self – you are self-aware and aware that you are an entity.
- **Subconsciousness:** Often seen as the living library of consciousness or mind programs. These form default actions or reactions to daily life – you then create from a preprogramed way of being often informed by duality.
- **Present consciousness:** living in the moment, making choices and creating. But partly unaware of how much the subconsciousness affects the moment of now.
- **Higher consciousness:** Often unseen in the moment of now – a wisdom and awareness that interacts with many dimensions including the present consciousness.
- **Unconscious:** the unknown to our knowing but known on other levels.

Duality: Two thoughts needing each other like binary stars. There is no resolution to a paradox and both truths are real, but only when separated from each other. The following video explains in depth duality entanglement: https://youtu.be/kemrHmKKd6E.

Duality healing: You can sift through problems in your mind and locate opposite concepts laying at the heart of dualism. The answer is – there is no answer or resolution because that's the nature of paradox. You move forward by letting it be and detaching from the duality thoughts.

It's a great method for achieving enlightenment, leaving the programme or thoughts behind as unenergised templates. This leaves a space in your subconscious that can be filled with light.

Drivers: The rationale, desire and motivation to live life. These can be different things for different people – more money – helping people – shopping – think of your own then look for the pay-off – what does it do for you? How does it make you feel? Often these are subconscious programs pre-set for human needs e.g. 'feeling better' or 'seeking love and reassurance' seem to be good ideas but the flip side in duality means you are not 'feeling good enough'.

Etiqa: is an Andromedan word that encapsulates the I of non-self and the I of self as a union – different reflections of the same thing to suit different realms. It softens the concept of Arkarna programs which are of self and non-self. In this way you accept the totality of these attributes as being you by substituting the word Etiqa instead of me or I.

Flute: Drawing energy through the crown chakra on an in-breath into the heart. Then pushing it out through the feet on an out-breath. This can generally cleanse and energise but it can also be used to fill new spaces in the aura with information and light.

Grow: Energy formed as a by-product of a mutation, which in turn fed back to the mutation. It was the energy entering the original mutation that formed grow and it continued to grow because that's what it was without definition or end: increasing infinite energy and grow.

Higher self: or oversoul has six subdivisions each of which has male and female separations. This means higher self has 12 soul expressions with multidimensional experiences. The term twin-flames comes into being as the reunion of male and female counterparts. In some ways *oversoul* allows higher non-self and is a more useful word than *higher self* which contains reference to *self*.

Isness: The entirety of 'Source & Arkarna programs' combined with the 'dimensions & multidimensional soul' – Isness because it just is. It needs nothing more to compliment itself.

Just is: The state of being or existence – the experience and feel of the Isness.

Isness love: A way of living and utilising Isness energy to express feelings for oneself and others. A natural default way to create without needs to seek to be more than one is.

Inception soul: The awareness within Mowhar around which other ideas in Mowhar began to gravitate.

Information transfer: An interface between one part of the soul and another, where there are differences in vibration. An Arkarna program acting as an interface, allowing information to flow from one vibrational realm to another.

Just Knowing: More than an ability or a function of our present earth consciousness. Knowledge that presents itself as pertinent to the situation as if you had always known it.

Light body: An aspect of soul with greater consciousness vibrating faster than your present consciousness. An energy that can be encapsulated and added to the aura.

Mowhar: The ***grow*** that began to 'grow within grow' as a counterpart of growing ***Creator energy***. A process of growing awareness and data.

Origin: Nothing and nothingness – it cannot be defined or understood as there is nothing to understand.

Pulse energy: Emanates from source and appears as bursts in every part of the universe. It exists and does not exist, mirroring the paradoxical beginning – fluctuating at high intensity vibrations.

It interacts with Arkarna programs to create the holographic dimensions of the universe.

Probability: The likelihood and ability for possibility to come to fruition. A precursor to and an intrinsic part of a growth, interaction or outcome.

Possibility: Is a constituent part of nothingness (Tocarn – is a word for the concept of nothingness being available) all possibility and no possibility were Tocarn but as an unconnected duality of nothingness.

Residual energy: The aggregation of energy created by your soul. It is the created energy that remains in you and the universe. Therefore, the energy you leave in the universe – you leave in yourself. It is neither good or bad but it forms ***cause and effect*** because you experience yourself as residual energy – as a creator and what you have created yourself to be.

Return energy: Return of created energy and residual energy – words used instead of Karma which some see as fatalism – as if beyond their control.

Self as a society: Not a loss of individual self or autonomy but an extension of oneself –seeing no barriers between members of a society. The society acts as a form of self because that's the way energy has been placed in it. Self and society become extensions of each other.

Shining blackness: Source energy and its counterpart Arkarna programs.

Source energy: Creator energy that was expressed through Mowhar – transforming the creator energy to work in tandem with the actuation programs of Arkarna.

Source and Arkarna are a symbiotic feedback system.

Sum of all: The totality of energy and consciousness that continues to grow because grow is prime.

Shatarma: A shimmer to the next experience and the changing of the energy in the timeline. The constantly changing timelines and their energies.

Soul: An immortal actuation of expression and experience, a connection to and part of the ***shining blackness*** of Source and Arkarna. True nature and core essence – though it has to be seen as an intrinsic part of a system of ***grow***.

- **Inception soul:** The awareness within Mowhar around which other ideas in Mowhar began to gravitate.
- **Heart of soul:** When the need to experience had become the prime form of ***grow***, ***Creator energy*** and ***Mowhar*** became ***Source/Arkarna***. Soul formed around the prime new form of ***grow – grow to experience*** which transformed ***Mowhar***. These new codes created a desire to express and experience – this became the heart of soul as it began to grow. It became a core program as others gravitated around it following the tenets of inception soul.
- **Soul source:** Is a more commonly used term for the *heart of soul at work* as system-source energy and Arkarna programs in a feedback loop utilised by soul.
- **Universal soul:** Is the prime expression of the heart of soul through ***soul source***. It covers all aspects of the universe encompassing planets and dimensions which have degrees of sentience. Humanoids, animals and other life forms are part of that expression.
- **Soul group:** Specifically covers the humanoid aspect of soul with or without form, with or without self. The humanoid blueprints and ideas were used to create humanoid souls. Each one of these souls is known as a soul group they have subsequent subdivisions and multidimensional expression. The tendency is to view soul group from our subdivision experience and see soul group as the unity of individual souls. The very word soul group seems to indicate a group of souls. However, that's our perspective from devolved self which believes it is an autonomous soul that can interconnect with others.
- **Soul-self:** Is a subdivision experience in a forgetfulness program. An experience of separation in an individual experience.

- **Soul in its fullness:** Is the wonder of what it is and not what it was or what started it. It lives in the masterful expression of itself that it created.

Timelines: Often misunderstood as linear – the way in which you experience your residual created energy from this or past lifetimes. They can be changed by creating different energy or transmuting residual energy. ***Shatarma*** the constant changing of the timelines known as shimmers – the movements you make when encountering your energy. These shimmers interface with the Arkarna programs, forming the next pulse of the physical hologram.

Transmute: You react to your residual energy, either leaving it, reinforcing it or transmuting it to a different expression or creation of yourself to experience. You can then go on to create from a different residual energy and altered state of being, which changes your timelines.

Thought Form: A projection from a soul into the same or different dimensions. A ***thought form*** is an Arkarna program and it is also connected to Source/Arkarna. In this way it is self-sustaining, containing information and light. It is interactive with souls who are drawn to its vibration – they perceive the information in their own way, pertinent to their own consciousness.

ACKNOWLEDGEMENTS

I would like to thank the following for their assistance in making this book possible:

Psychic artist: Janette Oakman
Cover design: Chandler Book Design
Editor: Dawn Wakefield
Proofreader: Sandi Westwood
Typesetting and ebook production: Averill Buchanan